The Perilous Bridge

The Perilous Bridge

Helping Clients Through Mid-Life Transitions

Naomi Golan

THE FREE PRESS
A Division of Macmillan, Inc.
NEW YORK

Collier Macmillan Publishers
LONDON

The Free Press
A Division of Macmillan, Inc.
866 Third Avenue, New York, N. Y. 10022

Collier Macmillan Canada, Inc.

Printed in the United States of America

printing number

1 2 3 4 5 6 7 8 9 10

Library of Congress Cataloging-in-Publication Data

Golan, Naomi.
    The perilous bridge.

    Bibliography: p.
    Includes index.
    1. Middle age—Psychological aspects.   2. Psycho-
therapy.   I. Title.
RC451.4.M54G65   1986   616.89'14   85-20522
ISBN 0–02–912090–X

*To our children, Jonathan Golan and Dalia
Ducker, who helped us negotiate our own
perilous bridge to late mid-life and who
offered support and friendship throughout*

"All of the world is a very narrow bridge (from birth to death). But the essential thing is not to falter."

Chassidic Folk Song

Contents

Preface   xi

Part I.   The Passage to Late Mid-Life   1

1.   Introduction   3

2.   Theoretical Approaches to Mid-Adulthood   10

3.   Bringing About Change: Treatment Indicators and Models   22

**Part II.   Potential Pitfalls En Route
           to Late Mid-Life**   33

     Introduction   34

4.   Biophysical Reactions   37

5.   Psychological Reactions   56

6.   Shifts in Work Patterns   78

7.   Relations with Adult Children   96

8.   Ties with Aging Parents   116

9.   Bonds with One's Mate   135

Part III.   Answering the Call for Help   **159**

Introduction   160

10. "They'll Be Better Off Without Me!"   163

11. "He's Kicking Me Out—Where Now?"   173

12. "I'm Redundant; No One Wants Me!"   182

13. "What's Happening to Our Family?"   190

14. "How Much Do I Owe My Parents?"   200

15. "What Can I Do for My Loneliness?"   211

Part IV.   Tying Theory and Practice Together   **221**

16. Putting It in Perspective   223

Appendix   231

Bibliography   237

Index   251

Preface

This book, conceived as my previous one, *Passing Through Transitions: A Guide for Practitioners*, was being completed, has been simmering on the back burner for more than three years, while I served as Dean of the School of Social Work at the University of Haifa and then went back to full-time teaching. Finally, in the fall of 1983, while on sabbatical at the University of Southern California, I was able to turn my full attention to examining the extensive clinical and research literature on middle age and recent developments in the area of transitional practice.

Since I wanted to do more than simply rehash existing material on the transition to late mid-life, I was finally able to narrow down my particular interest—with the help of colleagues at both schools and my editors at The Free Press—to an examination of what professionals, particularly social workers, *did* with clients who encountered difficulties at this particular life stage. Obviously the most direct way to find this out would be to ask them, and so the six "master case situations" in Part III were developed, using a study of professionals' reactions as background against which to present the treatment in each instance. I hope it will make some small contribution both to the understanding of the complexities of the stress-filled interval called the "perilous bridge" and to the explication of practice as it is currently being conducted in such situations.

While it is impossible to name everyone who has contributed to the production of this book, I should like to thank particularly the following: at the University of Haifa, Yechezkiel Taler, current Dean of the School of Social Work, and Relli Robinson, Executive Secretary, who were both very helpful in arranging conditions for me to carry out the preliminary part of this work. My colleagues there, particularly Nava El-Ad, Rachel Kats, Ruth Katz, Zmira Laufer, Sandra Levy, Anita Weiner, and my efficient assistant, Mina Kontas, were most receptive to my sharing my ideas, ruminations, and doubts with them.

At the University of Southern California, Dean Robert Roberts has been unfailingly supportive, both administratively and intellectually. Among the faculty, Kathleen Ell, Maurice Hamovitch, Lillian Hawthorne, Carl Shafer, and Barbara Star have been keenly responsive and helpful. Ruth Britton, the School Librarian, was a treasure of patience and potential source material, while Rebecca Amescua and Gloria Byrd efficiently smoothed away practical difficulties during my stay. In addition, Mrs. Byrd typed the final draft with amazing patience and efficiency, for which I offer her heartfelt thanks. Above all, I owe a special debt of gratitude to Helen Northen, whose keen insight and objective vision helped me adhere to my purpose and sense of direction in the final phase of writing.

A large number of professional colleagues and personal friends, from all points in the United States and Israel, helped me formulate my ideas and offered their own contributions, particularly in the area of social work theory and practice, which sparked new areas to be explored. Particularly helpful were Harris Chaiklin, Gertrude Conrad, Joyce Edward, Fern Katleman, Gertrude Katzenberg, Ralph Sherman, Charlotte Siegel, Phyllis Silverman, and Greta Stanton.

Although I have agreed not to identify individuals' responses or to make direct comparisons, I would like to list here alphabetically those who participated in the field study described in Part III and to convey my sincere gratitude to all of them for the considerable thought and effort they invested in reading the case material and in giving me their detailed reactions. The social workers from the United States and Canada who participated were:

Atashi Acharya, Ellie Amel, Bernice Augenbraun, Bert Barth, Madeline Birnbaum, Phillis Caroff, Harris Chaiklin, Helen Cohen,

Gertrude Conrad, Joan Dasteel, Joyce Edward, Claire Evans, Adele Fleming-Waltch, Bruce Fleming-Waltch, Anne Freed, Tovia Freedman, Alex Gitterman, Ann Hartman, Barbara Kaplan, Margot Kohls, David Kuroda, Gerda Lawrence, Mary Frances Lebassi, Anthony Maluccio, Mildred Mailick, Dorothy Mayer, Helen Mendes, Margrit Meyer, Marcia Mindell, Judith Mishne, Kathleen Olmstead, Genevieve Oxley, Howard Parad, Leela Pistake, Gloria Russell, Judith Schmir, Ethel Schy, Harry Sexton, Carl Shafer, Charlotte Siegel, Greta Stanton, Francis Turner, Esther Wald, Rena Waxman, Shirley Weiman, Rama Weizmann, and Reva Wiseman.

A partial list of the family agencies from which some of these workers came includes the following: Family and Children's Service of Minneapolis, Family Counseling Service of Hackensack, Family Service of South Lake County of Illinois, Family Service of Greater Boston, Family Service of Glendale, Jewish Family and Children's Service of Milwaukee, Jewish Family Service of Cincinnati, and Jewish Family Service of Los Angeles. Other agencies include the El Camino Mental Health Center, Coastal Community Mental Health Center, Conciliation Court of Los Angeles, and the Faculty and Staff Counseling Center of USC.

The five psychologists who served as a comparison group were Pat Armstrong, Lester Cohen, Lucy Ferguson, Gayle Mueller, and G. Tori. Their generosity in agreeing to take part in this study while knowing so little of the background is very appreciated.

Of the staff of The Free Press, I owe particular thanks to Gladys Topkis, who sparked off my initial interest in this topic and who left me feeling bereft when she left, and to Laura Wolff, who took over and patiently and persistently cajoled me along the path to completion.

Finally, I wish to thank my husband, Ezriel, who allowed the first years of his retirement to be spent soothing, supporting, and encouraging me as I struggled to carry out this project, and Dalia Ducker, who used her social psychology background to help me unravel theoretical "knots" and her research skills to help me work out some of the methodological difficulties in interpreting the data.

To all the other contributors to this book whom I cannot list by name, my sincere appreciation.

NAOMI GOLAN

PART I

The Passage to Late Mid-Life

CHAPTER 1

Introduction

Those of us who saw the *Time* magazine cover photo of Shirley Mac-
Laine effortlessly raising one long, shapely, black-stockinged leg
high over her head while smiling charmingly at us, were not surprised to read her words, "I love the idea of being 50, because the
best is yet to come. I am going to live to be 100, because I want to be
and I am going to go on learning. . . . This has been the best year of
my life!" (*Time*, May 14, 1984: 62).

Similarly, Gloria Steinem, senior stateswoman of the feminist
movement, in discussing her fiftieth birthday, recently said, "The
truth was that I kept . . . making assumptions about what being 50
would be like. Fifty was serious, grown-up, and finally old: a year
that would be a rite of passage, a transformation, and a proof of
mortality. . . . I am still trying to work up a healthy sense of panic
or at least concern about this birthday; behaving as if I were immor-
tal may cause me to plan poorly, to say the least" (*Ms*, June 1984:
109–110).

Is this what being fifty is like? Despite MacLaine's elfin charm
and Steinem's confident outlook, the reality for most of us is less
rosy. Our fiftieth year seems to find many of us in the midst of widespread changes in our life situations. If we define a transition as a
"process of change moving an individual from one relatively stable

state, through an interval of strangeness and uncertainty on the way to a new stable state," then the transition to late mid-life, which usually falls somewhere between the chronological ages of forty-eight and fifty-four, is probably the most complex and least understood of such bridging periods. A number of changes in sensitive areas, difficult to differentiate much less negotiate, must be dealt with before an individual—singly or as part of a couple—can settle down to enjoy the relative tranquility of the mid-fifties and early sixties.

This period, once discreetly referred to as the "change of life," is found to be an intricately interlocked mosaic of change and adjustment, during which a broad spectrum of biophysical, intrapsychic, and interpersonal conflicts surface. Because of the complexities involved and the numerous pressure points, each of which can trigger disequilibrium, I call it the "perilous bridge."

Many individuals, secure in their own self-image and personal relations, pass through this transition with relative ease. They experience little physical discomfort, make key decisions, rearrange priorities, and adapt to role expectations with a minimum of overt disruption. Others find themselves immobilized, enmeshed in agonizing dilemmas, engaged in maladaptive and even self-destructive behavior. What combinations of personality traits, interpersonal ties, and social support systems enable them to cross this bridge smoothly or to struggle and fall off into the morass?

A number of recent publications have examined the middle years from various viewpoints. Some, such as Eda LeShan's *The Wonderful Crisis of Middle Age*, Adele Nudel's *For the Woman Over 50*, and Edmond Hallberg's *The Gray Itch*, offer a combination of bracing practical advice and soothing emotional support to persons passing through this turbulent time. Other writers, such as Lillian Rubin in *Women of a Certain Age*, Anne Simon in *The New Years*, and Maggie Scarf in *Unfinished Business*, draw upon their clinical experiences to discuss the psychological implications and misconceptions associated with this phase. Still others present a bewildering array of psychological, sociological, and physiological research findings in volumes such as *Modern Perspectives in the Psychiatry of Middle Age* by John Howells, *Present and Past in Middle Life* by Dorothy Eichorn and her associates, and *The Second Season* by Estelle Fuchs.

Often these years are viewed as a lead-in period to late adulthood, and researchers in gerontological institutes or research foundations include them in their projects on aging and the aged, as reported in such works as *Transition of Aging*, by Nancy Datan and

Nancy Lohmann, and *Families in Later Life*, by Lillian Troll, Sheila Miller, and Robert Atchley.

This book, however, deals with still another aspect. Several years ago, in a previous volume, I voiced the hope that "further ordered descriptive studies of different types of transitional processes and practice in various settings with various types of clients" would ensue. In this volume I am picking up my own challenge and have singled out the entry into late mid-life for closer scrutiny of the issues involved, the obstacles encountered, and the specific approaches found helpful by and for practitioners.

Scope of the Transition

The use of the terms "middle age" and "mid-life" is in itself somewhat misleading. Developmental theorists such as Erik Erikson tended to clump together twenty-five to thirty years of adult living within one single life stage. Even writers who deal with the stressful aspects of the period tend not to differentiate: Barbara Fried speaks of the "middle-age crisis" and Nancy Mayer the "male mid-life crisis" when actually they are referring to disruptions over a wide range of time. More recently we have attempted to be more specific in our designations, since it is obvious that middle age is a rich and variegated stage, during which a number of expected and unexpected life events occur.

Daniel Levinson, whose views are discussed in Chapter 3, depicts two separate transitional periods as marking this stage: the Transition to Mid-Life, which he sees as occurring between the ages of thirty-eight and forty-three, and the Age-Fifty Transition, which takes places some ten years later. The first bridging interval seems to be primarily intrapsychic and existential in nature and to affect men more seriously than women, dealing with such issues as the awareness of approaching death and such questions as, "How much time do I have left?" and "Is this all I must settle for?". The second interval, which seems to be more biophysiological and psychosocial in nature, appears to affect women more deeply. It centers on menopause and on role changes in work and in relations with spouses, adult children, and aging parents.

However, this separation, in some cases, may be artificial. It appears increasingly evident, as we examine both the research and clinical data, that individuals become more differentiated as they proceed along the time span, and that their lives are growing increasingly fluid. One point stands out sharply in the theoretical discussion: The social clocks, to use Bernice Neugarten's term, are becoming more significant than biological or chronological ones.

One further distinction should be made. The second transition mentioned above has been designated by many researchers as the entry into "postparenthood." I find this term somewhat misleading since far more is happening during these years than merely changes in parent-child roles. I have therefore chosen to call it the "transition to late mid-life." For a while I quibbled over whether it should be "late" or "later," but decided the distinction was minor. It may be that, as the life span lengthens, the division into Erikson's usual eight stages will also change or the demarcations shift upward. Perhaps in another ten years, age fifty really will mark the entry into mid-adulthood, and the period between age thirty-five and fifty will be given a new designation.

In any event, what we find happening is a converging and, in some cases, a merging of the two transitions. Such situations make the bridge undoubtedly more perilous as individuals and families experience more disruptions concurrently or in close temporal proximity. This assumes clinical, as well as theoretical, importance if one remembers that stressful situations become crises through two types of processes. In the *shock crisis*, a sudden, often unexpected event in the social environment, such as the death of a spouse in an accident, may precipitate an explosive release of emotions that overwhelms available coping mechanisms. In the *exhaustion crisis*, the situation builds up slowly, as one difficult event (expected or unexpected) piles up upon another until the person's coping capacities become exhausted and he/she reaches the breaking point. In either case, disequilibrium and active crisis results.

What happens when this occurs or is threatened is the central question around which this volume revolves. As a teacher of social work practice—one of the disciplines most actively involved with clients having difficulties during the transition to late mid-life—I have long wondered about the nature and forms of help asked for and offered, and the extent to which such aid enables persons to proceed further along their life course with reinforced and renewed purpose.

Observations have shown that, when persons in mid-life turn to professionals for help, they usually do so at times of acute personal and/or familial distress. Often they are offered specific, crisis-oriented services, geared to relieving the immediate presenting problem, with little concern for the broader developmental issues that may have induced or influenced the stressful situation. In other settings, they may be treated by a variety of psychotherapeutic or social interventionist methods in which the mid-life issues are ignored or submerged. When effective, lasting assistance is given—in family service agencies, health or mental health settings, or in private practice—decisions and directions often appear to be based more on professionals' pragmatic practice wisdom, honed by years of personal experience in "what works," than on clear, well-articulated guidelines determined by tested theory.

Structure of Book

We shall examine the entry into late mid-life from the dual viewpoint of the men and women who are passing over this bridge and of the professionals to whom they turn, or are referred, for assistance. The book is divided into four sections:

Part I deals with significant theoretical perspectives on late mid-life, presenting several approaches as background material against which we can scrutinize the reactions of individuals and families to changes taking place in one or more persons that markedly affect the rest of the family system, and the tasks that must be accomplished in order to pass through this stage. Recent developments in helping persons deal with transitions are described.

Part II examines separately the potential difficulties that can arise during these years and the problems they engender within the individuals' biophysical and psychological areas. It also examines the shifts that take place in the individuals' work and career worlds, the pressures that alter their ties with their adult children, the realignments they must make to maintain their bonds with aging parents, and the events that upset their marital balance. Not only will theoretical and research findings be presented, but issues will be illustrated through the use of vignettes and descriptions based on six "master case situations" that have been developed from a bank of actual material collected over the past few years. Each vignette will highlight a particular aspect of the total "slice of life" with which the individual or couple is struggling at the time. (It should be stressed that these cases are edited, masked composites of real-life situations and do not represent actual, identifiable cases.)

In Part III the focus shifts from the various life situations in which individuals and couples may be experiencing difficulties to the ways in which they ask for and receive help. To illustrate what was and can be done, the six case situations are reassembled and presented in their entirety: First, a summary of the initial interview, in which help is requested, is provided. Then, in order to give an overview of the alternatives that can be used, we turn to a panel of experts, the "best practitioners we could find," who offer their opinions as to how such help should be administered. Finally, we present a condensed version of how aid was actually given and how it changed the client's situation.

Part IV attempts to put the theory from Part II and the practice from Part III together to consider the implications of using this view of the transition to late mid-life as the operational framework in which to deal with problems arising at this life stage. Certain conclusions will be offered that may have some influence on the way intervention can be carried out by professionals and on the way practice can be taught.

To my knowledge, although some transitions, such as the divorce process, widowhood, and retirement, have been considered within the crisis intervention framework, few authors have dealt with the interlocking and interacting aspects of complex transitional states within the adult life span, such as the bridge to late mid-life. An increasing number of writers in academic and professional journals, it is true, have begun to address the overall topic of transitional changes. For example, Nancy Schlossberg's *Counseling Adults in Transitions*, which I encountered after the writing of this volume was well advanced, offers a somewhat similar framework in discussing many of the issues raised here from the viewpoint of counseling psychology. Hopefully, we are now seeing the beginnings of a burgeoning literature on how professionals from various disciplines work with clients during periods of adaptation and change.

To whom is this book geared? I see it as potentially helpful to several different types of readers. First, for the intelligent middle-aged adult who may be puzzled or troubled by the stressful and conflictual changes within his/her own life situation and is looking for clarification and possible means of getting help. Second, for the serious, inquiring professional who is seeking to increase his/her understanding of client dynamics during this period of rapid change and to broaden his/her range of interventive skills. Third, for agency executives and directors of professional services to use as a tool in setting up and revising treatment priorities and practice guidelines. And finally, for schools of social work, departments of clinical and counseling psychology, and marriage and counseling programs, to help round out source material on practice with individuals and families during this particular transitional period.

References

DATAN, NANCY, and NANCY LOHMANN, eds. *Transitions of Aging*. New York: Academic Press, 1980.

EICHORN, DOROTHY H., JOHN A. CLAUSEN, NORMA HAAN, MARJORIE P. HONZIK, and PAUL H. MUSSEN, eds. *Present and Past in Middle Life*. New York: Academic Press, 1981.

FRIED, BARBARA. *The Middle-Age Crisis*, rev. ed. New York: Harper & Row, 1976.

FUCHS, ESTELLE. *The Second Season: Life, Love, and Sex for Women in the Middle Years*. Garden City, N.Y.: Anchor Press, 1978.

GOLAN, NAOMI. *Treatment in Crisis Situations*. New York: Free Press, 1978.

_____. *Passing Through Transitions: A Guide for Practitioners*. New York: Free Press, 1981.

HALLBERG, EDMOND C. *The Gray Itch: The Male Metapause Syndrome*. New York: Warner Books, 1977.

HOWELLS, JOHN G., ed. *Modern Perspectives in the Psychiatry of Middle Age*. New York: Brunner/Mazel, 1981.

LeSHAN, EDA J. *The Wonderful Crisis of Middle Age*. New York: David McKay, 1973.

LEVINSON, DANIEL J., CHARLOTTE M. DARROW, EDWARD B. KLEIN, MARIA H. LEVINSON, and BRAXTON McKEE. *The Seasons of a Man's Life*. New York: Knopf, 1978.

MAYER, NANCY. *The Male Mid-Life Crisis: Fresh Starts After 40*. New York: Doubleday/Signet, 1978.

NUDEL, ADELE. *For the Woman Over 50: A Practice Guide for a Full and Vital Life*. New York: Taplinger, 1978.

RUBIN, LILLIAN B. *Women of a Certain Age: The Midlife Search for Self*. New York: Harper & Row, 1979.

SCARF, MAGGIE. *Unfinished Business: Pressure Points in the Lives of Women*. Garden City, N.Y.: Doubleday, 1980.

SCHLOSSBERG, NANCY K. *Counseling Adults in Transition: Linking Practice with Theory*. New York: Springer, 1984.

SIMON, ANNE W. *The New Years: A New Middle Age*. New York: Knopf, 1968.

TROLL, LILLIAN E., SHEILA J. MILLER, and ROBERT C. ATCHLEY. *Families in Later Life*. Belmont, Calif.: Wadsworth, 1979.

CHAPTER 2

Theoretical Approaches to Mid-Adulthood

Several mainstreams of thought have merged to form the theoretical background against which we examine the transition of the entry into late mid-life. In this chapter, we mention briefly some of the significant theoretical perspectives.

Psychodynamic Perspective

Carl Gustav Jung. Once a close colleague of Sigmund Freud and later founder of his own school of analytical psychology, Jung paid particular attention to the second half of the life cycle. He speaks of middle age as the third of his four stages of life, lasting from about thirty-five until around sixty-five, when it merges into old age. During this period, the person works primarily on *individuation*, the process of becoming "more uniquely himself." Starting at about age forty, the "noon of life," he seeks to find a clearer and fuller personal identity and to become more able to utilize his inner resources and to pursue his aims. As the process goes on, the person develops clearer boundaries between self and the external world, forming a stronger sense of who he is and what he wants and a more realistic picture of what the world is like and what it can offer to and demand from him.

Using complex analogies based on various systems of mythology, Jung sees the middle-age crisis as an existential search for both wholeness and meaning. Through the process of individuation the individual nourishes the "archetypal unconscious," the inner source of self-definition and satisfaction, which can enrich his own life in ways hardly dreamed of in youth. Although individuation has its painful transitions and setbacks, it holds the possibility of continuing self-renewal and creative involvement in one's own and others' lives. Jung defines the task of middle age as that of relinquishing the heroic ego and returning to the unconscious, using the opposite side of one's personality—the feminine component, *anima*, for men and the masculine component, *animus*, for women—as a guide, in order to achieve wholeness. Once the individual integrates this as the later years approach, he can accept the diminished capacities and increasing losses associated with old age more realistically and philosophically.

Erik H. Erikson. The seventh of Erikson's eight epigenetic stages of life has been termed "the period of maturity," with *generativity versus self-absorption* as the psychosocial crisis and *care* as the key issue. Generativity is taken to mean the commitment to care for others and the willingness to offer guidance and counsel. This also implies selecting what one chooses to care for (and about) and to reject other issues from one's concern. For example, middle-agers may be concerned with just their own children or grandchildren or with the grooming of specific social heirs with whom they have formed special relationships. The extreme of this position may lead to feelings of stagnation and alienation, to focus only on oneself and one's spouse, choosing not to broaden one's social sphere or to engage in creative and committed activities in the larger community.

Robert C. Peck. Building on Erikson's stages, Peck sees middle age as the start of the second half of life, a period of psychological change and adjustment during which four major tasks must be mastered. First, *valuing wisdom versus physical powers* implies that older persons can accomplish more than younger ones through the ability to make more effective choices available: using their heads over using their hands. Second, *socializing versus sexualizing human relationships* is interpreted as the opportunity brought about by the climacteric to take on a new type of value in which men and women are seen as individuals and companions, rather than primarily as sex objects.

Third, *cathectic (emotional) flexibility versus cathectic impoverishment* implies the capacity to shift emotional investments from one person to another and from one activity to another. When parents die, or when children grow up and leave home, circles of friends and relatives begin to break up; individuals need the ability to shift their interests to other ties in their community and vocational worlds and to develop new relationships and pursuits. Fourth, *mental flexibility versus mental rigidity* deals with the question of whether one can gain control over one's own life or whether one must be driven by external events and experiences. Some persons learn to use their own experiences to achieve a degree of perspective and to solve new issues, while others grow increasingly inflexible in their opinions and actions and become closed to new ideas.

Developmental Perspective

Robert Havighurst.   Using a stage approach parallel to but independent of Erikson's, Robert Havighurst defines mid-life in terms of a set of specific developmental tasks that the individual must master if he/she is to mature successfully. For middle age, which Havighurst sees as lasting from thirty-five to sixty, he lists seven such tasks to be undertaken:

Achieve adult civic and social responsibility
Establish and maintain an economic standard of living
Assist teenage children to become responsible and happy adults
Develop adult leisure-time activities
Relate to one's spouse as a person
Accept and adjust to the physiological changes of middle age
Adjust to aging parents

Havighurst calls these developmental tasks the "markers of change" along the life span. Some are precipitated chiefly through biological maturation; others by social role change. Yet each encompasses biological, psychological, and sociological components. Each task has its optimal point at which it should be mastered; failure or delay in carrying it out interferes with successful resolution of the next task.

Bernice L. Neugarten. As perhaps the most influential researcher and theoretician in the area of middle age, Neugarten's thinking over the past twenty years has colored many of the present approaches toward this stage. In her early research on how adults in Kansas City and Chicago viewed middle age, she found a striking change in time perspective: Middle-aged adults restructure time in terms of time-left-to-live rather than time-since-birth. She noted a heightened self-understanding that came from observing, on the one hand, their aging parents, and, on the other, their young adult children. She also found a sense of expertise that accompanies middle adulthood, as well as a feeling of accomplishment that was not only appropriate but to be expected. She was impressed with the heightened importance of introspection in the mental life of these mid-life persons, the stock-taking, increased reflection, and restructuring of experience, as well as the use of this knowledge and expertise to achieve desired ends and to hand over to others the fruits of their experience.

When her respondents were asked about their awareness of middle age, she and her colleagues found that most women tended to define their age status in terms of the timing of events within the family cycle. For married women, middle age was closely tied to the launching of children into the adult world; even unmarried career women discussed middle age in terms of the family they might have had. Men, on the other hand, perceived the onset of middle age by cues presented outside the family context, often within the work setting. Some of the men's most dramatic cues were biological: Their attention to their health increased, they noticed more their bodies' decreased efficiency, and they became very aware of the death of friends of the same age. They became concerned with "body-monitoring," while their wives showed more concern over their husband's health than about their own.

Neugarten also found that entering the fifties represented an important change in most persons' lives in terms of new perceptions of self, time, and death. Introspection seemed to increase noticeably and contemplation, reflection, and self-evaluation became characteristic forms of mental activity, foretelling the importance of reminiscences in old age. She saw significant differences between men and women as they aged: Men seemed to become more receptive to affiliation and nurturance, while women grew more responsive to and less guilty about aggression and egocentricity.

An interesting concept offered is that of the *social clocks* that operate in various areas of people's lives. Men and women become aware of their own timing and can see themselves as being "early," "late," or "on time" with regard to familial and occupational events. Neugarten (1968) notes the importance of changing age-role identity and points out that the timing of life events provides some of the most powerful clues to adult personality.

Perceptions, expectations, and actual occurrences of life events tend to be socially regulated and often class-bound. Thus an upper-middle-class man may not see himself as middle-aged until almost fifty, while a working-class man may perceive himself as middle-aged by his fortieth year. The upper-middle-class man often describes middle age as the period of his greatest productivity and of major rewards, the "prime of life." The blue-collar worker, however, depicts it in terms of decline: slowing down, physical weakening, becoming a "has been." In general, middle-aged men and women see themselves as the norm-bearers and the decision-makers, the generation "in command." They also see themselves as the bridge between the generations, both within the family and in the wider contexts of work and the community (Neugarten and Datan, 1974).

In considering how the individual adapts over time, Neugarten notes that changes in the timing of the family cycle have been dramatic in the past several decades: active parenthood is becoming shorter, children are leaving home sooner, and grandparenthood comes at an earlier age; widowhood, on the other hand, tends to occur later. More than 50 percent of the women aged forty-five to fifty-four are now in the labor force, a trend that has definite implications for spousal relations during the lengthening postparental interval.

The life cycle tends to "fan out," to become increasingly fluid, with a greater degree of variability and a growing number of role transitions occurring. It takes on a new rhythm for those who marry, divorce, and then remarry. Large numbers of women are now rearing children in first two-parent, then one-parent, then again two-parent households. Women work outside the home, then stop to rear their children, then return to school part or full time, then go on to work again.

With all of the research carried out during the 1970s on stressful life events, Neugarten was one of the first to point out that normal, expectable life events do not in themselves constitute crises nor are they necessarily trauma-producing. They become *turning points*, markers that punctuate the life cycle and call forth changes in self-concept and sense of identity. They indicate the efforts to incorporate new social roles and precipitate new adaptations. On the other hand, unanticipated life events that occur "off time" are likely to evoke major stresses and crises as they upset the sequence and rhythm of the life cycle.

Daniel J. Levinson. Taking a different view of the life cycle from that of Neugarten, Levinson (1978) sees men's lives as proceeding in a series of sharply demarcated steps, with alternate periods of relative stability and stormy transitions. During middle adulthood, which he views as lasting from ages forty to sixty-five, he differentiates between two transitional intervals, the *Mid-Life Transition*, which lasts from roughly thirty-eight to forty-three and serves as a bridge from early to middle adulthood, and the *Age-Fifty Transition*, from about forty-eight to fifty-three, during which the structures formed in the mid-forties are modified.

Levinson views the first transition as the time when a male must work on three major tasks: *to terminate the period of early adulthood, to take the first steps into mid-adulthood, and to deal with the polarities that are the sources of deep division in his life.* These polarities may include resolving the young/old, destructive/creative, masculine/feminine, and attachment/separateness dichotomies. He becomes far less specific about the second transition, at age fifty, except that he sees it as a "second chance" to work on the tasks of middle age and to repair the crises that inevitably must occur:

> For many men, this transition is relatively smooth and undramatic. They use it to make minor changes in life structure but continue on the same general path. For other men, the Age Fifty Transition is a time of moderate or severe crisis. It is likely to be an especially difficult time for men who went rather smoothly through the Midlife Transition, without examining themselves or making necessary changes in their lives. At 50, the chickens may come home to roost. [1980, p. 287]

George Vaillant. Characteristic of a number of major longitudinal studies currently being carried out on the adult life cycle, Vaillant found evidence among the ninety-five Harvard men he studied that confirmed Erikson's stages, although he suggests placing an intermediate stage of *career consolidation* between Erikson's sixth stage of *intimacy versus isolation* and the seventh stage of *generativ-*

ity versus stagnation. He also predicted that another stage would appear in the mid-fifties, that of *keeping the meaning versus rigidity.* Like Neugarten, Vaillant feels that crises and major stresses are not an inevitable part of mid-life, unless unexpected events intrude.

Marjorie Fiske. * In examining how the concept of self changes over adulthood, Marjorie Fiske and her associates, Majda Thurnher and David Chiriboga, found that, as men approached postparenthood, they seemed absorbed in work-related problems: Conscious that their careers had peaked, they experienced pressures to provide sufficient income over the next ten to fifteen years to maintain a comfortable life-style at retirement. Many of their preoccupations and anxieties dealt with job frustration and/or economic and political factors beyond their control. About a third suffered from severe physical health impairments. Some were remorseful that they had not achieved closer ties with their children or wives. On the whole, they represented a picture of combined strain and boredom.

Over the next five years, however, they developed an increasing mellowness, social ease, and comfort with themselves, moving from their earlier concerns over instrumental activity toward greater emotional sensitivity and interest in interpersonal relations. Their mastery styles shifted from an active and aggressive coping with the social environment toward a more nurturant, sensual, and affiliative orientation.

The middle-aged women in this study, as they faced postparenthood, appeared to start out in a far more critical condition than their male counterparts. Many seemed to lack confidence and to feel both troubled and dependent. Although pleased that their children were leaving home, they felt negative and apprehensive about the future, anticipating an increase in marital problems.

Yet when interviewed five years later, many of the women reported themselves as happier than before. Some had achieved this through nurture of their husbands; others had initiated major changes in their lives through new training, new jobs, new houses, new husbands or boyfriends, or extensive trips abroad. In general, they seemed to be moving in the opposite direction from the men, toward assertiveness, mastery, and self-confidence. In terms of coping style, they were changing from a submissive and nurturing orientation to a more aggressive and self-centered one.

*Some of her earlier writing is presented under the name of Marjorie Fiske Lowenthal.

Sociological Perspectives

Family sociologists, who have long been interested in plotting the changes that take place over the family life cycle, find this task more complex than the depicting of individual life stages because different members of a family may be at different levels of development at the same time. Nevertheless, several paradigms have been developed that emphasize the changes in family structure and tasks to be carried out over the years.

Evelyn Duvall. Duvall sees the family life stage of the middle years as starting with the departure of the first child from the home and continuing until the retirement of the husband or the death of one of the spouses—a stage that may last from a few years to a relatively long span.

Within this interval, she lists separate developmental tasks for the postparental woman and the postparental man and for the two of them together as a family. The woman must:

Encourage young adult sons and daughters to be autonomous
Maintain a healthy sense of well-being
Enjoy career and creative accomplishments
Relate to aging parents
Keep her social life satisfying
Assume civic and community responsibilities

Similarly, the middle-aged man must:

Keep up his appearance and health
Pursue his job interests
Cultivate satisfying leisure-time activities
Carry community and political responsibility

The two-member family must also carry out a full complement of family developmental tasks:

Provide for comfortable, healthful well-being
Allocate resources for present and future needs
Develop patterns of complementarity
Undertake appropriate social roles
Assure marital satisfaction
Enlarge the family circle
Participate in life beyond the home
Affirm life's central values

Duvall sees the last task, the affirming of values, as reflecting the life-style the couple has worked out over their life together as well as influencing and being influenced by the values of previous and later generations.

Elizabeth Carter and Monica McGoldrick. Typical of the frameworks developed as the conceptual base from which to teach systems of family therapy, Carter and McGoldrick divided the life cycle into six steps. In their fifth stage, the launching of children and moving on, they see the key principle as that of accepting a multitude of exits from and entries into the family system. They see four "second order" or fundamental changes required in order to have the family proceed developmentally:

1. Renegotiation of the marital system as a dyad
2. Development of adult-to-adult relationships between grown children and their parents
3. Realignment of relationships to include in-laws and grand-children
4. Dealing with disabilities and death of parents (grandparents)

Women's Perspective

A chapter on theoretical approaches would not be complete unless we mentioned at least two of the considerable number of researchers who have studied mid-life women. While rather eclectic in content and thrust, the various authors share a common interest in differentiating women's developmental experiences, roles, and problems from those of men.

Carol Gilligan. Gilligan has made a lasting contribution to life span theory by pointing out that, since masculinity is defined through *separation* while femininity is defined through *attachment*, male gender identity is threatened by intimacy, while female gender identity is threatened by separation. Thus, men tend to have difficulties with relationships while women have problems with individuation.

The image of women arriving at mid-life childlike and dependent on others is belied by their previous activities in nurturing children and sustaining family relationships. Women, having reached this point with a psychological history different from men's, now face a different social reality, with different possibilities for love and for work and with a different sense of experience based on their personal knowledge of human relationships.

The events of mid-life—menopause and changes in family and work—can alter a woman's activities in ways that affect her sense of self. If mid-life brings an end to relationships, to the sense of connection on which she relies as well as to the activities of care through which she judges her worth, then the mourning that accompanies all life transitions can give way to the melancholia of self-depreciation and despair. The meaning of mid-life events for a woman reflects the interaction between the structures of her thought and the realities of her life.

Janet Giele.   Giele points out that some people experience distinct stages of adult development while others do not. Observers of lower-middle-class or blue-collar persons, for example, do not find the same clear patterns emerging as do observers of the upper middle class or professionals, on whom much of the research is carried out. Moreover it is hard to disentangle how much change over the life course is due to growth and development, how much to the times in which one is born and grew up, and how much to the historical conditions under which one lives at the moment.

Giele sees a new kind of "role package" emerging in women's middle years that enables them to meet competing obligations in a different way. New social norms have emerged that reveal more tolerant and supportive public attitudes toward women's work, with special programs and policies for equal employment opportunities, flexible working hours, child care, and pension coverage. Women also receive support from both family and their social networks of friends, and neighbors, which affect their choice of career and conditions of work. No single role—being employed or being a full-time homemaker—guarantees women a high sense of competence and self-esteem. Much depends on the structure of the role and the value attached to it, as revealed, say, in her husband's attitude or in what her mother would have preferred for her.

From the various theoretical approaches to mid-adulthood presented in this chapter, we obtain a picture of the complex, crucial changes that occur to both men and women during the last part of their forties and the early part of their fifties. These shifts may occur in specific areas, but they also affect how individuals view themselves and how they interact with their families and significant others. In the next chapter, we shall examine how these changes occur and how professional help givers can aid the process.

References

BORENZWEIG, HERMAN. *Jung and Social Work*. Lanham, Md.: University Press of America, 1984.

CARTER, ELIZABETH A., and MONICA McGOLDRICK. "The Family Life Cycle and Family Therapy: An Overview." In Carter and McGoldrick, *The Family Life Cycle*. New York: Gardner Press, 1980: 3–20.

CHIRIBOGA, DAVID. A. "The Developmental Psychology of Middle Age." In John G. Howells, ed. *Modern Perspectives in the Psychiatry of Middle Age*. New York: Brunner/Mazel, 1981: 3–25.

————, and MAJDA THURNHER. "The Concept of Self." In Marjorie F. Lowenthal, Majda Thurnher, David A. Chiriboga, et al., *Four Stages of Life: A Comparative Study of Women and Men Facing Transitions*. San Francisco: Jossey-Bass, 1975: 62–83.

DUVALL, EVELYN M. *Marriage and Family Development*, 5th ed. Philadelphia: J. B. Lippincott, 1977: 355–383.

ERIKSON, ERIK H. *Identity and the Life Cycle: Psychological Issues*. Vol. I, 1. New York: International Universities Press, 1959.

————. *Adulthood*. New York: W.W. Norton, 1976: 25.

FISKE, MARJORIE. "Interpersonal Relationships and Adaptation in Adulthood." In Peter F. Ostwald, ed. *Communication and Social Interaction*. New York: Grune & Stratton, 1977: 265–275.

————. "The Reality of Psychological Change." In L. F. Jarvik, ed. *Aging in the 21st Century*. New York: Gardner Press, 1978: 97–111.

————. "Changing Hierarchies of Commitment in Adulthood." In Neil J. Smelser and Erik H. Erikson, eds. *Themes of Work and Love in Adulthood*. Cambridge, Mass.: Harvard University Press, 1980: 238–264.

GIELE, JANET Z. "Unanswered Questions." In Giele, ed. *Women in the Middle Years*. New York: John Wiley & Sons, 1982: 1–35.

GILLIGAN, CAROL. *In a Different Voice*. Cambridge, Mass.: Harvard University Press, 1982.

————. "Adult Development and Women's Development: Arrangements for a Marriage." In Janet Z. Giele, *Women in the Middle Years*. New York: John Wiley & Sons, 1982: 89–114.

HAVIGHURST, ROBERT J. *Human Development and Education*. London: Longmans, Green, 1953: 257–283.

JUNG, CARL G. *Collected Works*. Vol. 7. Princeton, N.J.: Princeton University Press, 1966.

LEVINSON, DANIEL J. "Toward a Conception of the Adult Life Course." In Neil J. Smelser and Erik H. Erikson, eds. *Themes of Work and Love in Adulthood*. Cambridge, Mass.: Harvard University Press, 1980: 265–290.

———, CHARLOTTE M. DARROW, EDWARD B. KLEIN, MARIA H. LEVINSON, and BRAXTON McKEE. *The Seasons of a Man's Life*. New York: Knopf, 1978.

LOWENTHAL, MARJORIE F., MAJDA THURNHER, DAVID A. CHIRIBOGA, and Associates. *Four Stages of Life: A Comparative Study of Women and Men Facing Transitions*. San Francisco: Jossey-Bass, 1975.

NEUGARTEN, BERNICE L. "The Awareness of Middle Age." In Neugarten, ed. *Middle Age and Aging*. Chicago: University of Chicago Press, 1968: 93–98.

———. "Adult Personality: Toward a Psychology of the Life Cycle." In Neugarten, ed. *Middle Age and Aging*. Chicago: University of Chicago Press, 1968: 137–147.

———. "Adaptation and the Life Cycle." *Counseling Psychologist* 6 (1976): 16–20.

———. "Time, Age, and the Life Cycle." *American Journal of Psychiatry* 137, 7 (1979): 887–894.

———, and NANCY DATAN. "The Middle Years." In Silvano Arieti, ed. *American Handbook of Psychiatry*. Vol. 1, 3. New York: Basic Books, 1974: 592–608.

———, and LORILL BROWN-REZANKA. "Midlife Women in the 1980s." In *Women in Midlife—Security and Fulfillment*. Vol. 1. Compendium of Papers Submitted to Select Committee on Aging and Subcommittee on Retirement. Washington, D.C.: U.S. Government Printing Office, 1978: 25–38.

PECK, ROBERT C. "Psychological Developments in the Second Half of Life." In Bernice L. Neugarten, ed. *Middle Age and Aging*. Chicago: University of Chicago Press, 1968: 88–92.

THURNHER, MAJDA. "Turning Points and Developmental Change: Subjective and Objective Assessments." *American Journal of Orthopsychiatry* 53, 1 (January 1983): 52–60.

VAILLANT, GEORGE. *Adaptation to Life*. Boston: Little, Brown, 1977.

CHAPTER 3

Bringing About Change:
Treatment Indicators and Models

By the time most adults reach their late forties and early fifties, they usually see themselves as being in the "prime of life." While they may look enviously at their children, who still have most of their lives ahead of them, and may worry about growing older, they still, by and large, regard themselves as the generation in command. They have learned to make decisions, to adjust to new role demands, and to deal with the various social complications that are bound to arise. Any regrets over past roads not taken are tempered, for the most part, by the satisfaction of having learned to cope, with relative effectiveness, with life's challenges.

This is why the complications that arise during the transition to late mid-life often have such a drastic effect. Events that might have been taken in stride at other, more stable, life stages now trigger widespread disruptions, some rooted in severe external pressures, some rising out of internal personality or developmental complications, and some a combination of both. And these are set in the complex matrix of the various social systems of which the person in mid-life is a part and in which he/she has formed significant interactional ties: the occupational network in which he/she has been operating for the past thirty or so years; the marital system that might include, not only a living mate but divorced or dead partners with whom he/she still has unfinished business; and the intergenerational family networks peopled by children, grandchildren, parents, and even grandparents. Any transitional disruption immediately triggers responses and countertransitions on the part of these others. Bringing about change may become an arduous process involving negotiations and compromise.

Disruptions of Change

Several years ago, prize-winning journalist Ellen Goodman developed a scale of changes that occur during turning points in people's lives. These range from *lightweight changes*, which are clearly to our advantage and involve little risk or changes in central beliefs; *middle-range changes*, which produce growth and involve more risk and in which we have to let go some of the past in order to advance; and *heavyweight changes*, which seem to hinge on loss and often produce crises. These intense turning points may revolve around the death or departure of someone loved or depended on, the failure to achieve a counted-on goal, or the final frustration of some vital and cherished dream. Sometimes the crisis lies in the conflict between two kinds of loss, two opposing risks.

Along similar lines, David Kaplan, one of the early social work theoreticians on crisis, has recently introduced a new classification of human disturbances that he calls "disorders of change."* He defines these as the "brief personal struggles to adapt to changes in the psychological and social phenomena that affect individuals" and sees intervention in such disorders as affecting both the individual who undergoes the change and the significant others and social systems that are part of the impinging environment (Kaplan, 1982).

Kaplan offers several specific characteristics of such disruptions that are pertinent to our discussion. First, they involve problem-solving struggles in which successful outcomes are linked to the resolution of common, empirically determined coping tasks specific to each change. Second, problem-solving involves cognitive, affective, and decision-making elements that enable us to evaluate the adequacy of the coping struggle. Third, although the actual disorders of change may be brief and often bring about their own resolutions, they can also result in lasting complications for a significant number of persons undergoing them. Finally, outcomes can be either normal

*I would prefer the term "disruptions of change" because of the pathological implications of the term "disorders."

and adaptive or morbid and maladaptive. Intervention should be reserved, in Kaplan's opinion, for those who manifest maladaptive responses and cannot resolve the coping tasks effectively without help. The goal of professional treatment becomes that of helping the individual or family replace ineffective problem-solving methods with more effective ones.

Basic to all intervention in disorders of change, says Kaplan, is understanding what is involved in successful adaptation. Each situation involving change poses common coping tasks that can be identified, as well as specific behaviors that can be effective in resolving these tasks. Treatment thus becomes focused on *helping the person or family engage in the coping tasks that will result in a healthy, positive outcome, free of complications.* Other targets for intervention may be one or more of the *other persons* in the familial or social networks who are in a position to influence the individual undergoing the change or the *social systems* whose policies and personnel may affect the situation.

At this point, let us look more closely at ways in which transitional situations can be assessed and treated, in order to deal with these disruptions of change.

Types of Transitional Problems

Few persons asking for help indicate that they are in a mid-life transition. Instead, they come—or are sent—with specific problems in intra- or interpersonal functioning, which they can no longer manage either by themselves or with the aid of the various natural help givers to whom they may have previously turned for assistance.

What types of transitional problems do they bring? Often, we find persons or families struggling with:

1. *The inability to separate themselves from the past*, to put situations over which they have little or no control behind them and to distance themselves from earlier associations with persons, places, or work situations that are no longer pertinent or appropriate. An example might be a spouse's trying to hang onto a marriage that has already soured and where the partner has already made the choice to leave.
2. *The inability to come to a decision* as to which path to choose, which direction or role to take, and the implications inherent in the choice. A typical situation might be a mid-life

woman's need to find some area of central interest but feeling unable to choose between work, further schooling, or community involvement.

3. *The difficulties in carrying out the decision made,* in finding the appropriate resources available, in obtaining the right information as to the expectations of self and others in the new role, and in preparing oneself adequately to carry out the decision or to cope with the new conditions imposed by the choice. For instance, a widow might decide to try to become self-reliant, rather than depend on her children for support, but experiences difficulty in mobilizing herself to locate sources of training, funding, living arrangements, etc.

4. *The difficulties in weathering the period of adjustment,* in adapting to unfamiliar conditions and new role demands until the changes become stabilized and the person feels comfortable in his/her new life situation and has developed an adequate network of support systems. A former pilot with a newly developed heart disability may have a long and arduous time adjusting to the new position found for him, that of reservations clerk, with its lower prestige and limited sources of gratification.

While these problems are specifically tied to "stuck points" in the process of change and adaptation, other problems may be less directly connected with transitional adjustments. Nevertheless, even if a problem is not overtly part of the changes described in Part II, some aspects of the broader situation may have transitional elements that prevent resolution of the initial difficulty and deserve closer scrutiny. Some situations may be outcomes of maladaptive or inappropriate resolutions to earlier transitions that can now be renegotiated in order to help the person "get on with his life." For example, in Chapter 12, Mr. Carter's response to being fired from his executive position three years previously was to start drinking excessively. He presented his problem as that of his wife's desire to leave him, yet helping him resolve his employment issue was an important aspect in effecting change in his situation.

Assessment of the Transitional Elements

What needs to be examined when we suspect that an applicant for help seems to be at a stuck point? In working with persons who are in the forty-eight to fifty-three age bracket, or with families in which someone in this age group is involved, the initial interview should include obtaining the information and making the judgments needed to determine whether use of a transitional approach is appropriate.

This means asking certain types of questions and paying particular attention to certain aspects of the client's situation. Nancy Schlossberg, who has written extensively in the area of transitions, sees assessment of a transition as covering three sets of factors: the characteristics of the person or persons involved, the characteristics of the pre- and post-transitional environments, and the characteristics of the transition itself.

The characteristics of the individual that need to be taken into account would encompass such factors as his/her psychosocial competence (which would include attitudes about oneself, views about the world, and behavioral attributes), sex and sex-role identification, age and life stage, state of health, race and ethnicity, socioeconomic status, value orientation, and previous experience with transitions.

The attributes of the environment—which Schlossberg defines as including the interpersonal support systems, the institutional supports, and the physical setting—must also be assessed. The social support system would include three different types of bonds: intimate relationships, family units, and networks of friends. Institutional supports would involve occupational, religious, political, social welfare, and community networks. The physical setting would refer to climatic and weather conditions, urban or rural location, neighborhood features, living arrangements, and aspects of the workplace.

Examination of the transition itself would include perception of whether the person is engaged in a role gain or loss, whether the affect associated with the transition is positive or negative, whether the change is internal or external, whether it occurs on-time or off-time, whether the onset is gradual or sudden, and whether the transition is permanent, transitory, or of uncertain duration. In addition, some estimate of the degree of stress involved should be made.

In Schlossberg's view, adaptation to the transition would depend upon the individual's resources and deficits and upon corresponding differences in the environment and the various support systems involved. Transitions occur when an event or nonevent—something that should have occurred but didn't—results in a change in assumptions one makes about oneself and the world and a corresponding change in behavior and attitudes.

To return to our specific transition to late mid-life, the judgment that the transitional approach is appropriate should be made relatively early, and certain indicators can assist in the choice. The six master case situations that we shall be examining in Part III, which we have taken to be typical of many individuals and families at this time of life, all deal with very different persons, with different backgrounds, different complications in social functioning, and different presenting problems.* Yet they all have several factors in common.

To begin with, all of the persons concerned have had histories of adequate, positive coping and problem-solving patterns over their adult years. Thus Mrs. Alberts in Chapter 10, who might be considered to have made the most maladaptive adjustment in view of her suicide attempt, had evidently been a model wife, mother and housewife until her oldest son was killed some thirteen years ago. Even after that, until recently she continued to function fairly adequately.

Second, no entrenched pathology or long-standing, intractable social problems that would severely limit the ability to intervene seem to be present. All of the applicants for help came with relatively new escalations in difficulties that grew out of reality situations with which they had been actively struggling and which are resolvable. For example, in Chapter 15, Mrs. Farwell's dissatisfaction with her care-giver role, which underlies her difficulty in making a decision about moving to Florida with her employer, is fairly recent in origin and, though it has spread to dissatisfaction with her social relationships and her worry about what she will do in the future, seems to be stage-related, tied to her having passed her fiftieth birthday.

Finally, in all of these case situations the individuals involved are prepared to take an active part in changing their situation. Even Mr. Carter in Chapter 12, the most passively dependent of the clients, indicated his willingness to participate in the change process, even if only on a minimal level at the start.

---

*We regret that all of these cases represent essentially middle-class backgrounds. Virtually none of the appropriate cases in our case bank represent lower socioeconomic levels—which opens the gates to a number of speculations as to the relative importance of transitions in people's lives.

If all of these conditions can be met, it seems appropriate to use a transitional framework. If they are not, or if other overriding factors take preference, it is doubtful whether stressing this aspect will result in adaptive change.

The Transition Model of Treatment

Once the assessment is made that use of a transitional approach is indicated, intervention can be planned accordingly. At the outset, it should be emphasized that treatment may vary considerably, depending upon the nature of the setting in which it takes place, the degree of discomfort and the desire to change on the part of the client or client system, and the community resources available that can be called upon to buttress direct intervention.

The particular treatment approach is also inextricably linked to the professional style and values of the therapist, which have been built up over years of experience with *this* kind of person, with *this* type of problem, in *this* sort of place. While one practitioner can become very busy leading an upset, confused, or depressed client through the maze of steps that have to be taken before change can become effective, another will lean back, smile encouragingly, and ask, "Well, what do *you* think should be done?" Treatment strategies and techniques are very much a matter of practitioner preference as to "what works" for him or her.

Keeping all this in mind, a number of models have been developed in recent years that show promise for treatment in transitional situations. Many social workers find that versions of the task-centered model developed by William Reid and Laura Epstein (1972) can be adapted to their particular style, setting, and clientele. This model has already been recast for use in active crisis situations by Golan (1978: 84-94).

In this version, the *beginning phase* encompasses the practitioner's establishing contact, ascertaining the current situation, determining whether an active crisis exists, and setting up a working contract for further action. Initial focus is on the precipitating factor, the immediate incident or event that prompted the call for help. Once the person's subjective reactions to this event are elicited and explored, the social worker tries to establish the boundaries of the stressful situation by finding out the original point of change (hazardous event), the subsequent responses, earlier efforts to deal with the disruption and its effects, and the current dimensions of the situation: who is involved, how they are reacting, how this affects the client, how he responds, etc. Then, the clinician and client work out some form of initial agreement as to how and in which direction further intervention will take place.

In the *middle phase* of treatment, once the intense affective tone has been lowered, client and practitioner concentrate on certain central themes that appear to run through the case, such as loss or lack of appreciation, characterizing the client's interactions with others, both in the present and in the past. Where appropriate, the clinician may attempt to unlink past issues from present ones. Effort is focused on lowering affect, developing cognitive awareness, and bringing about behavioral changes; on the ways in which the person has tried to cope in the past with the same and similar situations; on how he/she can improve his/her coping patterns; and on the specific changes that need to be made. These are often phrased in terms of the tasks listed below, to be carried out by the client or by the social worker either with the client or on his/her behalf.

Finally, in the *ending phase*, the client and clinician make the decision that the former can continue on his/her own. They review their activities since the start of intervention, consider possible steps that the client can carry out independently and how he/she can use what has been learned. The overall message with which the client is left is that he/she has engaged in a constructive experience and has learned certain coping patterns that can be used during future stressful situations.

Treatment in developmental and transitional changes follows basically the same format, although the perspective is often broadened to cover a area broader than the immediate crisis (Golan, 1981: 251–271). Practitioners usually start with the present "stuck point," reach back to the disruption that triggered the upset or even back to the original marker event that started the process (for example, in the Alberts' case, to the death of their oldest son). Then they return to the present and immediate future as they concentrate on helping the client move beyond this stuck point, to master the impasse and achieve whatever goals have been set by working on specific coping tasks. The emphasis is on helping the person or family resume its forward momentum through the life span or to find a new, more appropriate direction.

At times, this joint work becomes fairly educative in nature as the clinician guides the individual or family into unfamiliar territory, teaching them to anticipate what may lie ahead during the fifties and sixties and to plan accordingly, helping them adapt to new role expectations, demands, and conditions. The use of support groups, geared to mutual aid in passing through difficult aspects of the transition, has been found to be helpful, particularly if combined with professional intervention.

Transitional Tasks

One of the most effective areas on which to concentrate during the intervention process is the coping tasks that each person or family must carry out in order to pass through the transitional process. These have been mapped out in a two-tiered series of specific steps that can be engaged in at the same time on parallel levels.

Material-arrangemental (instrumental) tasks refers to the obtaining of concrete resources and the setting up of substantive arrangements and services according to the following series of behavior-oriented tasks, the basis steps in problem-solving:

1. Recognizing the lack of supplies and services, the insufficiency or inappropriateness of the old conditions, and the need to do something about it.
2. Exploring available and possible solutions, resources, potential new or changed roles; investigating choices and options; weighing of alternatives.
3. Making a choice and implementing it by formal application for the solution, resource, or assuming the new role.
4. Starting to use the new solution or resource, to function in the new role; exploring expectations, limitations, requirements, conditions, etc.
5. Going through a period of adaptation and development of increasing competence until performance rises to acceptable norms and internal and external pressures decrease to manageable proportions.

Concurrently, the person/family may have to engage in the following *psychosocial (affective) tasks*, which are both cognitive and emotional in orientation.

1. Coping with the threat to past sense of security, competence, and self-esteem and dealing with feelings of loss and longing for the past.

2. Grappling with the anxieties and frustrations incurred in making decisions or in choosing the new solution, resource, or role with its accompanying feelings of pressure, panic, and ambivalence.

3. Handling the pressures generated in applying for the selected solution or resource, in taking on the new role, and in meeting the stress and frustration in implementation.

4. Adjusting to the new solution, resource, or role with its attendant shifts in position and status, feelings of inferiority and implied or overt criticism from others, and lack of initial satisfaction or perceived appreciation.

5. Developing new standards of well-being; agreeing to lessened gratifications, diminished satisfaction, and changed self-image until the level of functioning rises to acceptable norms and the person feels comfortable in the new situation or role, comes to terms with the new reality, and begins to seek different ways of gratification and enjoyment.

Many of these tasks, both arrangemental and psychosocial, are engaged in without conscious pressure or ambivalence; others may require considerable support, learning, and "girding of the loins." But they lie at the heart of the bridging process and can offer an appropriate guide by which the practitioner can help the client first examine and then cope with the complex process.

References

GOLAN, NAOMI. *Treatment in Crisis Situations*. New York: Free Press, 1978.

———. *Passing Through Transitions: A Guide for Practitioners*. New York: Free Press, 1981.

GOODMAN, ELLEN. *Turning Points: How and Why Do We Change?* New York: Fawcette Columbine, 1979.

KAPLAN, DAVID M. "Interventions for Disorders of Change." *Social Work* 27, 5 (September 1982): 404–410.

REID, WILLIAM J. and LAURA EPSTEIN. *Task-Centered Casework*. New York: Columbia University Press, 1972.

SCHLOSSBERG, NANCY K. "A Model for Analyzing Human Adaptation to Transition." *Counseling Psychologist* 9, 2 (1981): 2–18.

PART II

Potential Pitfalls En Route to Late Mid-Life

N OW THAT THE THEORETICAL FRAMEWORK for intervening in the transition to late mid-life has been set, we can examine the particulars of the dangers and difficulties that persons arriving at this stage in the life span may encounter.

We have separated the bridge into six parallel "lanes" (areas of concern), which will be examined independently, although it should be kept in mind that these lanes—to continue our metaphor— continuously intersect, merge, and diverge again. Moreover, we should recognize that the lanes, while separate, are inextricably bound together in the roadbed of a particular personality structure and are girded by familial, social, ethnic, racial, economic, and even political constraints.

The six areas that tend to affect middle-aged persons and their families are: biophysical reactions, psychological responses, shifts in work and career patterns, relations with adult children, ties with aging parents, and bonds with spouses. Each chapter in this part is devoted to a particular area, and in each we present theoretical material that appears pertinent and illustrate it with short incidents from the lives of six mid-life families: the Alberts, the Bennetts, the Carters, the Donnellis, the Eismans, and the Farwells. These examples have been "reconstituted" from information given in the case situations used as the basis for the treatment described in Part III.

Understandably, not all individuals passing through the transition to late mid-life experience any or all of the difficulties described. Nor are the ages forty-eight to fifty-four, the years of our bridging interval, sacred. Rather, we give them as approximations, general boundaries within which any, several, or all of these areas may be affected. Hopefully, readers will keep in mind that we are dealing with social rather than chronological calendars. Nevertheless, these are hazards that can and do occur. Persons who experience them do not always emerge unscathed; at times encounters with particular difficulties leave the victim permanently scarred and vulnerable.

But, as we learn more about these perils, we can learn as well how to deal with them, how to prevent further complications or mitigate the ones that have already ensued. This will be discussed in Part III.

One point should be mentioned at the outset. With few exceptions, which have been cited, the research findings often present a picture that is representative of the middle or upper class, largely white, elements in the population. Unfortunately, little identifiable material seems to be available on ethnic or racial minorities or lower socioeconomic classes that is relevant to our topics. Hopefully, as research continues in these areas, we may obtain a more representative picture.

CHAPTER 4

Biophysical Reactions

During the years of the late forties and early fifties, two sets of separate but interwoven physiological changes occur in both women and men that have a serious impact on their transition to late mid-life. The first is the various bodily reactions that come about as part of the lifelong aging process, while the second is the specific hormonal changes affecting sexual and reproductive functioning which escalate during these years.

The Aging Process

Bodily aging occurs gradually for both men and women, depending on a variety of genetic and environmental factors.* However, as late mid-life approaches, overt signs begin to appear—or become harder to mask. Sensory deficiencies, such as losses in hearing and sight, and the blunting of taste, smell, and touch sensations occur more often and to more people. Weight seems easier to put on and harder to take off; even when overall poundage may not increase, fat layers

---

*Because of the complexity of the material in this section, specific citations have been omitted, for the most part. Readers are referred to the references listed at the end of each chapter for details on sources.

tend to settle around the waist and hips. Hair starts to thin, gray, and grow brittle; hairlines begin to recede and "widow's peak" patterns in women and overall baldness in men become more prominent. Skin tends to become drier and more prone to wrinkles; faint lines around the eyes and mouth grow more evident; veins on the backs of hands begin to stand out and brown "liverspots" may appear. Varicosities along the veins of legs and thighs suddenly emerge.

Decreases in muscle strength and tone; aching limbs and swollen joints, particularly in damp weather; occasional breathlessness when climbing stairs and hills; digestive disturbances; and altered sleep patterns are common physiological complaints expressed at this stage. Irreversible changes in the central nervous system resulting from cell death, oxygen deprivation, and chemical changes in the cells themselves bring about a reduction in the efficiency of the brain's functioning and a gradual slowing down of reaction time.

Bodily illnesses that frequently occur at this time include essential hypertension (high blood pressure), cardiovascular accidents (strokes), diabetes, and cancer of various organs. Chronic complaints, such as arthritis, gallstones, and digestive disorders, tend to become aggravated. Changes in the cardiopulmonary system may result in complications such as asthma, chronic bronchitis, and emphysema. As the cardiovascular system undergoes physiological and pathological shifts, an increased tendency to arteriosclerosis (hardening and thickening of the arteries) and myocardial infarction (heart attacks) can be found. Excessive fatigue, palpitations, severe migraines, and insomnia are also reported.

One particular aspect that stands out is the psychosomatic nature of many of these physiological conditions. Medical researchers point out that disruptions in patterns of coping with psychosocial situations, such as shifts in roles and changes in social or professional statuses, tend to be highly correlated with these illnesses (Stein and Shamoian, 1981). Other determinants may be such high-risk factors as heavy smoking, elevated cholesterol intake, and obesity. Anxiety and depression have been found to be associated with such psychosomatic illnesses as peptic ulcers and heart disease. Immediate histories of intense conflict within families or at work are also frequently reported by patients. Research carried out by the Dohrenwends (1974) and by Holmes and Rahe (1967) and their successors has emphasized the significance of stressful life events on physical illness, which in turn increased the stress element, creating, in effect, negative feedback loops.

In general, age-related external and internal bodily changes and the emergence of life-threatening conditions and illnesses make middle-aged persons conscious that such changes can—and do— happen to them. Moreover, even if they do not experience the change themselves, they become more aware that disability and deaths are occurring among their contemporaries; they grow conscious of the irreversibility of the aging process and of their own eventual death.

While many of these biophysical changes occur equally to men and women, some aspects have been found to be particularly gender-related.

Men

In men, the gradual decrease in muscular strength is often experienced as "creaking" joints in shoulders, knees, elbows, and hips. Tossing a ball or playing body-contact games becomes more difficult and, despite widely publicized exceptions, marathon running and championship athletics must often give way to slower-paced sports—a major tragedy for those men whose social activities and self-image revolve around athletic performance.

Physiologically, mid-life men tend to become preoccupied with their internal bodily functions. Increased urinary difficulties, which sometimes lead to a gradual hypertrophy of the prostate and, in extreme cases, cancer, is a frequently expressed area of concern. Digestive processes are minutely monitored and self-medicated. Worry over the development of essential hypertension and heart attacks becomes prevalent.

Recent research has found that a rise in blood pressure does in many cases follow disruptions in coping patterns, such as often occurs during the transition to late mid-life. Similarly, myocardial infarctions, particularly in the form of atherosclerosis (damage to the inner surfaces of the coronary arteries) and coronary thromboses (blood clots) do rise sharply during this period. Such physical conditions have been found to be closely associated with anxiety and depression, although whether they were long-term prior conditions or immediate reactions to stressful life events remains an open question, say Stein and Shamoian.

One interesting series of studies by Friedman and Rosenman (1978) have attempted to work out personality profiles for individuals susceptible to heart attacks. They tried to differentiate between Type A persons, described as competitive, aggressive, hostile, restless, and pressured, and Type B persons, considered to be relatively nonaggressive, easygoing, relaxed, and noncompetitive. Type A men were found to be twice as prone to coronary heart disease as Type B men, with the factor of constant stress, which they tended to create for themselves and those around them, as the most significant factor.

This differentiation into personality types has aroused considerable controversy within the last few years, both on methodological grounds in terms of how the data were gathered, and because other factors, such as the existence of impinging situational or developmental circumstances, were not sufficiently taken into account. The reactions of the fifty-year-old men in one heart study, for example, clearly indicated that they were in the midst of the transition from the active orientation of youth to the more passive orientation of later years. The issue of whether personality traits can influence heart conditions is considered a promising area for study. Stress researchers such as Cohen and Lazarus feel that a considerable amount of work still needs to be done on both psychological and physiological components before the connections are conclusively established.

Physiological traumas often act as catalysts setting in motion chains of actions and reactions that have lasting impact on the lives of persons and families during the transition to late mid-life. The following incident portrays a dramatic but by no means unusual process:

In talking to a colleague, Robert Bennett described the effects of his first heart attack, which had occurred last year at age fifty-two, while he was lecturing at the university medical school. He is a prominent cardiologist and had long been aware that he himself was a potential "candidate." However, the continuous demands his extensive private practice made on his time and energies, his activities as head of the Cardiology Department at Meadowlake Hospital, and his work as a leading consultant kept him from paying close attention to his own condition until his first cardiac arrest. Once it occurred, however, he resolutely decided to simplify his life, as he always advised his middle-aged patients to do.

Dr. Bennett's interest in cardiology stemmed from his own family history: His father had a heart condition, along with other complications, as the result of an early bout with rheumatic fever. One uncle had died at a very young age of a cardiac infarction and a second had undergone bypass surgery twice. He recalls that last year, lying in his hospital bed, he had to confront himself; he knew that, with his family history, at his age, and with his numerous pressures, he had become a high-risk case. He didn't want to worry his wife, so he decided to make some changes himself.

Once back at work, he began cutting down on his practice and turned over a number of his cases to his partners. He also gave up most of his administrative duties at the hospital and the extensive community activities he had taken on over the years. He began to watch his diet and to play at least an hour of tennis each day and golf on weekends. He rearranged his weekly schedule so that he'd come to the office only three days, then would drive down to Boston to take part in a two-day research program on problems in heart transplantation, a topic in which he had long been interested.

Today, at fifty-three, he says he feels great. His own physician told him last week that his physical condition is better than it has been for years. He knows that he has to keep monitoring his "ticker," but he feels his most productive years still lie ahead, now that he has changed his style of life.

Women

The continuous struggle to ward off the inroads of the aging process, particularly when seen against the backdrop of the predominant emphasis in Western culture on the desirability and attractiveness of youth, assumes greater urgency for many women as they approach their fiftieth birthday. While modern developments in health, exercise, and diet patterns have placed the forty-year-old woman at the height of her vitality and sexual appeal, ten years later she is no longer able to hide the effects of aging. The appearance of her skin and hair becomes a source of constant anxiety. Decreased activity and lower metabolism reduce her need for a high-calorie diet so that, unless she modifies her eating habits drastically, she often gains weight. As already noted, her body fat becomes redistributed, as hips and waist grow thicker and "middle-aged spread" develops. Subcutaneous tissue along the upper arms thins out, giving them a flabby appearance; overall muscle tone lessens and the breasts, which have already started to sag, now lose more of their fullness, leaving them flatter and more pendulous. Body stature often shrinks and bones become more brittle. All of these external changes make women prime candidates for fad diets, cosmetic surgery, health farms, and aerobic exercise programs in the ongoing effort to keep themselves attractive and to slow down, if not halt, the erosion of the years.

The centrality of this concern over youthfulness and good grooming become evident in the following incident, which is the "other side of the coin" to the one presented above. It gains poignancy when a woman equates being desired and desirable with maintaining a youthful facade:

"It's not fair!"

The words kept echoing through Helen Bennett's head as she lay on the massage table, while Thelma, her favorite masseuse, pummeled her mercilessly.

She just cannot keep it up! After all the years that she's denied herself food, gotten up at ungodly hours to jog and play tennis, starved on Weight-Watcher diets, and wiggled for Jane Fonda . . . now she has to start all over again!

Bob had always told her how proud he was of her youthful, well-groomed, perfectly turned out appearance, of the high standard she set for young doctors' wives to follow. But he never knew how much it cost her, how great the effort was. Ever since she was a kid back on the farm in central Pennsylvania, she knew she'd only have herself to depend on to climb out of that rut. Since her only assets were a good face and passable figure, she decided to make the best of them. She remembered in college spending hours on her nails and her hair and her skin when she should have been studying or sleeping. Still, it paid off when she was chosen prom queen and met Bob. . . . Even though he hadn't any money, she recognized in him the same ambition to "make it" as she had.

So she never relaxed, never allowed herself to "let herself go." When the children were small, she'd do Canadian air force exercises while cleaning house and give herself a facial while preparing lunch. She remembered, later on, how proud she'd feel when strangers would take her for the girls' sister instead of their mother. When Bob and she would give dinners for visiting hotshots or community leaders, she could see how much her youthful appearance, her carefully casual outfits would impress them.

And then yesterday, as they were sitting on the patio before dinner, Bob calmly announced that he wanted a divorce, that he was giving her up so that he could marry his thirty-six-year-old assistant. Even now, the thought of it made her feel sick to her stomach. After all these years, after all her efforts, Bob was throwing her out like a worn-out pair of shoes. She tried to keep herself youthful and trim for his sake . . . and now he wants to start over again with a younger woman.

"But what about me, how can I start over again? I'm too old at fifty to get back into the rat race. . . . It's not fair!"

Many women at this age become preoccupied with a wide range of chronic physical illnesses, such as arthritis, gallbladder disease, digestive disturbances, and high (or low) blood pressure. They spend long hours in their physician's offices, recounting their combined physiological and psychosocial discomforts and receiving, in turn, soothing attention, symptom relief, and prophylactic treatment.

Considerable discussion and controversy exist over how many of the symptoms and physical reactions experienced during this period may be attributable to the overall aging process and how many are directly tied to changes in endocrine functioning. Marilyn Block (1981), for example, maintains that loss of skin tone and elasticity, resulting in facial wrinkles and sagging breasts, may be the direct outcome of estrogen deficiency, while other symptoms, such as thinning hair, weight gain, headaches, insomnia, dizziness, nausea, osteoporosis, and atherosclerosis, have not been proven to be directly related to menopause and are, rather, linked to other changes or to physiological problems.

In all probability, what is taking place is a combination of three factors: the overall effects of aging, physiological weaknesses associated with particular inherited propensities, and specific climacteric and menopausal changes that may emerge at this time.

The Climacteric

The biophysical changes uniquely associated with mid-life are collectively known as the *climacteric* or *climacterium*. The term, which comes from the Greek, means, literally, "rungs of a ladder" and refers here to the physiological process that begins around the mid-thirties, for both men and women, and lasts well into the fifties for women and somewhat longer for men. It centers around changes in the endocrine glands, which secrete their hormones directly into the blood stream. The endocrines most directly involved in the climacteric are the anterior lobe of the pituitary, located at the base of the brain; the adrenals, situated on top of each kidney; and the gonads, which refer to the ovaries in women and the testes in men. All of these endocrines are linked in a complex feedback process in which changes in any one affect the others as well.

While we shall not go into the physiological changes to any depth, in order to grasp the nature of the changes taking place, it may be helpful to identify the various hormones involved. The two hormones secreted by the anterior pituitary in both men and women are known as gonadotropins, which include the follicle-stimulating hormone (FSH) and the luteinizing hormone (LH). Their function is to stimulate the production of steroids, which are manufactured by the adrenals and the gonads.

In men, the climacteric process occurs somewhat diffusely and gradually, while in women it climaxes in menopause, which usually occurs between the ages of forty-eight and fifty-four and refers specifically to the slowing and ultimate cessation of the monthly menstrual cycle. Let us examine these two processes separately.

The Male Climacteric

Sexual functioning in men is regulated by the equilibrium maintained among the three hormones: the two gonadotropins of the anterior pituitary, FSH and LH (often called ICSH in men), and the gonadal steroid, testosterone. As the body ages, the production of both sperm and testosterone declines, affecting both fertility and potency. While the rate and age of change may vary individually over time, the shifting balance between the anterior pituitary, the testes, and the other endocrine glands affect both physical and emotional aspects of bodily functioning. Symptoms of this imbalance may include vasomotor and metabolic disturbances, exhaustion, emotional instability, loss of sex drive, and feelings of irritability and depression. Physical changes may include a lessening in the firmness of the testicles, enlargement of the prostate gland, weakening in the force of seminal ejaculation and lessening in the amount of fluid, slowdown in erectile responsiveness, and shifts during sexual arousal from specific genital sensations to more diffuse bodily sensations.

Masters and Johnson found that sexual inadequacies, particularly impotence (inability to initiate or maintain penile erection), take a sharp upturn at about age fifty. Moreover, the fear of losing sexual ability often results in a self-fulfilling prophecy: Even when sexual activity does take place, the normal male at this age may take double or triple the time a young man needs to achieve an erection after sexual stimulation. A man at this age ejaculates semen with about half the force of youth and may require up to twenty-four hours before experiencing another erection.

Symptoms of climacteric changes fall into three categories: physical symptoms, such as malaise, lassitude, weakness, easy fatigability, lethargy, and poorly defined pain or hypochondriasis; emotional symptoms, which range from variable degrees of depression, including somber and morose mood swings, feelings of hopelessness, self-depreciation, and withdrawal, to reactions of indecisiveness, anxiety, irritability and/or hostility, and even occasional panic episodes, outbursts of rage, or crying spells; and sexual symptoms, such as the reduction or loss of libidinal urges, inadequate erections, and occasional to total impotence. While only a small percentage of mid-life men may report such disturbances, their actual incidence is probably considerably higher, since men are culturally expected to be strong and not to complain.

Several sets of dynamic factors seem to be interacting in a circular pattern during the male mid-years. In addition to the endocrine changes directly attributable to the climacteric, men's overall physical slowing down and societal expectations as to how they should behave all feed into the process. The man on the threshold of his fifties finds that he is expected to show strength, be competitive, and display virility just at the time when he may be experiencing difficulties in his work, family life, and other personal relations. These difficulties become amplified by the inner feelings of anxiety, fear, and hopelessness with which he views his decreasing physical and intellectual functioning and the slowing down of his sexual prowess.

How does this look in actual life? The following episode reflects the complex cause-effect pattern expressed in terms of sexual inadequacy:

"Martha?"

Roy Carter whispered his wife's name as he opened the bedroom door. Martha had been unusually pleasant this evening. For the first time in weeks, she had come home from work early, put a roast in the oven, and served dinner in the dining room. She had been very attentive when he told her of his job interview that afternoon with the head of an eastern company who was looking for an area representative to distribute their computer software. Even though the guy hadn't promised anything, he asked for more particulars and Martha had even made a few suggestions to improve his résumé.

Then, after dinner, the Warrens, who lived next door, stopped in. They sat around on the patio and he and Jack swapped stories about the old days at Norton Aircraft, before the plant was sold—Jack had worked under him in administration. By the time they left, they had had several rounds of drinks and he was feeling very mellow. Martha had gone straight to bed because she had an early morning appointment, but he volunteered to load the dishwasher and empty the ashtrays. After a couple of extra drinks to "keep up the glow," he started up the stairs and then paused, leaning against the wall.

Martha and he hadn't been getting along well for a long time. Ever since Norton had folded and he hadn't been able to find another job, things had been souring. Oh, at first she tried to help and gave him a lot of encouragement. But since about a year ago, when she went out and got a job for herself, her message has been getting stronger: She doesn't need him anymore; she can get along without him; he's over the hump and no good to her. She's even accused him of becoming a drunk. . . .

Years ago they used to talk about how good it would be when the four kids were out of the house and they could be by themselves, do what they wanted to do when they wanted, for as long as they wanted. Sure, neither of them pretended a great undying love for each other, but it wasn't bad. One thing was for sure—they always had great sex.

But this last year Martha had changed. One thing he had always been able to count on: Even though she'd be mad at him, once he got her in bed things would become fine. But those great times were getting farther and farther apart. . . .

Now he slipped quietly into the room and stripped quickly, throwing his clothes down on the floor next to the bed. Feeling the

familiar tautness in his groin, he slipped into the wide bed, whispering again, "Martha?"

"Hmmmmm?" She turned over sleepily and Roy began to caress
her breasts. Automatically, she began to respond, her arms slipping
down around his back and along his thighs. Suddenly, fully awake,
she pushed his arms away and sat upright. "Roy . . . why, you old
fool! What do you think you're doing? Take your hands away . . .
you're not good to me, no good at all. You haven't been able to make
it for months! Maybe it's the drinking, maybe it's your age, but all
you do is to get me excited and then leave me hanging on the limb.
And you stink like a fish! Just stay away from me; that's all I want
from you. . . ."

Abruptly she turned her back and moved over to the other edge
of the bed. And Roy Carter, now flat on his back and suddenly so-
ber, felt his muscles grow flaccid and his penis limp. Just an old has-
been who couldn't even keep it up!

The Female Climacteric

As with men, sexual development in women is regulated by the anterior pituitary and endocrine glands. During the monthly menstrual cycle, the gonadotropins, FSH and LH, interact with the
ovarian steroids, estrogen and progesterone, first to produce ova and
then either to allow the fertilized egg to develop or to terminate the
cycle and start over again.

As part of the aging process, the functional capacity of the ovaries begin to diminish and the production of hormones, particularly
estrogen, starts to drop, usually after the age of forty. This, in turn,
upsets the endocrinal balance, resulting in a number of physical and
emotional symptoms. Among the most common ones reported during the forties are emotional and nervous upsets, fatigue, depression, vasomotor disturbances (such as sweating and hot flushes),
metabolic changes, headaches, insomnia, and irritability.

Between the ages of forty-five and fifty, the decline in the production of estrogen and progesterone usually reaches the point
where the menstrual flow becomes irregular, both in terms of the
amount of flow and the length between periods, until it stops altogether. At the same time, the ovaries begin to atrophy and cease to
produce eggs; the two processes, occurring concurrently, result in

the loss of reproductive capacity. Once the flow has stopped, the anterior pituitary gland tries for a while to correct for the lack of estrogen by overproducing FSH; eventually, this, too, is lowered and the adrenal cortex gradually increases the production of another steroid, similar to estrogen except for the ability to make eggs ripen in the ovaries. Hormonal stability is thus restored.

Physiologically, the vagina itself loses length and elasticity at this time and its lining becomes thinner; the lubricating glands atrophy and a decrease in vaginal wall secretions ensue. Secretions also become more alkaline, with the external vaginal lips becoming thinner and wrinkled, which in turn exposes the urethral and vaginal openings and the clitoris, resulting in irritation. Internally, the uterus shrinks substantially, the walls of the urinary bladder and the lining of the tube leading out from it become thinner, and the supporting tissues of the pelvic organs lose strength. This in turn may cause a sagging of the bladder, urethra, and rectum, so that urinary incontinence may be experienced after straining, coughing, laughing, sneezing, or even walking.

Menopause has been termed the *rite de passage* in women's transition to later life. The significance of this term, however, is somewhat blunted by the fact that it can only be recognized retroactively: The usual medical determination is that menopause has occurred if *no menstrual flow has taken place for the past twelve consecutive months*. The actual age at which it takes place is governed by hereditary, constitutional, racial, and social factors, with a daughter tending to follow the menstrual pattern of her mother. No relationship has been found between the age of onset of puberty and the age of menopause, although some data have shown that the earlier a woman starts to menstruate, the later she stops. Despite common myths, neither the number of children born nor the age of first sexual activity affect menopausal timing.

As already mentioned, the extent to which symptoms associated with the mid-life years can be attributed to hormonal changes that are part of menopause or to the overall aging process has been argued vehemently among gynecologists, general physicians, and feminists over the past quarter century, although the strident tone of the controversy has abated in recent years. According to Block, the Women's Medical Center of Washington, D.C. estimates that some 20 percent of women report no symptoms at all, 65 percent merely experience mild symptoms with which they can cope without medical intervention, and only 15 percent experience symptoms severe enough to warrant treatment.

Recent considered opinion seems to be that only two symptoms can be attributed *directly* to the declining hormonal production of the menopausal process: the thinning and loss of elasticity of tissue in the vaginal area and the so-called hot flashes. These hot flashes (or flushes) have been described as sudden feelings of warmth that pervades the upper part of the body, with the face becoming flushed and reddened and patches of red areas appearing on the upper cheeks, back, shoulders, and upper arms. They may be accompanied or followed by profuse perspiration. As the body temperature readjusts to its surroundings, the woman's body may feel cold and clammy. These symptoms may occur monthly, weekly, daily, or even every few hours and may last from a few seconds to over half an hour. They may occur during daytime or nighttime hours. The onset of such hot flashes is usually gradual and sporadic and may go unnoticed for several months or years. As actual menopause approaches, however, the flashes tend to become more frequent and intense; then, during the postmenstrual period, they gradually wane and disappear.

Complications of Menopause. Some evidence has been reported to show that the thinning of hair on a woman's head, while partially part of the overall aging process, becomes aggravated by the loss of estrogen, which also results in the receding of the hairline over the temples and the tendency to develop partial bald spots on the crown of the head. Similarly, without the inhibiting effect of estrogen, increased hair growth on the chest, chin, upper lips, and other parts of the body may occur. Most distressing to many women is the eruption of coarse hair along the chin line, making them acutely sensitive to their loss of femininity.

Medical authorities consider the most serious physical outcome of hormonal loss at this time to be osteoporosis, the thinning and gradually increasing porosity of the bones, which may eventually result in a tendency to bone breakage, particularly hip fractures. It may also lead, in some cases, to the so-called dowager's hump, an exaggerated forward curvature of the back due to the collapse of the anterior spinal vertabrae.

Many physicians, particularly gynecologists and internists, tend to prescribe estrogen therapy for their patients during the menopausal years and thereafter, seeing it as the only way to ameliorate and/ or prevent the disruptions of the later years.

On the other side of the ledger, some evidence has been produced by the American Cancer Society and other research sources that taking estrogen tends to aggravate or even cause cancer of the uterus, endometrium, or breasts, as well as increase the propensity for gall-bladder disease and clots in the cardiovascular system. Thus, physicians are now being cautioned as to the kind and dosages of estrogen they prescribe and to weigh the relative probabilities of the complications that may arise.

Some authorities go even further. They warn that estrogen therapy is *not* the universal panacea for aging and emotional disturbances. Its indiscriminate use as a fountain of youth, irrespective of the woman's symptoms, is unwarranted and may be dangerous.

Hysterectomy: Surgical Menopause. One of the most commonly performed surgical procedures in the United States is the removal of the female sex organs. This can take various forms—from a *simple hysterectomy*, where only the uterus and cervix are removed, to a *total hysterectomy*, in which the ovaries and the fallopian tubes are taken out as well. When the ovaries are not removed, ovulation still continues and menopause occurs at about the same time, or a few years earlier than expected.

Various reasons for engaging in such surgical procedures include the correction of pelvic relaxation or uterine prolapse, elimination of fibroid tumors within or on the surface of the uterus, endometriosis (growth of uterine tissue outside of the uterus itself), pelvic inflammatory disease, and sterilization. Although such operations are considered fairly safe, questions have been raised with increasing frequency as to their advisability in view of the physiological and psychological disturbances that may occur.

The performance of a hysterectomy as a prophylactic measure or to prevent ovarian cancer or other possible complications raises serious ethical questions among members of the medical profession. In general, current thinking seems to be that ovarian function should be preserved whenever possible in women under forty-five. In women over that age, ovaries should be periodically examined and, if any question arises, they should be removed. If the ovaries in a menstruating woman appear healthy, one or both may be left to ensure estrogen production. When postmenopausal women undergo hysterectomies and their ovaries are removed as a cancer prevention measure, the loss of estrogen secretion is far less serious.

Breast Cancer. Incidence of breast cancer peaks among women between the ages of forty-two and forty-seven. Then an eight-year plateau seems to occur before the rate starts to climb again in the early fifties. Recent research seems to indicate differences in the life histories between those who develop early breast cancer and those who develop it later in their life span: A family history of breast cancer and later age of the birth of the first child has been found to be more often associated with the disease in younger women, while breast feeding was thought to be a factor in its occurrence in older women, notes Block.

Breast cancer is usually treated surgically, and a mastectomy, the removal of a part or all of the breast, can have a strong psychological, as well as physical, impact. Postmenopausal married women who perceive their youth and sexual attractiveness as fading may be far more vulnerable to psychological problems than younger women in view of the other traumas that can occur at this age-stage. For example, losing a breast can have greater impact on women with bad or failed marriages than on those whose husbands are there to support them emotionally during and after surgery. When divorce occurs directly following surgery, it often becomes an excuse to get out of a situation that had already become perilous. (This point will be elaborated on in the next chapter.)

The following vignette reveals how a seriously ill woman reacts to her recent hysterectomy, which was performed in an effort to halt the growth of a malignant uterine cancer during menopause. Her medical problems are imbedded in a complex social situation that magnifies her distress.

Marie Donnelli lay on the sofa in the front room, a damp cloth over her aching eyes. From the bedroom she could hear the muted sound of the TV and the occasional rattle as Frank opened another can of beer. Sharon, in the kitchen, was trying to oversee the twins' supper while she fed the baby. The two-year-old boys kept asking querulously when they could go back home.

With a sigh, Mrs. Donnelli moved restlessly, the familiar nausea rising in her throat. She had just returned from another chemotherapy treatment at St. Vincent's outpatient clinic and still had three more to go to complete the series. But it never grew easier; in fact, after each treatment, the nausea grew worse. If only . . . Her mind drifted off along a well-worn treadmill. . . .

They had been such a happy family when the children were small. Frank really liked his job as investigator in the district attorney's office, though he was never able to go on to law school once he returned from the war in the Pacific. The children had come too fast: first Tom, then Sharon, then Lainey—Elaine, she corrected herself; she deserved more respect, now that she was the lawyer in the family. Paul came fourth; what a bad time she had at his birth! She never recovered completely and Dr. Perini strongly advised her not to have any more children, even offered to "fix her up" so she wouldn't become pregnant again. But their parish priest stood against it, so they tried to be careful instead. She had had her hands full raising Paul because he was such a delicate child, always ailing and clinging to her.

After he started kindergarten, however, she missed caring for him; maybe that's why she became pregnant again. This time she spent most of her pregnancy in bed, but once Joey was born, he turned out to be a tough little guy, always in trouble, but lovable, with a wonderful smile like his father's. But *so* spoiled; he could always get her to do what he wanted. . . .

Again her mind drifted . . . such a happy family; where had they gone wrong? Maybe it started with Tom's leaving for Canada. Frank had set such store by him, his first son. But the boy never would obey him blindly; more and more they argued—about politics, about Vietnam, about the draft. Then came that last terrible day when he didn't come home and they found his letter instead, saying he and two friends were hitching up north to cross the border. What a blow to Frank! He ranted and shouted that Tom had disgraced the Donnelli name forever and even threatened to call the FBI until she finally calmed him down.

Maybe that was the beginning. Things seemed to go better once Sharon got married, but her husband turned out to be a bum and a woman-chaser. Even the birth of the twins and, a year later, the new baby didn't keep him from drinking and beating her up. Finally Frank had to go up to Oakland and threaten him with the law. He brought Sharon and the children back with him and arranged for her to get a legal separation.

Again, Mrs. Donnelli shifted as she tasted the bitter bile in her mouth. She hadn't told Sharon about the tumors the doctors found in her womb six months ago, but she guessed anyway, being a nurse. She felt panicky whenever she forced herself to think about her illness. What would Frank do when she left him? She hadn't really been surprised, since her mother had died of it when she was forty-nine—just her own age. And Clara, her older sister, had had both breasts removed eight years ago.

She herself had been having irregular flows and severe abdominal cramps for the last four years and Dr. Perini had put her in the hospital several times. But once he discovered that the tumors in her womb were growing, he did a complete hysterectomy and then made her take chemotherapy treatments.

Now she's sure she will not recover; like her mother, she'll never see her fiftieth birthday. She doesn't mind for herself so much; she and Frank had had thirty good years together. He is *such* a good man, even though he sometimes has to act hard in the old Italian way. But once she's gone, how will he manage without her to soothe him and stand behind him?

And the grandchildren . . . she waited *so* long to see them. She just knows she'll never get to see how Sharon's children grow up. They're so little and lovable; she had already begun to dream of taking care of them, when Sharon would go back to work. But now . . . she was afraid. Silently Mrs. Donnelli began to cry once more.

The significant biophysical changes that occur during these transitional years, whether coming as part of the overall aging process or more specifically tied to hormonal processes as part of the male or female climacteric, add a complex dimension to the bridge to late mid-life, affecting all areas of intrapsychic and interpersonal functioning. The ripple effect of these physiological changes can be observed in the aspects discussed in the following chapters; the "change of life" has broad, interlocking ramifications.

References

BLOCK, MARILYN R., JANICE L. DAVIDSON, and JEAN D. GRAMBS. *Women Over Forty: Visions and Realities*. Vol. 4. *Focus on Women*. New York: Springer, 1981.

BOSTON WOMEN'S HEALTH BOOK COLLECTIVE. *Our Bodies, Ourselves*. New York: Simon & Schuster, 1976.

CHERRY, SHELDON H. "The Menopause and Postmenopausal Years (50–65)." In Cherry, *For Women of All Ages*. New York: Macmillan, 1979: 201–219.

COHEN, FRANCES, and RICHARD S. LAZARUS. "Coping and Adaptation in Health and Illness." In David Mechanic, ed. *Handbook of Health, Health Care, and the Health Professions*. New York: Free Press, 1983: 608–635.

COHEN, JESSICA, F. "Male Roles in Midlife." *Family Coordinator* 28, 4 (October 1979): 465–471.

DOHRENWEND, BARBARA S., and BRUCE P. DOHRENWEND, eds. *Stressful Life Events: Their Nature and Effects*. New York: John Wiley & Sons, 1974.

DONOHUGH, DONALD L. *The Middle Years*. Philadelphia: Saunders Press, 1981.

FRIED, BARBARA. *The Middle-Age Crisis*, rev. ed. New York: Harper & Row, 1976.

FRIEDMAN, M., and R. H. ROSENMAN. *Type A Behavior and Your Heart*. New York: Fawcett, 1978.

FUCHS, ESTELLE. *The Second Season: Life, Love, and Sex for Women in the Middle Years*. Garden City, N.Y.: Anchor/Doubleday, 1978: 193–216.

GUZINSKI, GAY. "Medical Gynecology: Problems and Patients." In Malkah T. Notman and Carol Nadelson, eds. *The Woman Patient*. Vol 1. New York: Plenum Press, 1978: 181–202.

HENKER, FRED O. "Male Climacteric." In John G. Howells, ed. *Modern Perspectives in the Psychiatry of Middle Age*. New York: Brunner/Mazel, 1981: 304–327.

HOLMES, THOMAS H., and R. H. RAHE. "The Social Readjustment Rating Scale." *Journal of Psychosomatic Research* 2 (1967): 213–218.

MASTERS, WILLIAM H., and VIRGINIA E. JOHNSON. *Human Sexual Response*. Boston: Little, Brown, 1966.

MORSE, DONALD R., and M. LAWRENCE FURST. *Women Under Stress*. New York: Van Nostrand Reinhold, 1982: 180–195.

MUSSEN, PAUL, JOHN J. CONGER, JEROME KAGAN, and JAMES GEIWITZ. *Psychological Development: A Life-Span Approach*. New York: Harper & Row, 1979: 410–445.

NACHTIGALL, LILA E., et al. "Estrogen Replacement Therapy I: A 10-Year Prospective Study in Relationship to Osteoporosis." *Obstetrics and Gynecology* 53 (1979): 277–287. Quoted in Donohugh, p. 133.

PERLMUTTER, JOHANNA H. "A Gynecological Approach to Menopause." In Malkah T. Notman and Carol C. Nadelson, eds. *The Woman Patient*. Vol. 1. New York: Plenum Press, 1978: 323–335.

SALES, ESTHER. "Women's Adult Development." In Irene H. Frieze, Jacquelynne E. Parsons, Paula B. Johnson, Diane N. Ruble, and Gail L. Zellman, eds. *Women and Sex Roles: A Social Psychological Perspective*. New York: W. W. Norton, 1978: 157–190.

STEIN, STEFAN, and CHARLES A. SHAMOIAN. "Psychosomatic Disorders in the Middle-Aged." In John G. Howells, ed. *Modern Perspectives in the Psychiatry of Middle Age*. New York: Brunner/Mazel, 1981: 266–278.

STRICKLER, MARTIN. "Crisis Intervention and the Climacteric Man." *Social Casework* 56, 2 (February 1975): 85–89.

WARING, JOAN. "The Middle Years: A Life Course Perspective: The Importance of Health." In Alvin C. Eurich, ed. *Major Transitions in the Human Life Cycle*. Lexington, Mass.: Heath, 1981: 471–489.

WEG, RUTH. "More than Wrinkles." In Lillian Troll, Joan Israel, and Kenneth Israel, eds. *Looking Ahead*. Englewood Cliffs, N.J.: Prentice-Hall, 1977: 22–42.

WILLIAMS, JUANITA H. *Psychology of Women: Behavior in a Biosocial Context*, 2nd ed. New York: W.W. Norton, 1983: 395–420.

CHAPTER 5

Psychological Reactions

Inextricably interwoven with the biophysical changes that occur during the transition to late mid-life are the perceptual, cognitive, affective, and behavioral adjustments that are taking place.

Perceptual and Cognitive Changes

As persons grow older, the acuity of their sensory perceptions tends to decrease. Visual ability must adjust to the physiological changes in the lens and other parts of the eye. Between the ages of forty-five and fifty-five, many adults become aware that they can no longer read clearly at their usual distance; they find they need glasses or, if they already wear them, they now require bifocals. Similarly, they may experience a gradual hearing loss in the high-frequency ranges, particularly if they have been exposed over the years to excessive amounts of noise. Some begin to lose their sensitivity to sweets and prefer sharper, tarter foods. On the other hand, smell changes rarely occur until after age sixty, while sensitivity to light touch and to temperatures remain relatively constant throughout life.

Considerable laboratory experimentation on the question of loss of cognitive functioning has been conducted by psychologists. Reaction time has been found to be slightly slowed down, although in practical performance this is rarely noticeable. Ability to carry out specific tasks may decrease somewhat and is often affected by such factors as anxiety, motivation, meaningfulness of the material, and interference in test situations. By late middle age, an individual seems to need slightly more time to get ready to learn, is slightly slower in actual acquisition of information and skills, tends to retain earlier learned patterns longer, and is slower in test performance.

Intellectual Abilities. The extent of intellectual changes during middle age has proved to be a highly controversial issue. While scores on such specific intelligence tests as the Wechsler Adult Intelligence Scale (WAIS) have shown a decrease in the middle years, considerable disagreement exists as to exactly what is being measured on such tests. James Birren, for example, found that older individuals did as well as younger ones on tests measuring general experience but poorer in those involving manipulative skills, perceptual functions, and the processing of new material. Others found that vocabulary scores tended to increase with age, while the ability to abstract remained relatively constant.

Moreover, measurements of intelligence have been found to be influenced by such extraneous factors as educational level, recency of learning, physical health, and socioeconomic status. Increased stimulation through occupational activities, travel, and the media also affect intellectual performance. Overall, Jack Botwinick finds, the most feasible conclusion at this time seems to be that measurable declines may not appear before the ages of fifty or sixty and that even then the extent is minimal.

Nevertheless, differences do begin to appear in the *kinds* of intelligence affected. *Crystallized* intelligence, which comes from the acquisition of information and skills, seems to increase throughout most of adulthood, while *fluid* intelligence, the abilities affected by physiological changes, does show a gradual but steady decline. Evidently, as the person grows older, he/she learns to substitute accumulated wisdom for the brilliance of youth.

Affective Reactions

As men and women pass through the several phases of mid-life, they react to life changes with a wide range of responses. Several general patterns emerge. At one level, say Neugarten, they view middle age

as being the "prime of life" and themselves as the "command generation." With the removal of a number of family responsibilities and
pressures they feel effective, competent, and at the peak of their
powers. At another level, however, individuals become aware of numerous losses, both intra- and interpersonally, and react with feelings of depression and desperation. They express it in a number of
ways: disruptions in their customary ways of functioning, depression, alcoholism, admissions to mental facilities, and attempts at suicide.

To look first at those who do well at this stage of life, Norma
Haan examined the overall personality attributes that were measured over the span of fifty years in the several longitudinal studies
carried out at the Institute for Human Development at Berkeley.
She concludes that, at middle age, participants were more cogni-
tively invested, nurturant, self-confident, open, and introspective
than they were in their younger years. As a group, they gave no concrete evidence of underlying mid-life crises; instead, their adaptation seemed to reflect the accrued wisdom of persons who had
grown tolerant, socially and psychologically:

> Undoubtedly, personal fluctuations in response to unexpected life
> events, fortunate and unfortunate—deaths, births, illnesses, divorces,
> marriages and remarriages, promotions and bankruptcies—attentuate
> estimates of stability and become reflected in individuals' changes, up
> and down. . . . [Yet] despite the unpredictable traumas and dramas
> visited on some persons' lives, the "generalized" middle-aged persons
> . . . appear to be equipped by reasons of past experiences both to savor
> and to deal with themselves effectively and comfortably. [1981, p. 151]

A good deal of attention has been drawn in recent years to the
shifts in affective reactions that occur in both men and women in
the decade between forty-five and fifty-five. Reflecting Jung's basic
contention, many of the studies by developmental psychologists
show a shift in men's orientation from an active, instrumental attitude in youth to a more affiliative, affective one in mid-life, while
women, on the other hand, show the reverse (Rossi, 1980). David
Gutmann found in his anthropological studies that, regardless of
their culture, as women age, they seem to become more tolerant of
their own aggressive, egocentric impulses while men, as they age,
react similarly to their nurturant and affiliative feelings.

One interesting distinction in personality type was drawn by
Florine Livson, who examined the data from the Oakland Growth

Study. She found she could divide her male subjects, who were predominantly urban, middle-class, white, and psychologically healthy, into two groups, the *traditionals*, who fit the customary male role expectations, and the *nontraditionals*, who showed a different pattern. The traditional men, at age fifty, were less emotional and more controlled than the nontraditionals. They appeared to be more intelligent in an analytic, logical, objective way. They valued intellectual mastery, rationality, self-discipline, and achievements. In contrast, the nontraditionals were found to be emotionally expressive, sensuous, talkative, gregarious, and outgoing. They seemed to be more extroverted, other-directed, and less controlled, with a strong sense of meaning in their lives.

By age forty, the traditional men had already established a balanced personality and achieved their main goals in life; they did not change much between forty and fifty. In contrast, the nontraditional men, by age fifty, had changed a great deal in the past ten years. At age forty, they had been often angry and defensive, tending to project their anger outward in a blaming, punitive fashion, but ten years later they had become emotionally expressive, sensuous, talkative, gregarious, and sociable. Having apparently resolved their identity conflicts, they were now able to give up their exaggerated masculine posture and move toward greater intimacy with others.

Livson found that women, too, could be divided into these two groupings. At age fifty, traditional women were relatively gregarious and nurturant, placing high values on closeness with others. They expressed their affiliative needs in trusting, protective relations with others, and their overall personality pattern was that of well-functioning, conforming women, well-suited to the traditional roles of wife and mother.

In contrast, nontraditional women, at age fifty, appeared to be more ambitious, intellectual, and unconventional. They were more expressive, more autonomous, and more in touch with their inner lives, coping with conflict by insight and direct expression rather than by conformity and repression. They were "doers," with intellectual and skill-oriented interests rather than social types.

Earlier, at age forty, the traditional women had evolved a repertoire of skills that met their core needs for sociability; they then maintained a steady course of growth so that by fifty, their gregariousness has taken on a more protective, giving quality that was manifested largely by nurturance. The nontraditional women at age forty had shown signs of inner conflict and displayed feelings of irritability and depression and seemed to have regressed in their search for identity. However, ten years later, these women seemed to have resolved their conflicts dramatically, with a rise in intellectual skills, insight, spontaneity, humor, and expressiveness.

Unfortunately, we have no similar data on other socioeconomic and ethnic groups, so we cannot see if parallel conclusions can be drawn. The San Francisco study, whose subjects were largely lower-middle- and working-class, found the same typical shifts in men's and women's intrapsychic orientation during later mid-life—from instrumental to affective for men and vice versa for women (Thurnher, 1976).

Emotional Problems of Men

In contrast to the positive picture presented above, many men at this stage of life do suffer from emotional difficulties. As mentioned in Chapter 4, physical and hormonal changes occur gradually with few dramatic signs. Their aging tends to be viewed tolerantly by society, which sees their graying hair as "distinguished," their thickening bodies as "masculine," and the wrinkles around their eyes as "laugh lines." On the other hand, the emphasis on their "machismo" image often pressures them to prove their virility and competence and to deny their bodies' warning signals of diminished capacity and longer reaction times. Some stubbornly refuse to recognize that they may no longer be "as good as they ever were."

Depression. Frequently, men suffer from depression during their late forties and early fifties. Some of this reaction occurs in response to an objective precipitating event such as the death of a parent, termination of a job, serious illness of a wife, departure of the last child from home, or the breakup of a marriage—experienced as an actual or impending loss. For others, the source may be more intrapsychic in nature and tied to generalized feelings of failure and personal malaise, triggered perhaps by a heart attack or lowered sexual performance. If the existential conflicts described by Elliott Jaques and elaborated by Daniel Levinson have not been resolved in the early forties, these doubts and fears may return ten years later as disappointments and losses multiply.

Depression and alcoholism have been found to be the most common types of problems experienced by middle-aged outpatients in mental health clinics. While women in such clinics tend to be diagnosed as depressed more often than men, the difference between the two groups may lie less in the extent of their underlying disturbance than in their different patterns of help-seeking. Middle-aged women tend to seek professional help more often than men for all types of medical and psychiatric disorders (including depression). However, men often drink to counteract their depression and do not ask for treatment until their reaction is so severe that they require hospitalization.

Moreover, when a depressed man turns for help, he is more likely to describe his problem as that of sexual impotence, work difficulties, or excessive drinking rather than sad moods and depressive reactions. Depression among men at this stage may lead to considerable impairment in daily functioning. Contrary to earlier theories, Jeffrey Boyd and Myrna Weissman believe depressed persons express increased, rather than decreased, levels of anger, irritability, and hostility to close family members. They perform poorly at work, are often absent, and tend to make decisions that reflect poor judgment.

From the following description, we can see how multiple losses can push a man to the breaking point:

Frank Donnelli, fifty-two, stared broodingly at the kitchen table, kneading an empty beer can in his hand. How much can a man stand before he breaks? This afternoon he had been summoned from a meeting with other department heads at the district attorney's office to take a phone call from Ben Stokes, the chief of police over in Gainesville. Joey, their youngest kid, not yet eighteen and still wet behind the ears, had been picked up with a couple of other young hoods for stealing two cars and staging a drag race down Main Street. Stokes refused to let him come over to see Joey, since he hadn't been arraigned as yet. They were holding him without bail, but he advised Mr. Donnelli to get hold of a "savvy" lawyer, since the old man they knocked down was in the hospital and still unconscious; if the man dies, the charge will be, at the least, manslaughter.

Mr. Donnelli shook his head angrily. After he hung up, he had felt so wound up, he never returned to the meeting, where he was supposed to present a plan to combat recent budget cuts. Instead, he called Sam Weber, a lawyer he knew from the courthouse, told him what had happened to Joey, locked his office door, and took off. He stopped at Mike's Bar for a couple of shots to calm himself and then decided to go home to tell Marie about Joey, her "baby," before she heard it on the afternoon news.

But when he got home, his stomach sour and his head pounding, Sharon's kids were making such a racket he couldn't even talk to his wife. So he shut himself up in the bedroom and watched T.V. and drank beer with vodka chasers, all he could find in the house. When Sharon called him for dinner, he just said he wasn't hungry. Only after the kids were put to bed did he come out to join Marie, who was preparing a batch of pasta in the kitchen.

But how could he tell her about it? She had been through another series of treatments at St. Vincent's and looked terrible, like death warmed over. She was such a little, frail thing to start out with, and now Doc Perini warned him that she had just a couple of months left—at the most, a year. After thirty years together . . . what would he do without her? Sharon was here now, doing most of the housework, but she had her hands full with the three small kids; besides, she never could take her mother's place.

It's been just one thing after another . . . first his father's stroke, then Sharon's leaving her husband, then the news about Marie . . . and now, Joey. . . . Goddamn God for doing this to him!

Rising, his eyes filled with tears, Mr. Donnelli grabbed the chair on which he had been sitting and heaved it through the open kitchen window.

Alcoholism.   Alcohol addiction, which is often considered a "depressive equivalent," is usually measured by the five primary criteria of length, amount, and pattern of drinking (steady versus episodic); resultant social problems (loss of job, divorce, traffic violations, arrests, etc.); psychological dependence signs (loss of control, preoccupation); physiological dependence symptoms (tolerance to high blood alcohol levels, withdrawal syndrome, tremors, hallucinations, delirium tremens seizures); and medical complications (liver damage, upper gastrointestinal bleeding, etc.), according to Peter Murkin and Roger Meyer.

Within the last decade, the entire subject of alcoholism has received increased attention. Two different patterns have been found among middle-aged alcoholics. The more traditional pattern is that of men who have habits of long-standing alcohol abuse, often dating back to youth and early adulthood. The second is that of men who started drinking in their forties, largely in response to depression, bereavement, early retirement, loneliness, marital stress, or physical illness. Men in this second group experience a variety of pressures, such as problems in driving, job performance, and marital difficulties; usually they ask for treatment because of specific health problems rather than because of the drinking itself.

Alcoholism during the bridge to late mid-life may develop as a maladaptive coping mechanism to deal with changes within the family structure or, conversely, shifts in the family structure may unmask previously covert alcohol abuse.

While women may seize the opportunity at this time to seek a second career outside of the household, men feel that they may have peaked in their jobs and begin to want closer involvement with their wives and children at a time when the latter are less involved and seeking distance. However, if the man already has a drinking problem that was previously tolerated by his wife, the transitional shifts taking place at this time may precipitate a crisis.

A typical example of this situation can be seen in this vignette:

In the darkened living room, Roy Carter stared down blearily at the small heap of coins and crumbled bills on the coffee table. Seven dollars and thirty-two cents! All the cash he had in the world until the end of the month. Abruptly, he switched off the television set, where a well-dressed, middle-aged man, radiating confidence, was urging him to pick up the phone and book in to an alcohol abuse treatment center. They talked as if all he had to do was to call and all his problems would disappear. His wife would love him again; his children would come around to hug him; his boss would offer him his old job back. . . .

But what did that character know about it? His shaking hand groped for the bottle of cheap white wine standing next to his chair. Martha just let him know this morning, before she left for work, that her lawyer wanted to see him about a property settlement. She'd been sending messages for months: First she refused to cook his meals; then she moved into another room, claiming he "stunk" and was no good to her in bed; then last week she filed divorce papers on him. Now she wants to take him for everything he has.

Not that he has much left. Since he was laid off by Norton Aircraft, after the company was taken over by competitors three years ago, he hasn't been able to find a decent job—*any* job for that matter. All of his stock options and retirement benefits at Norton were wiped out. By now, they've used up their joint bank account and all their convertible assets. Even the house, which they bought when they married sixteen years ago, had been put in Martha's name years ago for tax purposes; now she'll probably sell it. Everyone is against him; even his own kids stayed far away. They refuse to side with him, claiming he had messed up their lives with his drinking.

Moodily, he gulped another drink, splashing the front of his shirt. Was it his fault that he lost his job? He had obeyed all the company rules, had been a good corporation man all those years, pushed all those brash young brats from Cal Tech up the ladder . . . and then he was paid back by being fired. Even afterward, he kept making the rounds, kissing the bottoms of men once junior to him, only to be given the brush-off and told he was either too old, too overtrained, or out of date. Sure he drank; at Norton the three-martini lunch was the way he snared contracts and customers. And now it was the only way he could get through the day, waiting for the telephone that never rang and the mail that never brought the right answers.

For a while there, he had been riding high, but in the last three years everything had turned sour: his job, his marriage, his relations with his kids, even his health. So what was left for him? He was just a has-been. He took another drink from the almost empty bottle, then laid his head down on his arms and began to sob.

Suicide.   The dynamics of depression and suicide often overlap; in fact, taking one's own life can be considered the most extreme reaction to adversity. Boaz and Eva Kahana found, however, that men and women show different overall patterns: While the suicide rate for men tends to increase steadily with age from childhood to old age, the rate for women gradually escalates to the decades of the forties and fifties, and then declines. In most Western societies, suicide is the act of an older person, frequently male, suffering from a serious physical or mental illness, often widowed, separated, or divorced, who may be socially isolated or have recently moved, and who may himself have lost one or both parents during early childhood.

A difference has been found between successful and unsuccessful suicide attempts. Those who actually commit suicide are usually men who are middle-aged and older, while those who attempt to take their own lives but fail are most often younger women. Because of the lack of clarity in reporting deaths, some suicides fall into a gray area between accident and suicide and escape detection. Nevertheless, when a middle-aged man talks abut taking his life, he should be taken very seriously. Such a man often chooses more violent means, with a greater assurance of lethality, such as a gun, while a woman may more frequently ingest pills, which allows a greater possibility of being rescued, say Burrows and Dennerstein (1981). They also note that a majority of those who succeed in killing themselves have seen a physician during the previous month and have told someone, either overtly or in a disguised form, that they intend to commit suicide.

Emotional Responses of Women

Like men, women's most frequent reaction to the vicissitudes of the transition to late mid-life is depression, ranging from mild unhappiness to severe psychosis. As discussed in Chapter 4, their evaluation of their self-image may be tied to feelings about their fading facial or bodily attractiveness and to fears concerning the aging process. The sight of each new wrinkle or sag will start them worrying about become unexciting, boring, or unattractive in the eyes of their husbands, other men, and even other women. And they compound the process by blaming themselves or feeling guilty for having let it happen.

Women's depressive reactions in response to stressful life events during the bridging process will be explored more specifically in the chapters on changes in their social roles. But whatever the external reality, depression and the "change of life" have long been considered synonymous, to be treated as either a medical or psychiatric problem.

Medical Treatment of Depression. Traditionally, depressed mid-life women have consulted their family physicians, who see them in their offices and treat them symptomatically with a "listening ear" and mood-elevating or tranquilizing drugs. If the depression is viewed as an inseparable outcome of an endocrine imbalance, the physician may, in addition to Valium, prescribe estrogen as the treatment of choice. The extreme of this viewpoint, still held by some physicians, is that postmenopausal women tend to become unattractive and "nuisances" to their husband unless they take replacement estrogen therapy for the rest of their lives.

Since so many physiological, psychological, and social factors interplay in this phase of the life cycle, it is difficult to pinpoint a single causal factor for women's depression. Their reactions to the pressures they feel may, indeed, emerge in the form of emotional lability and instability, crying spells, apprehensiveness, nervousness, fatigue, irritability, depression, insomnia, decreased memory, and an inability to concentrate. Treatment of these symptoms, regardless of their cause, by administering tranquilizers or mood-elevating medication may result in feelings of well-being and even euphoria and thus help some patients. Unfortunately, this level of treatment rarely deals with the underlying difficulties, the reasons why these women became depressed in the first place.

When a mid-life woman's physical health conditions are imbedded in a complex of emotional and familial complications to the extent that she attempts suicide, a family physician may well feel that, while he can treat her medically, getting at the underlying causes or even dealing with the familial components of the situation is beyond his area of competence or comfort.

The following incident reflects what happens when a patient views her physician as the only one who understands her situation. When he, appropriately, wants to lessen his involvement, she sees it as a desertion in her hour of need:

Jessie Alberts, fifty-three, lay in the high hospital bed staring drearily at the opposite wall. She felt closed in, imprisoned: both of the bed's sidegates were raised, and one tube was stuck into her left forearm and attached to an intravenous drip while another was taped to her right arm and connected to a wall monitor over her head.

Dr. Manton, her family doctor, has just left. Usually he was so kind; he always seemed to understand just what she was going through in her family life. But this time he sounded really angry as he looked over her chart and read the notes in it. Brusquely he had asked her where she had gotten all those sleeping pills she had swallowed and why had she tried to kill herself? She attempted to explain that she wanted to get some sleep. She had received a very upsetting phone call the other night from her daughter, Diane, and it gave her a terrible migraine. She had tried to reach him in his office but was told he was out of town. So she remembered these pills her neighbor once gave her and just kept taking them until she fell asleep. . . . Dr. Manton shook his head and said that maybe he better refer her to some place where they could help her more than he apparently could. He didn't even say goodbye as he left the room.

Actually, thought Mrs. Alberts, she couldn't recall much of what had happened, how she came into this place. She remembered feeling very upset when Diane phoned from school to tell her that she was moving in with her boyfriend. That's when she tried to reach Dr. Manton. Then she tried to call her husband, who was up in Green Bay at some business meeting. But his snippy young secretary answered instead, saying that Mr. Alberts was unavailable and would call her back.

She remembered lying in bed for hours waiting for him to call, but he never did. The thought kept running, over and over through her head, that no one seemed to care about her, that she was losing everything, and that the world would be well rid of her. Finally—it must have been almost morning by then—she felt desperately that all she wanted to do was sleep . . . and she thought of the pills hidden in her dresser. So she took two and lay down on the living room sofa. But they didn't seem to have any effect, so she kept swallowing more until . . .

The next thing she recalled was a nurse slapping her face and telling her to wake up. She was lying on a stretcher in the Emergency Room and they were doing terrible things to her. Some young doctor in a white coat kept trying to make her throw up; finally he stuck a tube down her throat and began to pump her stomach. She touched her throat where it still felt sore.

It must have been hours before they brought her up here and let her go back to sleep. She remembered waking up once to find Paul standing next to the bed with Diane. He was very angry and upset, said he had found her on the sofa. He then shouted at her—what was she trying to do, kill herself? She tried to explain in a whisper that she hadn't meant to; all she wanted to do was sleep. But he didn't even listen, just said he had to get back upstate and that Diane would stay with her until he returned.

Poor Diane; she must really have been frightened. Whenever she woke up during the night, she found her daughter sitting next to her bed. But this morning, when Dr. Manton came in to check her, after the hospital got in touch with him, he made her feel guilty all over again. He sounded as though he was blaming her for trying to get him into trouble.

Slowly, Mrs. Alberts shook her head. What a mess she'd made of things. All she had been trying to do was to get out of other people's lives; she had become just a nuisance to everyone . . . to Paul, to Diane, even to Dr. Manton. Now everyone was mad at her and she'd be more alone than ever. Why couldn't they have let her die?

Psychiatric Treatment of Depression.   Psychiatrists, as well as physicians, had long considered depression to be an inescapable part of menopause; in fact, "involutional melancholia" or "involutional depression" was once the label routinely applied to the severe depressive episodes seen in middle-aged women. In the last two decades, however, increasing discomfort with this classification has been expressed and the current manual of psychiatric disorders no longer even lists it or considers menopause to be a contributing factor in major depression.*

Myrna Weissman, one of the most active psychiatric researchers in the field of depression, offers the following working description:

> A typically depressed woman [in a psychiatric facility] will talk of feeling sad, hopeless, and empty, will complain of a loss of interest and pleasure in activities, and will report crying spells. She will look sad, speak in a sad voice, appear to be slowed down, and will lack energy. . . . Typical symptoms of depression include depressed mood, changes in appetite, disturbed sleep, loss of pleasure, loss of interest in work, decreased sexual interest, decreased ability to concentrate, feelings of helplessness, anxiety, feelings of guilt and shame, pessimism and hopelessness, bodily complaints, and thoughts of death. [1980, p. 309]

None of these, she points out, are primarily associated with middle-aged women. The age bracket at which hospitalization for depression occurs to the greatest extent is that of twenty to forty-four years of age. From then on, its prevalence decreases. Others have pointed out that researchers have often drawn faulty conclusions about the relationship between depressive symptoms and menopause because they were looking at the skewed population of middle-aged women patients found in both medical and mental health outpatient clinics and hospitals who represent only a small percentage of the total population in this age group.

From the psychoanalytic viewpoint, menopause has been considered a potential danger to a woman's mental health in that it poses a threat to her feminity, sexual attractiveness, and reproduc-

---

*See the *Diagnostic and Statistical Manual of Mental Disorders*, 3rd ed., of the American Psychiatric Association (1980: 210–224), commonly known as the DSM-III and used in almost all psychiatric and mental health settings.

tive potential. Helene Deutsch, whose views epitomized this approach, held that the climacteric is a narcissistic mortification during which the woman loses all she has gained earlier during puberty; it becomes, in effect, the "closing of the gates." Thus, almost all women inevitably experience a short- or long-term depression at this time.

Therese Benedek also saw menopause as a difficult developmental stage for women, similar to puberty and pregnancy, but offered a more hopeful outlook. While the psychological symptoms that accompanied menopause may have been rooted in the woman's previous psychosexual history, if her adaptive capacities had not been exhausted by previous neurotic processes, she could recapture the psychic energy released by the end of her reproductive role to provide the impetus for her flexible ego to engage in new learning and socialization.

The view frequently expressed in current analytic literature associating menopause with an excess of symptoms of depression and irritability is probably a function of patient selection, as previously noted. According to Barbara Ballinger, those women seeing psychoanalysts or psychotherapists who manifest difficulties in adaptation to menopause are probably not characteristic of mid-life women as a whole.

Menopause as a Normal Life Event.   As opposed to the view that menopause is a pathogenic event producing depression, many developmental psychologists, sociologists, and researchers on women's issues maintain that women's problems at this stage of life stem most frequently from such external causes as role strain or role loss, devaluation because of perceived lessening of sexual attractiveness, economic disadvantages, or social exploitation. While menopause may become a marker event, reactions of depression, anxiety, and nervousness are often reality-based in their current life situations. The cogent question to ask at this time is, "What are these women depressed about?" Neugarten and her associates (1968) were among the first to challenge the view that women feared or had negative attitudes toward menopause. In one study of women aged forty-five to fifty-five, of whom 75 percent were currently experiencing the "change of life" or had completed the process, the majority felt that elimination of the fear of pregnancy and the bother of menstruation were the most positive aspects of menopause. Although they were somewhat uncertain of its effect on their sexuality, they reported having better relations with their husbands and increases in energy and feelings of well being. They also indicated that they were far more worried about such concerns as widowhood, children leaving home, possibilities of contracting cancer, and the aging process itself than about menopause.

Sociologically, the relationship between depression and menopause tends to vary by social context. Pauline Bart, for example, found that certain changes in women's status after menopause were associated with structural arrangements and cultural values in different societies (1978).

Improved status at middle age was found in those societies where a strong tie to family of orientation was maintained, the extended family system was valued, the grandmother and mother-in-law roles were institutionalized, maternal bonds were maintained in later life, and postmenstrual women were valued above younger ones. Among the various ethnic groups within our own society, Bart found that actual or impending role loss was associated with depression to varying degrees. Housewives seemed particularly vulnerable to these effects. She found that Jewish women showed the highest level of depression; Anglos, an intermediate amount; and blacks, the lowest degree.

In another cross-cultural study, Nancy Datan compared how women from five subcultures in Israel viewed mid-life changes. She found great similarity in how all the women felt about menopause and the loss of fertility; whether they came from a Central European, Turkish, Persian, North African, or Arab background, all welcomed it. Regardless of the number of children they had borne, they looked forward to the postmenopausal years.

Datan had predicted that the traditional women would welcome the changes of menopause, which would bring an end to childbearing and menstrual taboos and raise their social statuses to those of matriarch, mother-in-law, and grandmother; while modern women would resist and regret menopause, which signified the loss of youth and child-bearing potential, or conversely, would be better prepared to deal with the changes of menopause because they had already actively coped at earlier stages and would bring a broad range of tested coping skills into middle age.

Both of these predictions turned out to be half right. The balance between the degree of modernity and self-reported psychological well-being appeared to hold true for the two end groups, the Central Europeans, the most modern of the five cultures, and the Arabs, the most traditional, while psychological well-being seemed lowest among Persian women, who represented the midpoint along the continuum from traditional to modern.

In one recent, practice-oriented study of the effect of menopause on women's affective states, Cleo Berkun found it difficult to separate women's reactions to the cessation of menstruation from their overall concerns about other mid-life changes. The sixty women in her support-group project tended to be traditional and family-oriented in their outlook, putting the needs of their husbands, children, and other close family members above other considerations. Although these women were all in relatively good health, their most frequent complaint about their own bodies was their inability to control their weight; second was their dislike of faded, wrinkling skin. A strong theme prevailed that "if they had been properly 'good' or 'moral,' then muscles would not sag, weight would behave, unexplained twinges would stop, and they would look and feel wonderful."

These women expressed little real concern over loss of their mothering role and did not regret the ending of their reproductive ability (including those who had had early hysterectomies). To them, cessation of menstruation meant freedom from worry over pregnancy and other uncomfortable symptoms. If they felt depressed, they related this to external factors in their environment, such as the harsh social and economic reality that women over forty must compete with younger women for the same jobs. They tried very hard to control their lives, seeking security through husbands, jobs, close friends, and a dependable body. What they wanted most was reliable, detailed information to help them sort out their controllable from their uncontrollable physical and mental reactions.

Loneliness in Mid-life.   People are lonely, Jules Henry, the anthropologist, once said, because they are vulnerable and they are vulnerable because they are alone. They are vulnerable when they are without love and when they have it. Personal vulnerability and loneliness are inseparable; they are often merely different ways of looking at the same thing.

Actually, many women enter the transition to late mid-life vulnerable to loneliness. They may have already sustained serious losses that have changed the course of their lives. Often remembrances of such past events color and define their current reactions, making adaptation to new losses difficult, even threatening.

Maggie Scarf found in her intensive interviews with women hospitalized for depression that loneliness often lay at the core of their reactions to the loss of a significant person or role. However, she differentiates between ordinary loneliness and depression. Persons may try to rid themselves of their loneliness by seeking out a new relationship or trying to regain a former one. If they are successful, their feelings will change and their loneliness is dissipated. In depression, on the other hand, individuals surrender to their distress. They often withdraw, unwilling to impose their unhappiness on others. Or they may be so immersed in it that they cannot be reached by others who offer them new relationships.

At times, a milestone event, such as the advent of one's fiftieth birthday, can trigger feelings of loneliness and awaken a soul-searching review of past losses and fear of what lies ahead:

Charlene Farwell got up restlessly from her armchair and looked at the row of birthday cards propped up along the mantelpiece: an elaborate, flowery one from Homer, her gentleman friend; a sleekly sophisticated one from her older son, Earl, which she was sure his wife, Lucinda, had chosen and mailed for him; a sentimental one from her sister, Mattie; and comic ones from her cousins, Ruby in New York and Dorothy in Houston. Nothing from her younger son, Sherman; she'd be lucky if he remembered to call before the month was out. She peered down at the old-fashioned bowknot watch pinned to her blouse, which Mrs. Campbell had given her that morning with a gracious little speech about how much she and Mr. Campbell had appreciated her having worked for them these past thirteen years.

Fifty years, she thought with a sigh—a lot of living had gone into those years. Now more than half of her life was over, if you believed in the Good Book. But what did she have to show for it? She looked around the room; each piece of furniture had a history of its own, some going back to when George and she had moved here to Chicago's near North Side with their two little boys more than twenty-five years ago. George had been promoted to sergeant and transferred to the regular army barracks near Navy Pier, so he could come home nights. She was working at the box factory then, but she was always there to welcome him; she could still recall the sound of his whistling, "Oh, You Beautiful Doll," as he bounded up the stairs. The boys would drop their toys and stand at attention, facing the door to salute him as he came in.

Things were never the same after his regiment left for Vietnam in 1967. He wasn't much for letter-writing, but she'd receive a card every now and then and twice he managed to get leave. She still had the kewpie doll he won for her in Honolulu when she met him there the last time. When his colonel came to tell her that George had been killed in the rice paddies in the spring of 1970, just two months before he was supposed to come home, time seemed to stop for a while. It took every bit of strength she had to get up in the morning. Oh, everyone was very kind to her. Reverend Peabody would come to pray with her and the church ladies were always bringing in food. Mama came to stay for a while, but Charlene had no patience with her complaining. She felt so restless and uprooted—just an "emptiness" that went down deep.

Finally she took her life in her hands again. The boys were gone by then, so she just quit her job and went on a trip to Washington. It was too late for the cherry blossoms, something George had been promising for years to take her to see, but still it made her feel better. When she came back, she decided she was tired of boxes; she needed to be with people. So she took this course in practical nursing, which was something she had been doing anyway for her family, and then found a job with the Campbells. She had been there ever since, but now she'd have to decide about that soon. Mrs. Campbell wanted to move for good to Florida and asked her to come along. It would be nice to get away from Chicago's snow and that windy walk to the bus each day. And yet . . . two aging widows, sitting in the sun. . . .

Mrs. Farwell went into the kitchen to put on the kettle. She didn't know what was the matter with her tonight. Maybe her change of life was coming on. Or maybe she was just feeling lonely. Homer had wanted to come over for dinner, but she had told him she was busy this week. He was a nice man, but he kept pushing her about going back to Nashville with him. The trouble was, she didn't know *what* she wanted. It must be this fiftieth birthday that had upset her. So many years still to go; how was she going to fill them?

Reactions to Environmental Conditions. The benign or adverse influence of enviroment on mid-life women should be viewed against the background of the observation that those women who live in "unsustaining environments" are prone to depression. In looking at this issue more closely, Janice Wetzel found a difference between those depressed women who were dependent and saw their environments as low in supportiveness, and those who were independent and did not perceive their environment as controlling. Moreover, while the independent depressed women seemed to be unhappy and resentful about their relationships with their husbands or other male partners with whom they lived, they indicated that they had full responsibility for the home and children. Many other factors, such as personality characteristics, seem to enter into the development of depression beyond environments that did not support women's needs.

Changes in the social environment over time can also affect mid-life women. Sophie Loewenstein reports that many women who had grown up with one set of assumptions about their role in society now face another set of values that undercut their earlier ones, and often experience a sense of deep betrayal. They tend to feel that their earlier conformity did not bring about the rewards in middle life that they felt had been initially promised and expected. Now, when they see their daughters living by another set of values, they feel cheated and depressed. Such bitterness about betrayal is particularly acute in those women who become single in mid-life, not through their own choice but because they have been abandoned through death or discarded by divorce. (This point will be explored further in Chapter 9.)

Some never-married, childless women's reactions to menopause indicate that they suffer poignant regret that they had never borne children, feeling this loss more deeply than that of never having married. Such women tend to become favorite aunts to their relatives' or friends' children or big sisters to children in need of parenting, Loewenstein observes.

In general, the psychological adaptations to late mid-life that begin during this transition contain both positive and negative components. On the one hand, individuals feel more independent and confident of themselves and their abilities to cope; on the other, they find the ravages of time overwhelming and become depressed and dissatisfied with what they foresee as lying ahead. While work changes affect men more adversely than women, role shifts in family life seem to influence women more than men, as we shall see in the chapters that follow. As the individual adjusts to specific changes, however, the central existential question arises again and again, "What am I going to do with the rest of my life?"

References

BALLINGER, C. BARBARA. "The Menopause and Its Syndromes." In John G. Howells, ed. *Modern Perspectives in the Psychiatry of Middle Age.* New York: Brunner/Mazel, 1981: 279–303.

BART, PAULINE B. "Depression in Middle-Aged Women." In Vivian Gornick and Barbara K. Moran, eds. *Women in Sexist Society.* New York: Basic Books, 1981: 99–117.

————, and MARILYN GROSSMAN. "Menopause." In Malkah T. Notman and Carol C. Nadelson, eds., *The Woman Patient.* Vol. 1. New York: Plenum Press, 1978. 337–354.

BENEDEK, THERESE. "Climacterium: A Developmental Phase." *Psychoanalytic Quarterly* 19 (1950):1–27.

BERKUN, CLEO S. "In Behalf of Women Over 40: Toward Understanding the Effect of Menopause on Women's Affective State." Paper presented at NASW Professional Symposium, November 1983, Washington, D.C. Reproduced.

BIRREN, JAMES E. "Toward an Experimental Psychology of Aging." *American Psychologist* 24 (1970):124–135.

BOOTH, RICHARD. "Toward an Understanding of Loneliness." *Social Work* 28, 2 (March-April 1983):116–119.

BOSTON WOMEN'S COLLECTIVE. *Our Bodies, Ourselves.* New York: Simon & Schuster, 1976.

BOTWINICK, JACK. *Aging and Behavior.* New York: Springer, 1973.

BOYD, JEFFREY H., and MYRNA M. WEISSMAN. "The Epidemiology of Psychiatric Disorders of Middle Age: Depression, Alcoholism, and Suicide." In John G. Howells, ed. *Modern Perspectives in the Psychiatry of Middle Age.* New York: Brunner/Mazel, 1981: 201–221.

BURROWS, GRAHAM, D., and LORRAINE DENNERSTEIN. "Depression and Suicide in Middle Age." In John G. Howells, ed. *Modern Perspectives in the Psychiatry of Middle Age.* New York: Brunner/Mazel, 1981: 222–250.

CHIRIBOGA, DAVID A. "The Developmental Psychology of Middle Age." In John G. Howells, ed. *Modern Perspectives in the Psychiatry of Middle Age.* New York: Brunner/Mazel, 1981: 3–25.

DATAN, NANCY, AARON ANTONOVSKY, and BENJAMIN MAOZ. *A Time to Reap: The Middle Age of Women in Five Israeli Subcultures.* Baltimore: Johns Hopkins University Press, 1981.

DEUTSCH, HELENE. *The Psychology of Women.* New York: Grune & Stratton, 1944.

Diagnostic and Statistical Manual of Mental Disorders, 3rd ed. Washington, D.C.: American Psychiatric Association, 1980.

EICHORN, DOROTHY H., JANE V. HUNT, and MARJORIE P. HONZIK. "Experience, Personality, and I.Q.: Adolescence to Middle Age." In Eichorn, et al., eds. *Present and Past in Middle Life*. New York: Academic Press, 1981: 89–116.

FRIED, BARBARA. *The Middle-Age Crisis*, rev. ed. New York: Harper & Row, 1976.

FUCHS, ESTELLE. *The Second Season*. Garden City, N.Y.: Anchor/Doubleday, 1978.

GIESEN, CAROL B., and NANCY DATAN. "The Competent Older Woman." In Nancy Datan and Nancy Lohmann, eds. *Transitions of Aging*. New York: Academic Press, 1980: 57–72.

GILLIGAN, CAROL. *In a Different Voice*. Cambridge, Mass.: Harvard University Press, 1982.

GOLAN, NAOMI. "The Transition to Postparenthood: Ties Between Physiological and Psychological Changes in the Lives of Middle-Aged Couples." *Proceedings of the 5th World Congress on Sexology*, Jerusalem, June 21, 1981. Amsterdam: Excerpta Medica, 1982.

HAAN, NORMA. "Common Dimensions of Personality Development: Early Adolescence to Middle Life." In Eichorn, et al., eds. *Present and Past in Middle Life*. New York: Academic Press, 1981: 117–151.

HENRY, JULES. "Loneliness and Vulnerability." In Joseph Hartog, J. Ralph Audy, and Yehudi A. Cohen. *The Anatomy of Loneliness*. New York: International Universities Press, 1980: 95–110.

HORN, J. L., and RAYMOND B. CATTELL. "Age Differences in Fluid and Crystallized Intelligence." *Acta Psychologica* 26 (1967):107–129. Quoted in Donald L. Donohugh, *The Middle Years*. Philadelphia: Saunders Press, 1981.

JAQUES, ELLIOTT. "Death and the Mid-Life Crisis." *International Journal of Psychoanalysis* 46 (1965): 502–514.

KAHANA, BOAZ, and EVA KAHANA. "Clinical Issues of Middle Age and Later Life." In Felix M. Berardo, ed. *Middle and Late Life Transitions*. Annals AAPSS 464 (November 1982):140–161.

LEVINSON, DANIEL J. "The Midlife Transition: A Period in Adult Psychosocial Development." In Lawrence D. Steinberg, ed. *The Life Cycle*. New York: Columbia University Press, 1981: 280–298.

LIVSON, FLORINE B. "Paths to Psychological Health in the Middle Years: Sex Differences." In Dorothy H. Eichorn, et al., eds. *Present and Past in Middle Life*. New York: Academic Press, 1981: 195–221.

LOEWENSTEIN, SOPHIE F. "Toward Choice and Differentiation in the Midlife Crises of Women." In Carol L. Heckerman, ed. *The Evolving Female: Women in a Psychosocial Context*. New York: Human Sciences Press, 1980: 158–188.

LOWENTHAL, MARJORIE F., MAJDA THURNHER, and DAVID CHIRIBOGA, et al. *Four Stages of Life: A Comparative Study of Women and Men Facing Transitions*. San Francisco: Jossey-Bass, 1975.

MAYER, NANCY. *The Male Mid-Life Crisis: Fresh Starts After 40*. New York: Doubleday/Signet, 1978.

MIRKIN, PETER M., and ROGER E. MEYER. "Alcoholism in Middle Age." In John G. Howells, ed. *Modern Perspectives in the Psychiatry of Middle Age*. New York: Brunner/Mazel, 1981: 251–265.

NEUGARTEN, BERNICE L. "Adaptation and the Life Cycle." *Counseling Psychologist* 6, 1 (1976):16–20.

————, VIVIAN WOOD, RUTH J. KRAINES, and BARBARA LOOMIS. "Women's Attitudes Toward the Menopause." In Neugarten, ed. *Middle Age and Aging*. Chicago: University of Chicago Press, 1968: 195–200.

NOTMAN, MALKAH T. "Midlife Concerns of Women: Implications of Menopause." In Elizabeth Howell and Marjorie Bayes, eds. *Women and Mental Health*. New York: Basic Books, 1981: 385–394.

NOWAK, CAROL A. "Does Youthfulness Equal Attractiveness?" In Lillian E. Troll, Joan Israel, and Kenneth Israel, eds. *Looking Ahead*. Englewood Cliffs, N.J.: Prentice-Hall, 1977: 59–64.

ROSSI, ALICE S. "Life Span Theories and Women's Lives." *Signs* 6, 1 (1980):4–32.

SCARF, MAGGIE. *Unfinished Business: Pressure Points in the Lives of Women*. Garden City, N.Y.: Doubleday, 1980.

THURNHER, MAJDA. "Midlife Marriage: Sex Differences in Evaluation and Perspectives." *International Journal of Aging and Human Development* 7, 2 (1976):129–135.

WEISS, ROBERT S. *Loneliness: The Experience of Emotional and Social Isolation*. Cambridge, Mass.: M.I.T. Press, 1973.

WEISSMAN, MYRNA M. "The Treatment of Depressed Women: The Efficacy of Psychotherapy." In Carol L. Heckerman, ed. *The Evolving Female: Women in a Psychosocial Context*. New York: Human Sciences Press, 1980: 307–324.

————, and EUGENE S. PAYKEL. *The Depressed Woman: A Study of Social Relationships*. Chicago: University of Chicago Press, 1974.

WETZEL, JANICE W. "Depression and Dependence Upon Unsustaining Environments." *Clinical Social Work* 6 (1978): 75–89.

WILLIAMS, JUANITA H. *Psychology of Women: Behavior in a Biosocial Context*, 2nd ed. New York: W. W. Norton, 1983.

WILSON, R. A. *Feminine Forever*. New York: Evans Press, 1966. Quoted in Berkun, 1983.

WINOKUR, GEORGE. "Depression in the Menopause." *American Journal of Psychiatry* 130 (January 1973): 92–93.

CHAPTER 6

Shifts in Work Patterns

Work is a major area of concern in the lives of both men and women. When they have reached their middle and late forties, most men and an increasing number of women spend a considerable part of their weekdays in factories, offices, trucks, or other occupational settings. The large majority of these workers, whether operating independently or as part of a regulated workforce, have stable position and like their work. In fact, Joan Waring found that most persons feel they would continue to work even if they had enough money to live comfortably without doing so.

Since men and women perceive and enact their work roles differently, the two will be considered separately.

Men's Work Role

Climbing the Work Ladder

It should be kept in mind that a man's identity is uniquely set by his work role. Not only is work a source of income and sustenance, but it is also the clock by which he assesses his life's achievements and decides whether they are on time, successfully early, disappointingly late, or woefully not forthcoming.

Except for those who have chosen careers requiring lengthy preparation, by the time most men have reached the transitional years—forty-eight to fifty-four—they have been engaged in income-producing work for twenty-five years and more. Levinson has devoted considerable time in *The Seasons of a Man's Life* to discussing occupational activity over the years of adulthood. After a series of false starts, the man lays the foundation, makes his decisions, and becomes involved in "making it" up the career ladder. By his late thirties and early forties, he becomes more senior and increasingly "his own man," eventually rejecting the mentor who advised and guided him over the years. Occasionally, when he finds his work no longer interests him, he may give it up entirely and shift to a new occupational interest. However, by the time he reaches his late forties, starting anew is rarely a viable option and he may have to live with work decisions and structures made at an earlier stage.

A typical picture of the men who function well at age fifty in their work role is given by John Clausen who reviewed the longitudinal data from the Oakland Growth Study. Of the one hundred participants, nearly half were high-level executives or in the major professions. Some had prepared for professional careers and moved immediately into high-prestige positions, but almost half started in lower-level jobs and worked their way up. A number of executives had begun in minor administrative jobs, while a third of the men in sales and clerical positions had started in blue-collar jobs. Greatest job stability was found among the blue-collar workers. More than half of them saw security as the most important feature of their job, while less than 20 percent of the white-collar workers valued this aspect—perhaps because they took it for granted. In general, the higher status a worker, the more heavily invested he tended to be in his work—and the more hours he worked.

By this time, most of the Oakland men felt they had reached the peak of their occupational attainment. They saw their current jobs as satisfying and their careers, on the whole, rewarding. Some 30 percent felt their work truly represented what they wanted to do, while another 45 percent saw it as approximately what they wanted. Less than 5 percent expressed active dislike of their occupation. Most of the men at all job levels felt they probably would remain in their present type of work and with their present employer;

only 20 percent said they expected to advance beyond the level of their present job.

Reaching the Top

In general, by the time men turn fifty, they have usually climbed to the top of their occupational ladder. Except for such "free" professions as law, medicine, and, to some extent, academia, where opportunities for·advancement may continue through the fifties and even the sixties, men now find themselves either on the highest rung or can see the steps ahead that will lead to their goal.

Some, of course, reach a plateau partway up and remain there. They have neither the organizational capability nor the psychological toughness needed to fight their way up further and may choose or resign themselves to stopping there, despite feelings of stagnation and boredom. Many men at this age choose to settle for job security and, even though their work is no longer challenging, will seek other sources of gratification in their family or community roles, while plugging along at this level until retirement.

If a man works in a factory or similar type setting, he may have become by now a foreman or at least an old and experienced hand, with special prerogatives accumulated through years of seniority. If he is a professional, he probably has become a member of the establishment and a mentor for those coming up from below. If he is an executive, he undoubtedly wields considerable administrative power and is involved in making and executing key policy decisions. At this level, he may even be asked to transfer, by virtue of his success, to a senior position in a rival company or to a bigger arena. In any event, the majority of men at this age feel secure and unthreatened, counting on their years of experience and expertise to carry them through.

However, many successful men at this stage in their work careers become "workaholics," spending long hours, evenings, and weekends at their desks or work tables, either because they enjoy the challenge or because they become anxious that their position or competence may be challenged by younger, more recently trained men.

The following vignette illustrates how one successful middle-aged professional, forced by health impairment to change the nature of his work role, was able to restructure it in a more gratifying way, since he could take advantage of one of the options still open to him:

As he drove back from Boston, Dr. Robert Bennett thought with satisfaction of the letter in his pocket from the head of the research facility at Pilgrim General Hospital offering him a full-time appointment and a generous grant to continue his project on heart transplantation. Pretty good for a guy his age, with all the fierce competition from the young hotshots straight out of research specializations. Maybe his years of active practice in the field of cardiac surgery did count for something. . . .

Reflectively, he thought of the long road he had traveled to reach this point. Even as a young kid, he had wanted to be a doctor; he remembered reading Paul de Kruif's *Microbe Hunters* and dreaming that someday he'd make some spectacular medical discovery. When he was a teenager, he saw his dad shrivel up after his heart condition made his boss transfer him from the production line to a dead-end spot as a storeroom clerk; he had vowed then that he'd find some way to help his father—and people like him.

Unfortunately, when Dr. Bennett completed his medical training, there just weren't any research jobs open. Besides, he felt obligated to his wife, Helen, who had been carrying the major financial burden while he finished school. Also, their first child, Meg, had already been born and Helen was pregnant with their second. And both their parents were looking to them for help by this time.

So he opened his first practice in Granville. He remembered how the pressures increased: He always seemed to be either in surgery, attending staff meetings at the hospital, or moonlighting elsewhere. Then, when the local hospital closed after a series of scandals, he and several of his colleagues decided to open their own facility, which later became Meadowlake Hospital. For its first ten years, he recalled, he had to be the administrative director as well as heading the Cardiology Department. Fortunately, eight years ago, they became affiliated with the University Medical School and he could begin to share the load. Also by that time, they were pretty well fixed financially.

Maybe, if he hadn't had his own first heart attack last year, he would have continued the rat race, probably going on to become president of their local Medical Association . . . he already heard hints about it. But he took himself in hand and decided to shift his direction completely, to return to his first love: research. He cut down on his practice and began going down to Boston each week to take part in a research seminar; soon he became an active member of the team.

Dr. Bennett's mind switched back to the current research project that he had started with one of his colleagues. Within the next few months he expected to wind up his affairs in Granville entirely and move to Boston. Then they could really move into high gear.

Work Stresses

The climb upward is by no means a smooth or easy one. As men move up occupationally, some find themselves experiencing increased pressure, disappointment, and frustration. Part of this strain is related to the work itself: They may feel the new job is too heavy, too demanding, too boring, or too nonproductive. Some experience role ambiguity in that they are not sure of what is expected of them, what the scope or boundaries of their work are, and how much decision-making power they will be allowed. They may worry about the new responsibilities thrust upon them and the outside involvements that their positions demand. They may find themselves caught in a vertical press between management and the work force or a horizontal one between the conflicting interests of different departments or factions.

In a study he conducted, Cary Cooper found two major clusters of potential work stressors felt by middle-level managers at this stage in their careers: (1) lack of job security, fear of redundancy, obsolescence, or early retirement; and (2) status incongruity, under- or over-promotion, and frustration at having reached one's career ceiling. Many came to feel that "luck" and being in the right place at the right time played a major role in their advancement.

Leaving the Job

A third alternative to climbing further or remaining at the same level may be to leave the job. As already noted, however, while men at fifty or more may feel dissatisfied with the limitations and frustrations of their work, few seriously consider changing either their position or their occupation at this stage. While in their late thirties and early forties they may turn to other fields if pressed hard enough, by the time they pass the fifty-year mark, their options have narrowed and they become more cautious. They may dream and even talk about moving to that "little chicken farm in New Jersey," but they rarely act on it. Few men at this age can allow themselves the luxury of simply walking away from their job. Fears of losing fringe benefits and endangering pension rights deter some, while others may not be able to afford the loss of a regular paycheck, the cost of a retraining program, or the initial investment for some independent venture with an uncertain future.

Of course, some men have no choice in the matter; they may have been fired or have given up working altogether. Sometimes the reason is intrinsic to the job situation itself. In this era of rapid technological change, a position or department may have been declared obsolete, replaced by a computer or a new step-saving process. Sometimes the man's own educational or mental capacities cannot keep abreast with new developments. Since in all probability it would be difficult to find him a new spot in the organization, he may be forced, for lack of choice, to remain at home in what is euphemistically called early retirement. Or he may putter about in a series of makeshift, temporary jobs, far below his previous position and level of competence, until retirement age is reached.

Sometimes the reasons for a man's giving up his job may be extrinsic to the work situation, lodged in factors such as health problems that can both cause or result in difficulties and may require him to slow down or change the type of work he does. He may be hemmed in by family obligations that prevent him from working a particular shift or moving to another community when the workplace is transferred.

Fiske points out that, when a man confronts the realization that his occupational career has peaked, not only is he likely to feel anxious and insecure, but he may be prompted to reflect on his work in terms of such questions as, "What is it all for?" Such men often attribute their plans for early retirement to a disparity between their own values and ethics and those of the organization for whom they work.

The combination of age plus occupational obsolescence can become a lethal combination during the bridge to late mid-life, as the incident below demonstrates:

Roy Carter squirmed in the uncomfortable chair and stared down at the questionnaire before him. Around him, men and women sat at the long tables in the State Unemployment Office, busily writing or whispering to each other. He didn't know what he was doing here, he thought bleakly, his shaking hands scarcely able to grasp the pen. At fifty-four, who was going to hire him? After three years out of a job, he had finally gotten the message. But okay, might as well get it over with, so he could say he tried.

"Occupation?" Well, what was he? Once he had been a pretty good aeronautical engineer. He got his M.S. from Carnegie Tech, waltzing through on the G.I. Bill after World War II, and then headed out west with the rest of the "whiz kids" to the booming aircraft industry on the West Coast. For a while he hopped from one job to another, but then he met Blanche and settled down at Norton Aircraft in their Seattle plant. After they were married, things went along easily for him: he moved up the ladder, became a section head, had his own group of younger men under him whom he helped to climb up with him. He really was riding high in those days, even received a couple of sizeable bonuses for some breakthroughs in design that had given Norton an edge over their competitors for a few years.

"Years with Previous Employer?" Let's see, there were those ten years in Seattle. Then, after Blanche died, he moved with the two kids down to the L.A. area when he was transferred to the Pasadena plant. By that time Norton was moving into aerospace projects and he had his own team. He stayed with one big project for another four years . . . yeah, it was 1967, right after he married Martha, his former secretary, that he shifted over to the administrative side. She had heard on the grapevine that there was an opening in sales, so he got in touch with Frank Holden, one of the V.P.'s who was an old classmate of his. Before he knew it, he had entered the corporate rat race, all of the way up to "Vice President in Charge of New Projects."

Oh, at first it was exciting, traveling around the country, talking to prospective customers, keeping an eye peeled for new developments, getting together with "opposite numbers" at Kennedy and Houston. Since his job involved the promotion of new projects, much of his week was spent entertaining procurement officers from the Pentagon and reps from all over Europe and the Mideast. Gave him a real feeling of power, all that wheeling and dealing . . . yeah, it was a long trip up, those twenty-seven years at Norton.

"*Reasons for Leaving?*" Well, how do you squeeze that into four lines? He remembered those last weeks back in 1980, during that big recession, when rumors began to float that Norton might go under. Then the day came when Holden, who had just become president in an internal shake-up, called the senior executives together to inform them that Norton had been bought out by Amalgamated Industries of Philadelphia. They were taking over the plants on the West Coast and their outstanding contracts, but Norton itself was finished . . . just like that.

Things really began to move fast after that; within a week half of the offices in the Administration Building were emptied out. Some of the junior execs were kept on or moved over to other plants, but at his level, everyone was fired. At first he was sure his own job was secure, but one morning he came in to find that his nameplate had been removed from his door and a curt note on his desk requested him to vacate his office immediately. When he tried to call his pal Holden for an explanation, an impersonal recorded message said that Mr. Holden was unavailable, out of town indefinitely. And no one answered at his home phone. So there he was, out on his ear.

"*Previous Efforts to Find Employment?*" Well, at first he took it easy, letting it be known in the industry that he was available. But it was a bad time in the aerospace field and Norton's collapse made other companies wary of their own chances of survival. He got the message pretty quick, the familiar "Don't call me; I'll call you" from guys he had helped up the ladder and who owed him one. He even registered with a couple of companies guaranteeing to relocate executives, but nothing ever came of that.

He then decided to try to get back into engineering. But he soon realized that aeronautical engineering was now a completely different ball game. First of all, they were looking for Ph.D.'s in computer technology these days, and newly trained ones at that. Then, when he tried to take some refresher courses, he found he didn't even know the language; the technological revolution had changed the nature of the field and he was hopelessly out of date. Neither his head nor his hands could keep up. So he kept on sending out résumés and either getting no answer or receiving quick turndowns, no matter what he tried: too old, too qualified, not qualified enough. This last year he had even given up trying—what's the use? No question about it; he's a has-been.

"*Current Sources of Income?*" Mr. Carter thought of the two part-time jobs he found helping a couple of small businessmen in the neighborhood balance their monthly accounts. Money from Martha or his two kids . . . what a laugh! Suddenly he rose, and with an angry gesture, tore the application form in half and tossed it in the wastebasket.

"The hell with it! What I need is a drink!"

Traditionally, the "good provider" role was a man's chief responsibility to his family, Jessie Bernard has observed. Whatever his other qualities, if he could support his wife and children well, or even adequately, everything else was considered secondary. Success in this role was taken to define masculinity itself; part of the proof that one was a "real man" lay in the ability to be a successful breadwinner. Even today, many men tend to view their wives' working with ambivalence. On the one hand, it allows the family to enjoy greater amenities and a higher standard of living; it also acts as a cushion against his losing his job. On the other hand, it challenges his dominance as head of the family and reflects on his "macho" image. During the transition to late mid-life, this issue assumes real significance, partly because of what is happening to the man's work role and partly because of changes in the woman's work world at this stage.

Women's Work Roles

Patterns in Mid-Life

While men's work involvement remains clear and relatively unidirectional, commanding a high priority from early adulthood until retirement, women's paid work activities tend to move in a more irregular pattern throughout their adult years. Although U.S. Labor Department statistics and other sources show that a higher proportion of women are working today than ever before,* such figures should be viewed with caution. On closer scrutiny of the course of women's lives, we find that most women's participation in the work force follows several patterns, depending on family priorities and other pressures that may prevent or limit the kind and extent of outside work they do.

Both Block and Goodman note that probably the most common path among both working- and middle-class families is for a woman to work for a while after she finishes high school or even un-

*Los Angeles Times, September 4, 1984.

dergraduate college; to marry and have children; then, when the children are a little older, to go back to part-time work in order to supplement her husband's income. As the children begin to leave home, the woman goes back to school for some updating of earlier skills or for a retraining program so she can take a full-time paid job in her late forties and early fifties, when she is relatively free of familial responsibilities.

For the professional or career woman, the picture tends to be somewhat different, since she has more invested in keeping up her professional skills and regards it as part of her core identity. Four career patterns among professional women have been identified by Margaret Paloma: (1) *regular*: the woman who pursued her professional training immediately after graduation, who began to work and continued to do so without interruption or with minimal interruption throughout the years; (2) the *interrupted career*: the woman who began as in (1) but interrupted her career for several years, usually for child-rearing, and then went back full time; (3) the *second career*: the woman who only started her professional training near or after the time the children left home or after a divorce; and (4) the *modified second career*: the woman who started her professional training while the children were still at home but old enough not to need full-time mothering, then started to work, possibly part time, until the last child left home or became independent, when she shifted to a full-time career.

Why women go back to work during the transition to late midlife has been the subject of considerable speculation. What stands out is that the reasons are rarely simply to earn money, although in those families where the husband has become ill or disabled or, for other reasons, is no longer able to keep up his breadwinner role, the salary is undoubtedly the primary motive. Many older women enter the labor force for lack of choice, when they are confronted with the need to help support themselves and their families. However, boredom, loneliness, and the desire to find new interests may also play a part.

Whatever the overt and covert reasons, we find that, where in previous generations women in their late forties and early fifties tended to fill in the gap created by the departure of the children from home with "good works" and voluntary activities in women's organizations, today an increasing number are going out, or returning to, full-time paid employment. At fifty, they display a new burst of energy, enrolling in a school of social work, taking a course in computer programming, or studying for a real estate broker's license. While they may attempt to justify this new departure in terms of keeping themselves busy and their husbands from working so hard, actually they rarely hide the zest and gratification with which they leave for work each morning and bank their paychecks, often opening up a separate checking account for the first time in their own name. In fact, the trend to "dual career couples," so prevalent in their children's generation, is also penetrating into this age group.

Complications in Going Out to Work

While women who enter or reenter the work force in their forties and fifties may find it a revitalizing process, offering freedom, independence, and economic self-sufficiency, it can also justify unloading tedious household chores onto other members of the household. Moreover, point out Atchley and Corbett, they have to be careful how they present their jobs:

> Those women who are highly committed to being at a job are likely to be punished in one way or another. . . . The norms of our society do not so much discourage women from developing commitments to jobs as they discourage the development of such commitments to the *exclusion of other things*. [1977: 123]

Frequently the matter of the middle-aged woman's taking and holding a job comes down to the cost-benefits issue. On the one hand, delayed entry into the labor market might offer such benefits as improved family income and the freedom to schedule work without worrying about child-rearing obligations. On the other, its costs would include starting at the bottom in terms of skill, seniority, tenure, and savings for retirement. Women who are late entrants into the labor force tend to be concentrated in lower-status jobs and in low-wage industries and may find it difficult to accrue satisfactory benefits such as social security entitlements, note O'Rand and Henretta.

Those women who have been out of the labor force for some time or who may never have held a paying job until this stage in their lives may discover to their dismay that their preparation is inadequate, outdated, or too general or diffuse. (One woman put it despairingly, "Who needs a B.A. in French literature, thirty years late?") Often the nature of the work to be undertaken is a significant factor. Although, as Janet Giele points out, employment may serve

as an antidote for depression, it has to be the type of work that supplies adequate earnings, rewards competence, and generally rein-
forces a sense of self-direction and personal control. Otherwise, it
simply becomes more drudgery.

Moreover, the advantages of the new job may have to be weighed
against the additional costs of the different type of clothes to be pur-
chased, the hiring of outside housework help, the use of fast or pre-
packaged foods instead of home-cooked meals, and the trimming of
hours available for leisure or social pursuits.

Often the issue boils down to the question of conflicting role demands. Unlike her daughter, who at the start of her marriage may
have negotiated with her husband the allocation of such housekeeping chores as cooking, cleaning, shopping, and doing the laundry,
the mid-life woman who returns to work on a full-time basis may
find that she is working a second evening shift after she comes home.
Women frequently report that their husbands have agreed to their
working on the condition—often unspoken—that the balance in
family life remains the same.

Others come to recognize that, regardless of how much they earn
or how important their job may be, their husbands still consider
their work to be secondary and their earnings the equivalent of their
mothers' "egg money" or "pin money." Should the husband be transferred or his hours be changed, should the illness of parents or the
demands of adult children interfere, they find that their own job
immediately becomes downgraded in status and, if no accommoda-
tion can be found, may have to be curtailed or given up entirely.
Relatively few couples who are now in their late forties and early
fifties regard theirs as a "dual career" marriage with work decisions
to be made jointly or on the basis of equal consideration.

This combination of positive and negative reasons for working is
clearly illustrated in the following vignette, again the counterpart of
the situation described earlier in this chapter.

Martha Carter, dressed in a smart, tailored gray suit, impatiently
awaited her turn as the group of middle-aged women completing
the adult education course, "Real Estate Selling as a Mid-Life Challenge," discussed their reasons for returning to work and their plans
for the future.

She had always worked, she said, ever since she was a kid. Back
in Omaha, where she was born and raised, her father was a chronic
alcoholic who used to beat up her mother and the nine kids every

Friday night after he stopped off at the tavern to "tank up." She decided to get out as soon as she could and, while still in high school, worked part time as a cashier. She went back to the restaurant to work full time the day she graduated, and that's where she met her first husband, Bobby Butler, a jazz drummer. Once they moved up to Chicago, she immediately found a new job, this time as a waitress. She held on to it through the birth of her two sons because Bobby would travel most of the time and would only "stop over" when the band was in town.

Then one day she found a note saying that the band was moving east and he wouldn't be back. To make sure of it, she gave up her job, packed their belongings into her thirdhand car, and, with the two small kids, traveled to the West Coast, stopping off in Reno for a quick divorce. She found a job in Los Angeles as a telephone operator, working nights, after finding a nursery school that would take both kids together and arranging for a neighbor to put them to bed after she left for work.

Once the boys were in school for the full day, she took a secretarial course and eventually started to work in the typing pool at Norton Aircraft. She moved up in the secretarial network until she became private secretary to one of the sales executives. Her boss was a quiet, soft-spoken widower with two children of his own; she would organize his work for him and "keep him on his toes" in the company jungle. Eventually they decided to get married; by that time she was managing a good part of his home life as well. They bought a big house in Pasadena and settled down with their four kids. She had to give up her job than because it was against company policy for executives' wives to work.

For the next thirteen years, Mrs. Carter related, she was a company wife, entertaining the right people, showing up with Roy at the right places, organizing and running the household—which wasn't easy with four teenagers. She had to work hard to keep the kids in line, but she eventually pushed and pulled all four of them through high school and even college. Roy's son and daughter both moved out of town; they had never gotten along with their father. Her own two sons are also on their own; Gary is an assistant movie producer at Universal Studios while Roger runs a "hard rock" radio station in Vegas.

Things settled down at home once the kids were gone; she and Roy partied a lot and sometimes she would travel with him on company business. Suddenly, about three years ago, the axe fell. The aircraft industry was suffering a recession and Roy's company was taken over by competitors from the East. Without warning, in spite of his connections in the firm, he was fired.

Mrs. Carter said she tried to help him as much as she could; she worked up his job résumé and sent out dozens of letters to other companies for him. She tried using her own connections in the industry, but unfortunately employment opportunities for a man of Roy's status and age were drying up. Since he had been so long in administration, even his previous training as an aeronautics engineer was out of date. Besides, he took his firing very hard and began to drink heavily. She'd come home from shopping or golf and find him sitting in the den with a drink in his hand instead of going out to chase down employment leads. She knows he always had had things made easy for him, first by his mother, who pampered him as an only son, and then by his two wives, who in turn propped him up and kept his life running smoothly.

She, on the other hand, had learned to take care of herself, to be a survivor. So, after more than two years of patting Roy's hand, she realized he had just run out of steam and probably would never be able to get a decent job again. She decided it was up to her, so she did a quick inventory of what she had to offer and decided she'd probably do best by going into business for herself. That's when she noticed the ad for the course and decided to enroll.

Her plans now? Well, as they know, she already passed her realtor's exam and has started to sell property in the Bel-Air section. She's now thinking of moving farther up the coast, maybe to Santa Barbara. She doesn't have much to tie her down, since she and Roy are on the verge of splitting up—but that's another story.

Starting the Second Half of Life

A number of writers have pointed out that women's childbearing and child-rearing stages are shrinking both in actual years and in the proportion of the life span they cover. As women live longer, the number of years between the time their children leave home and the time they retire tends to increase. A growing number of women are looking to full-time employment not only as a way to fill up these years, but as sources of enjoyment and regeneration.

Even those who maintained their careers throughout their child-rearing years and who consequently experienced intense conflict between their loyalty and commitment to their families and their interest in their work, now find that the conflict abates and they can experience gratification and fulfillment during their fifties. Loewenstein found that those who entered traditional female occupations earlier now regret that they had not set their sights higher toward less predictable, more innovative directions.

But what about the woman who has never married or who is no longer married? While this will be discussed more fully in the latter part of Chapter 9, it should be noted here that even when a woman no longer feels the conflict between her role as a paid worker and her other social roles, her entry into late mid-life still brings about anxiety over change.

Often the anxiety may be tied to some milestone, such as her fiftieth birthday, which brings home the realization that the years are passing. She must acknowledge that her job or career is her primary interest and, as such, may feel the need to make it a meaningful one. The following incident illustrates this point.

Charlene Farwell waited with the filled-out questionnaire in her hand until the vocational counselor called her name. Then she sat quietly while the well-groomed young woman, black like herself, skimmed the pages quickly.

"I see you've been working as a licensed practical nurse for the past thirteen years, Mrs. Farwell. Why do you want to change now?"

Mrs. Farwell began to explain. "I really like working; I've done it since I was seventeen. But actually, I've only had two jobs in those thirty-three years. I'm like my father, I guess; he worked almost fifty years in one steel foundry in Gary before he retired three years ago. I started to work in 1950, when I was still in high school in just a 'hole in the wall,' folding paper boxes. When I left in 1970, I was supervising thirty women on the production line at Amco, one of the largest carton companies in the Midwest. We just grew up together.

"By that time, I wanted a change, so I answered this equal opportunity ad for black women to take a six-month course to become licensed practical nurses. I learned a lot then; it was a stiff program. But I always liked nursing and my whole family used to call on me when they needed that kind of help—they still do. Once I completed the course, the LPN Placement Service wanted to send me out to Cook County Hospital, but I preferred something more personal, with less pressure. So they placed me with the Campbells in Evanston—Mrs. Campbell had just broken her hip. And I've remained there ever since. I nursed Mr. Campbell through two strokes until he died last year."

The counselor prompted, "But why do you want to leave *now*?"

Mrs. Farwell hesitated, then smiled apologetically. "I guess I have a big decision to make and I want to know my choices. You see, my employer just told me that, with her husband gone, she wants to give up the big house in Evanston and move down to Palm Beach for good. She wants me to go along with her. Don't get me wrong; we get along fine. She's a kind lady and gives me all the time off I want or need, and I guess it would be good to get away from the snow and cold here in Chicago. But i would mean giving up my church and my friends here. And well, Mrs. Campbell is almost eighty, so how much time would I have with her?"

She paused and then added, more decisively, "Besides, maybe it's time for another change. I've been getting into a rut, just the two of us alone. Maybe I need something more challenging, like working with handicapped children, the way they show on TV. Yes, maybe that would be the answer. . . ."

As for the future, Bernice Neugarten (1978) predicts that most mid-life women will continue to balance work and family responsibilities in the latter part of their lives. For an increasing number, this will involve working throughout adulthood and moving up the career ladder; others will seek flexibility in part-time work without sacrificing the opportunity for interesting and responsible activities, as more jobs are specially arranged to match the capabilities of mature and experienced women. Still others will choose nonrenumerated work in their communities and a wider range of service opportunities, possibly as husband-wife undertakings. Regardless of their eventual choice, the transitional period of the early fifties is the time when many women set the direction for their future work course.

References

ATCHLEY, ROBERT C., and SHERRY L. CORBETT. "Older Women and Jobs." In Lillian E. Troll, Joan Israel, and Kenneth Israel, eds. *Looking Ahead*. Englewood Cliffs, N.J.: Prentice-Hall, 1977: 121–125.

BERNARD, JESSIE. "The Good Provider Role: Its Rise and Fall." *American Psychologist* 36, 1 (January 1981):1–12.

BLOCK, MARILYN R., JANICE L. DAVIDSON, and JEAN D. GRAMBS. *Women Over Forty: Visions and Realities.* New York: Springer, 1981.

CLAUSEN, JOHN A. "Men's Occupational Careers in the Middle Years." In Dorothy H. Eichorn, et al. *Present and Past in Middle Life.* New York: Academic Press, 1981: 321–351.

COOPER, CARY L. "Middle-Aged Men and the Pressures of Work." In John G. Howells, ed. *Modern Perspectives in the Psychiatry of Middle Age.* New York: Brunner/Mazel, 1981: 90–102.

FISKE, MARJORIE. "Changing Hierarchies of Commitment in Adulthood." In Neil J. Smelser and Erik H. Erikson, eds. *Themes of Work and Love in Adulthood.* Cambridge, Mass.: Harvard University Press, 1980: 238–264.

GIELE, JANET Z. "Women's Work and Family Roles." In Giele, ed. *Women in the Middle Years.* New York: John Wiley & Sons, 1982: 115–150.

GIESEN, CAROL, B., and NANCY DATAN. "The Competent Older Woman." In Nancy Datan and Nancy Lohmann, eds. *Transitions of Aging.* New York: Academic Press, 1980: 57–72.

GOODMAN, ELLEN. *Turning Points: How and Why Do We Change?* New York: Fawcett Columbine, 1979.

LEVINSON, DANIEL J., et al. *The Seasons of a Man's Life.* New York: Knopf, 1978.

LIDZ, THEODORE. *The Person: His and Her Development Throughout the Life Cycle*, rev. ed. New York: Basic Books, 1976: 504–506.

LOEWENSTEIN, SOPHIE F. "Toward Choice and Differentiation in the Midlife Crises of Women." In Carol L. Heckerman, ed. *The Evolving Female: Women in a Psychosocial Context.* New York: Human Sciences Press, 1980: 158–188.

NEUGARTEN, BERNICE L., and LORILL BROWN-REZANKA. "Midlife Women in the 1980s." In *Women in Midlife—Security and Fulfillment*, I. Compendium of Papers submitted to the Select Committee on Aging, Subcommittee on Retirement, U.S. House of Representatives, December 1978. Washington, D.C.: U.S. Government Printing Office, 1978: 25–38.

———, and GUNHILD O. HAGESTAD. "Age and the Life Course." In Robert H. Binstock and Ethel M. Shanas, eds. *Handbook of Aging and the Social Sciences.* New York: Van Nostrand Reinhold, 1976: 35–55.

O'RAND, ANGELA M., and JOHN C. HENRETTA. "Women at Middle Age: Developmental Transitions." In Felix M. Berardo, ed. *Middle and Late Life Transitions.* Annals, AAPSS 464 (November 1982): 57–64.

PALOMA, MARGARET M., BRIAN F. PENDLETON, and T. NEAL GARLAND. "Reconsidering the Dual Career Marriage: A Longitudinal Approach." In Joan Aldous, ed. *Two Paychecks: Life in Dual-Earner Families.* Beverly Hills: Sage, 1982: 173–192.

SULLIVAN, JOYCE, and KAREN G. ARMS. "Working Women Today and Tomorrow." In John G. Howells, ed. *Modern Perspectives in the Psychiatry of Middle Age.* New York: Brunner/Mazel, 1981: 71–89.

TAMIR, LOIS M. "Men at Middle Age: Developmental Transitions." In Felix
M. Berardo, ed. *Middle and Late Life Transitions.* Annals, AAPSS 464
(November 1982): 47–56.

WARING, JOAN. "The Meaning of Work." In Alvin C. Eurich, ed. *Major
Transitions in the Human Life Cycle.* Lexington, Mass.: Heath, 1981:
457–470.

Chapter 7

Relations with Adult Children

Persons approaching late mid-life are frequently referred to as the "sandwich" generation, caught between the opposing pressures of their adult children on the one hand and their aging parents on the other. In this chapter we examine the first of these intergenerational bonds: ties to grown-up children who, by this time, have already left the family home to live independently, to work or build their careers, to go on to university and graduate school, to marry, and/or to form their own personal relationships.

Emptying the Nest

The family sociologist, Evelyn Duvall, was probably the first to use the term "empty nest." She sees the departure of grown children from the home as a turning point for each member of the family, as well as for the family as a whole. New patterns must now be established and former habits abandoned. Duvall agrees that, when the empty nest comes at the expected time, it represents an adjustment to a normal aspect of the sequence and rhythm of the family life cycle rather than a crisis.

Not that all family ties are broken at this time. A series of studies in both the United States and England amply established that, far from being thinned out, bonds with adult children tend to increase, particularly after they marry and even more so after they become parents. Although children may move out physically, they continue to maintain close, ongoing relationships, popping in frequently to borrow the family car, use the washing machine, negotiate a loan until next payday, or ask for help in financing a major home appliance. Even when they are separated by geographic distance, children continue to phone, write letters, and visit their parents on family occasions and to celebrate holidays—sometimes to a greater extent than the parents anticipated. LeShan quotes one parent:

> "When Alice got married, we thought, 'Oh, how great—we're really alone at last.' Two weeks later she called and said she missed us and could they come for the weekend. Then it got to be two or three weekends a month, at a time in our lives when we have expected to have some time along together." [1973: 24]

Parents' expectations as to how their own lives will change, once the last child leaves, are often quite unrealistic. The transition to the children's departure can cover a prolonged period, during which the parents have to integrate their past images with current reality, as Ellen Galinsky notes:

> The wish builds and builds into an image for many parents that there will be a day, somewhere in the future, when the parent can return to the carefree, daring, impulsive, indulgent person he or she remembers being—the kind of person who can sleep all day Saturday or spend an outrageous amount of money on something luxurious or jump into a swimming pool with his or her best clothes on. . . . Then the dreamed-of day comes . . . and the parent is supposed to be free of the job of parenthood. [He/she] finds that this image will never totally come true. . . . Parents do remain involved in their children's lives. [1981: 294]

Parents do not stop caring, being concerned, worrying, or even thinking about their children once they depart. But because many had expected, unrealistically, to do just that, they struggle with the suspicion that something may be wrong with them or that they are different. Galinsky defines the central task at this time as that of loosening their control so that their grown-up children can become responsible for themselves without giving them up. One way of retaining the bond between them is by continuing or establishing customs and rituals that can still connect them, such as the regular dinner or Sunday morning telephone call, the weekly letter, and the joint celebration of birthdays, holidays, and family events.

After Departure.   Most parents continue to serve as role models and help in decision-making even after the physical separation is finally made. Since children may not have resolved decisions about occupation and marriage even though they have already left home, their parents remain a source of advice and support as these late adolescents and young adults experiment with new roles and lifestyles. Often they use their parents as sounding boards or "jousting partners" at this time.

Considerable differences in how middle-aged parents and their young adult children view each other after the latter leave have been discerned. Parents often continue to speak of their children as "family," while married children refer to their parents as "relatives," notes Joan Aldous. Parents tend to emphasize similarities, while children maximize differences. While this may be attributed to the parents' need to continue their "developmental stake" in the children by minimizing the gap, some intergenerational ambivalence or even hostility may be necessary on the part of the children so that they can "prove" to themselves and to outsiders that they can perform competently without their parents' aid.

Parents tend to respond in different ways to their children's efforts to become independent adults. Some are extremely proud of the accomplishments and personal qualities of their offspring, feeling that they have attained goals that hold meaning and value for them and thus contribute to their own feelings of accomplishment. Others may find their children adopting life-styles and goals that are contrary to their own hopes and plans and realize that, if they want to maintain the bonds between them, they may have to learn to live with this difference. Still others view their adult children as inadequate, immature, and even failures and feel disappointment and a strong sense that they themselves have failed. They are haunted by the question, "Where did we go wrong?"

But what happens when children don't leave at the expected time? Nancy Datan speaks of the "crowded nest," the period when the children are grown but not yet out of the parental home. While this situation may be based on such reality factors as lack of suitable employment or struggles to find adequate housing, it may also lie in adult children's inability to break the psychological bonds holding them at home. When this occurs, the outcome for one or both parents is frequently discomfort and often outright anger and a sense of exploitation.

Cultural Differences. Sometimes ethnic values serve to continue such patterns. Generations of Spanish-speaking or Asian-American extended families often cluster together for economic, social, and psychological support long after the adult children could viably leave. In black families, Saundra Murry and Daphne Harrison points out, many mid-life women face the reality of the "full nest," the necessity, either alone or with husbands, of providing shelter and economic support to their adult children. One recognizable cause of depression among mid-life black women has been the failure of children to leave when expected.

Sometimes difficulties in the process can be attributable to class differences. Most middle-class parents, for example, know when the big break will come, usually when the child leaves for college, so they can prepare in advance for the big event. In working-class families, however, children are usually expected to live at home until they marry, often contributing to the family's support. Since the age of marriage is not clearly fixed, the time of departure is also indefinite—for both parents and children. Even after their daughters marry, traditional working-class mothers and daughters in London, for example, were found to spend a good deal of time together, shopping, having afternoon tea, visiting one another, sharing meals. "Mum" helped when daughter gave birth, provided child care, and took over the major responsibility for household tasks when others in the family were at work.

Effect on Women

The departure of the last child from the parental home usually affects women to a greater extent than men. Until this stage, the mother, regardless of what else she did, spent a considerable part of her waking hours preparing meals, laundering clothes, and taking care of the children's daily needs, as well as showing them love and affection. Now she has to carry out one of the primary developmental tasks of the postparental years, that of encouraging them to become more autonomous. As Duvall puts it:

> She must convert the formerly dependent mother-child relationship into one of mature interdependence, in which she and her grown chil-

dren mutually support and encourage one another without intruding into one anothers' lives. . . . She must learn to stand by, offering assistance only as it is requested. She must avoid hovering over [them] with too much smothering attention. [1977: 358]

Some of the mid-life women in the San Francisco Transition Study said they had anticipated the youngest child's leaving home and were experiencing little stress in adapting to the change. Others seemed to feel that a total reorganization of their life-styles, including adjustments in behavior, attitudes, and relationships, would be required. Most of the women felt that their children's success would be the criterion measure of their own success or failure as mothers.

Some sounded quite tentative and pessimistic; they look forward to their last child's independence but were less confident of their ability to manage on their own, according to Donald Spence and Thomas Lonner. Others were resentful, feeling that their mothering role had stunted their own personal growth, that their other interests and involvements had been shunted aside for the children's sake. Now they found themselves at a loss; though they expressed vague desires to help their husbands prepare for retirement, to travel, to do volunteer work, to renew long-ignored artistic interests, or to see their grandchildren, they felt themselves ill-prepared for what lay ahead. Still others felt no need to change; they saw themselves as being actively involved in their children's lives long past the time when they would marry and have children of their own.

In an effort to pin down what constituted a child's leaving home, Elizabeth Harkins found that going away to school, moving to a separate residence, and getting married all rated higher as indicators of the child's leaving home than simply graduating from high school. She also observed that, while women initially experienced a period of maladjustment, they eventually readjusted to the new situation and worked out new roles and patterns of interaction with their offspring.

Depressive Reactions. Sophie Loewenstein has noted that women who have invested all their energies in their maternal role, or who view their children as narcissistic extensions of themselves, tend to become emotionally drained and even clinically depressed at this time. Nevertheless, Pauline Bart found that even hospitalized depressed women continue to find some satisfaction if their children fulfill their expectations, either by the son's obtaining a good job or by the daughter's making a good marriage.

The effect of a youngest daughter's announcing that she plans not only to change her life-style but to leave her parents' home as well can have a devastating effect on a mother who is already depressed by other losses in the family:

Jessie Alberts closed her eyes and leaned back against the wall, tears rolling down her cheeks, the phone lying unheeded in her lap. Diane, their youngest, had just called from the state university to say that she was moving out of the dormitory. Carl, her boyfriend, had asked her to share his off-campus apartment and she was in the midst of packing her things. She was sending home her collection of glass miniatures and the stuffed animals that had lain on her bed since she was a little girl; somehow she couldn't see them in Carl's place.

Without giving her mother a chance to reply, Diane excitedly rushed on to say that they've been making plans and expect to move down to West Texas when he graduates in June. Mrs. Alberts managed to ask, "To get married?" Diane answered carelessly, "Well, we haven't gotten that far in our plans. Maybe when we leave school, or maybe we'll wait till we see how it works out down there, first." In any event, she probably wouldn't be coming home so often now. Both of them feel they should spend some time together outside of school days, so they're going away for the weekend. She'll write her details.

My God, thought Mrs. Alberts, after her daughter hung up. She's leaving me, too. . . . Four children, all gone. . . . Diane is the last one! What's happened to them? They had been such a perfect family when the children were small. Her days were filled with taking care of them, cooking and baking and taking the boys to Cub Scouts and Diane to ballet class . . . when did it start to fall apart?

Oh, she knows when it started, when Paul Jr. was killed in that car accident on graduation night. He was going to enlist in the Marines the next day, like his dad, and she always blamed his father for letting him take the big car that night. She remembers how she screamed at Paul that he was a murderer; it took her a long time to get over her grief.

They must have neglected the other kids during those first months. Frank, the second boy, dropped out of high school for a while and started hitchhiking around the country; finally he met a girl out west and settled down in Oregon with her. They're married now and he manages a supermarket, but they almost never hear from him—he's lost to them in his own way. And Jim, their youngest boy . . . what a lot of trouble he had in school before he transferred to Pope Pius High School where the classes were smaller. When he finished there, he told them he wanted to join the Catholic church, and now, at twenty-six, he's studying to be a priest in a seminary in the East. Paul becomes furious when she even mentions his name.

And now Diane, her only daughter, is going. How will she be able to bear it? Paul's wrapped up in his business and she'll be alone . . . all alone. She felt the familiar migraine pressure building behind her eyes.

And how would she tell her family? Ma always blamed her that the children had turned out so bad. And her sister, Cora, would certainly crow; she always flaunts her two daughters who are married to successful businessmen and have already given her five grandchildren. After they hear that Diane isn't getting married, she'll never be able to hold her head up in church again.

By now, she felt herself growing nauseous. Maybe she better call Dr. Manton.

Some authors reject the contention that the departure of the children results in depression and anxiety, insisting that the cultural stereotype of the depressed mother rests largely on data from clinical or hospitalized patients. The normal, healthy women whom Lillian Rubin interviewed for her study felt, on the whole, that their children's departure from the home was a distinct relief. Those who did seem to suffer were the ones who were disappointed in their children, whose previous relations with them had been unsatisfactory, and whose disapproval of their children's life-style made their interactions with them difficult and tenuous. Many of these mothers felt that they had aborted their own hopes and career plans for their children's sake. Now they felt disappointed and saddened in the way things had turned out.

Indeed, some women are puzzled, confused, and even guilty that they feel so good once their children leave home. They may even consider themselves "abnormal" because they feel "better than ever," and now have free time in which to explore themselves, take classes or workshops, or even enter the job market. Undoubtedly, what we are seeing here reflects, to some degree, the influence of the women's movement in the 1960s and 1970s on changing mores and standards as to how women ought to feel about their adult children. But it also demonstrates a more realistic approach toward the increasing span of time that women have left to live, once the last child has left home.

Mother-Daughter Bond. "A son is a son till he gets him a wife, but a daughter's a daughter the rest of her life."

This old folk rhyme typifies the ongoing nature of mother-daughter ties. Recently, Grace Baruch and Rosalind Barnett found that the relationship with the mother and the role of daughter provide emotional gratification important for psychological well-being, particularly when the daughter lacks other social roles. In those cultures where the young wife customarily has to move to the home of her husband (usually within *his* parental home), the marriage of a daughter usually represents an almost complete separation between mother and daughter, observes Therese Benedek. However, in cultures such as ours, daughters often move to or remain in close physical proximity to their mothers, particularly as they become mothers themselves. Despite their vaunted independence, few young women voluntarily forego their mother's presence during the birthing process and in the first anxious weeks after they return from the hospital or maternity home. From then on, if they do not see their mothers every day or at other frequent intervals, they maintain an active telephone link with them. Much of the interaction is centered on the daughter's learning the mothering role. She turns to her own mother for advice and guidance on such weighty matters as how to differentiate in the color and consistency of the baby's stool, how much burping is sufficient, and how to tell whether the crying baby is sick or just fussing.

In a study aimed specifically at examining this bond, Lucy Fischer notes that the daughter's transitions—first to marriage and then to parenthood—demand a redefining of the relationship in terms of roles, statuses, and family constructs. She found that both mothers and daughters tended to reevaluate each other while at the same time becoming more involved in each others' lives. Particularly after they have had children, the daughters tended to idealize their mothers' ability to mother and both consciously and unconsciously tried to echo this behavior. The daughters expressed a desire to be closer to their mothers and to continue the ties, both for themselves and for their children. On the other hand, a number of the mothers, while pleased with their grandchildren, felt that they did not want to become too involved, too entangled in demands for such services as baby-sitting or childcare.

When mid-life women experience clashes between their role as mothers and other significant ties, they are often called upon to re-order their priorities, as reflected in the following incident, seen through the daughter's eyes:

Marilyn Freeman hung up the phone slowly. Her mother, Betty Eis-man, had just called to tell her apologetically that she wouldn't be able to take the boys for two days next week as she had promised. Dad and she were going out of town on an extended business-vacation trip for at least three weeks.

Absently Marilyn began to pull clothes out of the dryer and fold them. She had been counting on Mom to help out with Donald and Danny so that she could go with Hank to St. Louis to have him fitted with a new back brace. She hadn't gone into details with Mom, just said it was a "shopping trip" because Hank didn't want them to fuss or interfere. But Mom should have known it was important to her.

Funny about Mom—they never used to get along when she was a teenager; maybe it was because she resembled Dad more. Carole, who's four years younger, takes after Mom: petite and gentle and interested in "wifely" things, especially now that she's had her new baby. Mom and Dad hadn't approved of Hank when she met him seven years ago as a freshman at the University of Chicago. He was a political activist who had dropped out of law school during the Vietnam protest days and returned to campus to recruit volunteers for the '76 presidential campaign. They took to each other at once and have been together ever since. Her parents didn't like it, but at least they didn't interfere.

When she became pregnant five years ago, after she stopped taking the Pill, they decided to get married. Since then she spent a lot of time taking care of first one baby and then, two, while Hank traveled around the country, running political campaigns. It was pretty lonely for her, but Mom had come down to stay for a couple of weeks each time, and they spoke on the phone at least twice a week . . . she really came through when Marilyn needed her. And when she would try to thank her, Mom would remind her of the saying in her family when she was young, "All for one and one for all!" Marilyn would laugh at her for being so naive and sentimental, but it gave her a warm feeling all the same.

Marilyn piled up the folded clothes and took them into the boys' room. As she sorted them into dresser drawers, she recalled what had happened last year when Hank slipped in the rain on some rickety platform and almost broke his back. He spent most of the next month in traction in the hospital and then almost half a year in a wheelchair before he could use his legs again.

Mom and Dad had been wonderful at that time. They insisted that she pack up her family and come back to Minneapolis with them. For the first few months they lived at home, until Hank's disability allotment came through and his rehab program was approved. Dad even found them a ground-floor apartment and Mom helped her furnish it with things from the attic back home. Now Hank's enrolled at the university, finishing the law school program he had dropped out of ten years ago, and she's working full time as a market research associate. But, even though the kids are in a day-care center, Mom's been terrific about stepping in when arrangements fall through and she needs a rescuer.

About that phone call, mused Marilyn. . . . This is the first time Mom has ever said "No" when she's asked her to take the kids. She never thought about Mom and Dad wanting to go off by themselves. Maybe she and Carole ought to think more about that. They've been leaning on her pretty heavily these last years—probably taking her too much for granted.

An interesting variation in the mother-daughter bond occurs when a mid-life women in her mid- or late forties gives birth to a last child at the same time that her daughter has her first. Whether one attributes this late pregnancy to cultural patterns, to a desire to ward off the end of the active mothering role, or simply to a miscalculation based on the irregularity of the premenopausal menstrual cycle, it poses an unusual situation in which mother and daughter really close the generation gap as both carry out their mothering role side by side.

Mother-Son Bond. The second half of the jingle quoted above supposedly represents the "ideal" situation in which the grown son separates from his parents to go off on his own and, in time, marries and takes on primary responsibility for his own wife and children.

For him not to do so is considered socially aberrant and emotionally unhealthy; often it is attributed to the inability to individuate and separate or it is placed within the Freudian context of the Oedipal conflict. While such overclose bonds do occur, these ties often represent continuing social attachments and obligations, says anthropologist Estelle Fuchs. In some societies, the older woman's status improves only when her son grows up and brings home wives to do the menial work. Her primary attachment is not to her husband but to her children, while her husband's primary bond is to his blood relatives and his own mother.

Even in our own society, sometimes mid-life widows or divorced women suffer loneliness when their sons fail to continue an ongoing relationship or maintain only nominal ties. In the short vignette below, the thinness of such a mother-son bond can be detected:

Earl Farwell waited impatiently while his secretary dialed his brother's number in Chicago. "Hi, Sherm? How's it going in the Windy City? Yeah, my law firm is giving me time out to work on the presidential campaign; good p.r., you know. . . . Lucinda is fine, busy working on her Ebony Art Project and getting us settled in our new place in Georgetown.

"How are things going? Heard from Ma that your trucking firm is making a lot of money these days. I guess it helps to have been an all-American back when it comes to making good connections. Hey, have you gotten tied down yet? Twenty-nine isn't too young, you know. . . . How *is* Bettina? . . . Oh, it's Jackie these days, is it?

"Sherm, the reason I'm calling is to ask about Ma. Have you seen her lately? Last week was her fiftieth birthday. I guess you forgot. Well, Aunt Mattie called me last night from New York; she's kind of worried about her. Said she sounded pretty down when she spoke to her last.

"No, it's not a question of money. You know Dad's army pension and insurance set her up fine, and she gets a good salary from Ol' Lady Campbell. Whenever I send her a check, she just sends it back. Yeah, I *know* you can afford it, but that's not what she needs.

"Look, Sherm, maybe someone better look in on her. She's all alone in that dinky apartment over on the North Side. . . . I know she's got a boyfriend, but it's not like it was with Dad. It'll be hard for me to get away these next few months, so how about you? I know you're a busy man, Hotshot. . . . Well, how about a call? Remember, she's all we've got and we promised Dad we'd keep an eye on her."

Effect on Men

While more attention has been paid to the effect on women of the last child's leaving home, men, too, are affected, particularly when this occurs during the transition to late midlife. According to one study by Michael McGill, men who are deeply involved in their parenting role can react strongly to the emptying of the nest. Many middle-aged men express frustration in their attempts to pass on traditional work, family, and personal values to their children. Others fear that what their children have learned at home will be threatened and undermined by their outside experiences, and they try to protect them as long as they can from those external forces.

The loss of the active father role may call forth a broad range of responses. The most common reaction, says McGill, may be passive acceptance and subsequent depression, resulting in a diminished sense of self. Other men may act out against their children, rejecting both them and their behaviors. Or they may go to great lengths to postpone the loss of their influence, refusing to let the children depart, keeping them at home by whatever means available, even if it requires interfering in their children's career or work opportunities, trying to break up their marriages, or becoming physically ill.

Some men respond with anger and aggression, which becomes generalized against other young people as well; they harbor a simmering rage that can boil over at the slightest provocation. Others go in the opposite direction; they tend to avoid involvement with young people altogether. Possibly the most positive type of reaction is that displayed by those men who reconcile themselves to their own loss by becoming interested and involved as leaders in youth groups or activities where they can continue to act as father figures. Of course, one possible danger may be that they seek out father-daughter relationships with younger women, which develop complications that can directly affect their marital ties.

As children grow up and depart, the father's role as their provider, protector, and shaper of attitudes and beliefs diminishes and often disappears. Many middle-aged men cannot deal with this loss because the role of father is the one role that has been important to them. The empty nest leaves behind an "empty man," sums up McGill.

Other researchers found that, while the majority of postparental fathers felt either happy or neutral when their last child left home, almost one quarter of them reported feeling unhappy. These were apt to be the same men who felt most neglected by their wives, received the least amount of understanding from them, were most lonely, were least enthusiastic about their wives' companionship, and had the least empathic wives.

These men tended to be those who had the most to lose. They were older fathers with the fewest children and had more to give up emotionally with each child's leaving. They foresaw such men as continuing in rather bleak marriages for the next sixteen to eighteen years after the last child departs unless some intervention in the form of anticipatory socialization to the postparental role and changes in the marital balance could be carried out.

Rubin stresses a different aspect of the father-child separation process. She sees the father's previous involvement in his family as primarily working to ensure that they will be economically secure in the event of his death. While a mother fears leaving her children before they're emotionally ready, a father worries that he will leave them before they are financially set. She also sees fathers, more often than mothers, wanting to hold back the clock and keep the children at home for just a little longer:

> He's not there to watch their development, to share their triumphs and pains. Then suddenly, one day it's too late. One day they're gone . . . even before he had a chance really to know them. Long ago he promised himself he would [relate more and differently]—some day, when he wasn't so busy, wasn't so tired. But there was never the time, never the energy, and besides, he never quite knew how to relate to them, what to say—how to play with them when they were little, how to talk with them as they grew. [1979: 36]

Now, just when the children are old enough to be talked to like real people and he's beginning to notice what he missed, they leave.

Father-Son Bond.   Particularly with their adult, independent sons, some mid-life fathers tend to experience a sense of loss and guilt over having missed so many opportunities to be with them during the growing-up stage. Sometimes unresolved conflicts from their own adolescence, which had emerged when they were in their early forties, still have not been resolved. New conflicts, related to the battles they fought with their own fathers in their own early adulthood, arise around such issues as career choice, life-style, and "carrying on the torch" in the family business. Fathers are apt to view their sons at this stage as extensions of themselves and see in them the possibility of a second chance to work out their own unmet hopes and disappointments. Even when physically distant, they remain emotionally bound to them.

Returning Home Again

Even more traumatic than for adult children to remain in the crowded parental nest after the expected time for them to leave, is for them to return once the break has been made. This may occur for a number of reasons: economic setbacks, physical illness, divorce, widowhood, or some similar disruptive event in the life of either the parent or the child. But when it happens after parents have already made—or are making—the adjustment to late mid-life and have modified their physical surroundings, such as moving from a large house to a compact apartment, the situation can become stressful. Moreover, when they have made basic changes in their daily routines, such as the mother's having returned to work or started a new career, the parents may resent the return as an imposition, a reversal of their life course.

Sometimes the parents may welcome the child's return, but other factors complicate the situation as in the following vignette, seen through the returning daughter's eyes:

Sharon Metzger sat huddled at the foot of the bed, cradling the baby, Cindy, in her arms while trying to quiet the two-year-old twins, Tommy and Stevey, who were squabbling over the blanket they were supposed to share. From the other room she could hear her father, Frank Donnelli, shouting at her mother about the trouble her brother Joey had gotten into with the police.

"Trouble"—that had a familiar ring! She herself had known nothing but trouble since she met that good-for-nothing bum, Kenny Metzger, four years ago. She had been on nursing duty in the hospital where he had been admitted for a cocaine cure. He made a big play for her, said he couldn't live without her, and, when she refused to go to bed with him, insisted they get married. She thought she could straighten him out, but it didn't take long for her to find out her mistake. She even got pregnant—twice, yet—in the hope he'd grow up and get his old job as a TV announcer back, so he could support them.

But nothing helped; he'd just go chasing after each new pretty face he saw. And when he was high on whatever combination of stuff he picked up on the street, he'd come home and beat her up. Finally, when he started on the kids, she decided she had enough and came home to her parents. They were against divorce, being strict Catholics, but they didn't say a word, just turned Joey's room over to her and the kids.

She had been so busy with her own misery, she hadn't realized how sick Mama was until she came home. But one look at her and she knew; she remembered enough from her nursing days to recognize the signs. She checked with Dr. Perini and he warned her the prognosis was not good. With the history of cancer in her mother's family and her refusal to admit it when her pains first began, it had already spread into her intestines by the time he started her on chemotherapy. Now she probably had less than six months left. . . .

Sharon began to cry silently. They had made such wonderful plans together: Mama would look after the grandchildren while she went back to work. Lainey, her sister, would handle the divorce for her and Pop would get the police to keep a watch out so that Kenny wouldn't come after her. But now she knew Mama would never live to see her daughter's life straightened out. Pop, she could tell, was going crazy with worry, even though he tried to hide it from Mama. He was tearing himself apart and hitting out at everybody; she'd never seen him drunk until tonight.

Poor Mama . . . she'd had nothing but trouble these last years from her kids. . . . Sharon choked back a sob as the baby stirred restlessly. Now that her own marriage was breaking up, she could see what Pop and Mama had together.

Under less traumatic conditions, the adjustment to returning home on the part of adult children and their mid-life parents can still be difficult for both sides. With the best goodwill in the world, it is hard to turn back the clock. Children may have been living independently for years, making their own decisions, building their own relationships, experiencing their own triumphs and disappointments. Now they are, literally, forced to regress to an earlier developmental period, to assume a familial role they have already given up.

Even when parents can forgo such reproaches as "I told you it wouldn't work out," they rarely have the objectivity to view their returning children as adults and tend, instead, to act as if they had remained at home continuously, as if their earlier role as daughter- or son-of-the-house is still ongoing. Even more destructive is for the parents to feel that, since their son/daughter is now dependent upon them financially, this entitles them to interfere in other aspects of their child's life. Women who have returned home during or after divorce have spoken at length of this debilitating aspect of the situation. Even young widows, who come home without the social stigma of divorce, report that they rarely can stay there for more than a few weeks without friction arising.

Sons, returning home under similar conditions, usually tend to react to the experience more positively; they even may enjoy the decreased responsibility and increased pampering that this invites. Parents, too, are likely to respect their sons' privacy and independence more, even though they are under the parental roof. The return is usually considered a "temporary setback" rather than a personal failure on their son's part.

Becoming Grandparents

Because we are dealing with persons who are now in their late forties and early fifties whose last child has left or is on the verge of leaving home, we also include some who already have grandchildren by their older children. Rather than fitting the classic image of the sweet, white-haired, bespectacled "Granny," grandmothers of the 1970s and 1980s are often still very active, with careers and multiple interests outside of the home.

As mentioned earlier, traditional men and women often pass smoothly from the role of active parent to that of involved grandparent, treating it as a continuation of their parenting function. Duvall quotes one man in his early fifties as observing,

> What's all this about the empty nest? The old nest here is bursting at the seams, with five wonderful grandchildren and two sons-in-law extra, besides the two daughters who used to roost with us! [1977: 376]

Grandparenthood has been interpreted as giving a new lease on life because grandparents (particularly grandmothers) can relive the memories of the early phases of their own parenthood as they observe the growth and development of their grandchildren. However, reminds Benedek, it is one step removed. Relieved of the immediate stresses of motherhood and the responsibilities of fatherhood, grandparents appear to enjoy their grandchildren more than they enjoyed their own children; their love is not as burdened by doubts and anxieties as when their offspring were young. Grandparents offer their grandchildren undemanding love, giving them a sense of security; in return, they receive the message that they are needed, wanted, and loved, even while the specific emotional content of the grandparent role varies with the cultural and socioeconomic variations in family structure.

Psychologically, if mid-life adults show little interest in becoming active grandparents, this may signal, not a desire for distance, but a shift toward their own individuation and an attempt to redefine their relations with their own children. Moreover, since grandparenthood is one of the few life roles that an individual does not elect, it may be experienced as a narcissistic injury to the self, especially in persons already sensitive to effects of aging.

Of the meager research on grandparenthood, one early study by Neugarten found that middle-aged grandparents tended to be funseekers (informal and playful, seeing their grandchildren as playmates and sources of enjoyment) or distant figures (busy persons who emerge from the shadows only on holidays and special ritual occasions, such as birthdays) rather than fulfilling the more functional formal care-giving task or acting as reservoirs of family wisdom as grandparents of previous generations did. With women experiencing the emptying of the family nest, the marriage of their children, and the birth of grandchildren at earlier points in their lives then their own mothers had, many look forward to grandmotherhood as a welcome, pleasurable event.

Middle-class grandparents appear to fill an ambiguous "roleless" role, with little evidence of active participation in the family unit, notes Sylvia Clavan. In poorer families, however, grandparents take a far greater role in the family's daily life. Working-class grandmothers frequently run the household and care for children while the other adults in the family are at work. Among blacks and other ethnic groups, a widowed grandmother is an extremely functional family member. Within the urban black community, the maternal grandmother frequently socializes and nurtures her grandchildren and runs the house while the mother works, becoming in effect an extended, surrogate mother and an important part of the natural support network.

In situations where the child's mother is a single parent, the grandmother's role may be pivotal. Even young, upwardly mobile adults who set up dual-career marriages may find that the timing and size of their family may depend on whether either one of the couple has a mother willing and able to take on care of the grandchildren, full- or part-time in case of emergencies.

Nevertheless, the grandparent role is a contingent, peripheral one, according to Lillian Troll (1983). The tie to grandchildren is indirect and mediated through the adult parent who, at least for young grandchildren, often sets the nature and tone of the relationship. In cases of separation, divorce, or widowhood, the parents of the noncustodial or deceased adult child may have to negotiate their grandparental rights with in-laws. Moreover, if they have had serious estrangements with their own children, this can, of course, have a ripple effect on their ties with their grandchildren: They may never even get to know them.

With all this, it seems difficult for middle-aged adults to rely on grandparenthood to fulfill a central role during and after their transition to late mid-life.

References

ALDOUS, JOAN. *Family Careers: Developmental Change in Families.* New York: John Wiley & Sons, 1978: 286–288.

BART, PAULINE B. "The Loneliness of the Long-Distance Mother." In Joseph Hartog, J. Ralph Audy, and Yehudi A. Cohen, eds. *The Anatomy of Loneliness.* New York: International Universities Press, 1980: 204–219.

BARUCH, GRACE, and ROSALIND C. BARNETT. "Adult Daughters' Relations with Their Mothers." *Journal of Marriage and the Family* 45 (1983): 601–606.

BENEDEK, THERESE. "Parenthood During the Life Cycle." In E. James Anthony and Therese Benedek, eds. *Parenthood: Its Psychology and Psychopathology.* Boston: Little, Brown, 1970: 185–206.

CLAVAN, SYLVIA. "The Impact of Social Class and Social Trends on the Role of Grandparent." *Family Coordinator* 27, 4 (October 1978):351–357.

DATAN, NANCY. "Midas and Other Midlife Crises." In W. H. Norman and T. J. Scaramella, eds. *Midlife: Developmental and Clinical Issues.* New York: Brunner/Mazel, 1980.

DUVALL, EVELYN M. *Marriage and Family Development*, 5th ed. Philadelphia: J. B. Lippincott, 1977: 353–383.

FISCHER, LUCY R. "Transitions in the Mother-Daughter Relationship." *Journal of Marriage and the Family* 43, 3 (August 1981):613–622.

FUCHS, ESTELLE. *The Second Season: Life, Love, and Sex for Women in the Middle Years.* Garden City, N.Y.: Anchor/Doubleday, 1978.

GALINSKY, ELLEN. *Between Generations: The Six Stages of Parenthood.* New York: Times Books, 1981.

GERSON, MARY-JOAN, JUDITH L. ALPERT, and MARY SUE RICHARDSON. "Mothering: The View from Psychological Research." *Signs* 9, 3 (1984): 434–453.

GORLITZ, PAULA, and DAVID GUTMANN. "The Psychological Transition into Grandparenthood." In John G. Howells, ed. *Modern Perspectives in the Psychiatry of Middle Age.* New York: Brunner/Mazel, 1981: 167–186.

HARKINS, ELIZABETH B. "Effects of the Empty Nest Transition on the Self-Report of Psychological and Physical Well-Being." *Journal of Marriage and the Family* 40, 3 (August 1978): 549–556.

HESS, BETH B., and ELIZABETH W. MARKSON. "The Family in Later Life." In Hess and Markson, eds. *Aging and Old Age.* New York: Macmillan, 1980: 258–260.

HOWELL, ELIZABETH. "Psychological Reactions of Postpartum Women." In Elizabeth Howell and Marjorie Bayes, eds. *Women and Mental Health.* New York: Basic Books, 1981: 340–346.

KRYSTAL, SHEILA, and DAVID A. CHIRIBOGA. "The Empty Nest Process in Midlife Men and Women." Research Report, Langley Porter Institute, University of California, San Francisco. August 1978. Reproduced.

LESHAN, EDA J. *The Wonderful Crisis of Middle Age.* New York: McKay, 1973.

LEWIS, ROBERT A., PHILLIP J. FRENEAU, and CRAIG L. ROBERTS. "Fathers and the Postparental Transition." *Family Coordinator* 28, 4 (October 1979): 514–520.

LOEWENSTEIN, SOPHIE F. "Toward Choice and Differentiation in the Midlife Crises of Women." In Carol L. Heckerman, ed. *The Evolving Female: Women in a Psychosocial Context.* New York: Human Sciences Press, 1980: 158–188.

McGILL, MICHAEL E. *The 40-to-60-Year-Old Male.* New York: Simon & Schuster, 1980.

MENAGHAN, ELIZABETH. "Marital Stress and Family Transitions: A Panel Analysis." *Journal of Marriage and the Family* 45, 2 (May 1983): 371–386.

MURRY, SAUNDRA, and DAPHNE HARRISON. "Black Women and the Future." *Psychology of Women Quarterly* 6, 1 (Fall 1981):113–122.

NEUGARTEN, BERNICE L., and KAROL K. WEINSTEIN. "The Changing American Grandparent." In Neugarten, ed. *Middle Age and Aging.* Chicago: University of Chicago Press, 1968: 280–285.

NEWMAN, BARBARA M., and PHILIP R. NEWMAN. *Development Through Life: A Psychosocial Approach.* Homewood, Ill.: Dorsey Press, 1975: 291–339.

NYE, IVAN F., and FELIX M. BERARDO. "The Role of Grandparents." In Laurence D. Steinberg, ed. *The Life Cycle.* New York: Columbia University Press, 1981: 325–330.

ROBERTS, CRAIG L., and ROBERT A. LEWIS. "The Empty Nest Syndrome." In John G. Howells, ed. *Modern Perspectives in the Psychiatry of Middle Age.* New York: Brunner/Mazel, 1981: 328–336.

ROBERTSON, JOAN F. "The Significance of Grandparents: Perceptions of Young Adult Grandchildren." *Gerontologist* 16 (1976): 137–140.

ROSSI, ALICE S. "Transition to Parenthood." *Journal of Marriage and the Family* 30, 1 (1968):26–39.

RUBIN, LILLIAN B. *Women of a Certain Age: The Midlife Search for Self.* New York: Harper & Row, 1979.

SPENCE, DONALD L., and THOMAS LONNER. "The 'Empty Nest': A Transition Within Motherhood." *Family Coordinator* 20, 4 (October 1971): 369–375.

SPREY, JETSE, and SARAH H. MATTHEWS. "Contemporary Grandparenthood: A Systemic Transition." In Felix M. Berardo, ed. *Middle and Late Life Transitions.* Annals, AAPSS 464 (November 1982): 91–103.

STEVENS-LONG, JUDITH. *Adult Life: Developmental Processes.* Palo Alto: Mayfield, 1979: 289–298.

TROLL, LILLIAN E. "Family Life in Middle and Old Age: The Generation Gap." In Felix M. Berardo, ed. *Middle and Late Life Transitions.* Annals, AAPSS 464 (November 1982): 38–46.

———. "Grandparents: The Family Watchdogs." In Timothy H. Brubaker, ed. *Family Relationship in Later Life.* Beverly Hills: Sage, 1983: 63–76.

———, SHEILA J. MILLER, and ROBERT C. ATCHLEY. *Families in Later Life.* Belmont, Calif.: Wadsworth, 1979: 108–120.

YOUNG, MICHAEL, and PETER WILLMOTT. *Family and Kinship in East London.* London: Routledge & Kegan Paul, 1957. Quoted in Fuchs, 1978.

CHAPTER 8

Ties with Aging Parents

At just about the time that mid-life men and women are struggling to redefine their relationships with their adult children, they often become caught up in another intergenerational shift: that of readjusting their bonds with their own parents, who by now are usually in their late seventies and eighties. Since people are living longer and remaining active later, this bond with one or both aging parents may continue for twenty or more years after the last child leaves home. In fact, the four-generation family, once a rarity, is now commonplace. Moreover, the intergenerational ties are viable and ongoing.

In a far-ranging, three-country study of family support networks for the aged, Ethel Shanas (1979) found that four out of five elderly, noninstitutionalized persons had at least one living child. While only 18 percent of these parents actually lived with their children, more than half lived within ten minutes of them and three-quarters lived within half an hour's distance. More than half of the parents reported that they had seen their children within the last two days and about 75 percent had seen them within the past week. Only one out of ten had not seen their children in over a month.

To back this up, Troll found that aging parents and their middle-aged children not only see each often, but, if they live too far apart for regular visits, maintain ongoing contact by telephone and letters and then get together for extended visits or on special occasions such as holidays, birthdays, and family ritual events such as weddings and funerals. Otherwise, visits may be very brief, often just a short conversation to "catch up on the time of day" or to check that all is well, and much of this brief contact is done via the phone, even if they live near each other.

For most middle-aged children and their elderly parents, the relationship tends to be fairly smooth and comfortable. In one recent study, Victor Cicirelli found that 87 percent of the adult children questioned felt close to their fathers and 91 percent close to their mothers. As expected, daughters felt closer than sons, while lower-class children felt closer than those at higher socioeconomic levels.

What is the nature of these bonds? Two concepts dominate the discussion in this area, that of *filial responsibility* and *filial maturity*. Filial responsibility defines Alvin Schorr, usually refers to the child's obligation to meet the concrete, operational needs of his/her aging parent(s) and centers around such issues as protection, physical care, and economic support. Filial maturity, on the other hand, is a more abstract concept first developed by Margaret Blenkner to allude to the developmental stage during mid-life when the child achieves a sense of personal growth at which he/she realizes that the aging parent has become dependent upon him/her and is able to offer assistance in a nonthreatening, mutually helpful way.

These two issues assume tangible proportions in the increasingly long stretch of years between the first recognition that parents can no longer manage without help to their eventual death. The road is usually punctuated by a number of stress-laden turning points that sometimes erupt into crises. They are often triggered by a medical problem, deterioration of a neighborhood that makes living alone hazardous, the thinning out or lack of household help, or the need to institutionalize. Whether or not they personally care for their elderly parents, children are usually intensely involved. Generally, many adult children are able to accommodate to the changing needs of their parents and are both willing and eager to help them face the loss of independence. Others, swamped with the demands, not only of their aging parents but of their own mid-life adjustments and the competing needs of their children and spouses, feel caught in the intergenerational squeeze.

Let us examine these two areas separately.

Filial Responsibility

Studies of how help is given within families have shown that it usually flows in a downward direction: parents give to their children who give to *their* children. Only as the first generation becomes very old or when illness and infirmity impinge do those in the first generation begin to receive as much or more than they have given.

What Parents Want

Recently, it has been found that, generally, with social security programs, Medicare, pension plans, and savings of various types, most older persons do not need financial assistance from their children. Only when serious illness wipes out their resources do they turn to them. Bernice Neugarten (1975) reports that, while most old people would prefer to be independent of their families as much as possible, when they can no longer manage financially for themselves, they expect their children to come to their aid. Sometimes, even when they may need it, some elderly parents will feel reluctant to ask for it, possibly fearing that children will use gifts of money as substitutes for attention and other gestures of caring.

Of course in those ethnic or religious subgroups that have strong familial values, asking for such help is considered both appropriate and acceptable. In the Chicano culture, for example, David Maldonado observes that the family is seen as a lifelong system of emotional support and, at times, of material help, particularly in regard to the expected obligations toward elderly parents. While Chicano parents tend to de-emphasize their dependency upon their children, a universal value in this culture is that offspring will provide for their parents when they reach old age and always respect them.

In his study of older parents' expectations of their children, Wayne Seelbach separated these expectations into six categories: (1) married children should live close to their parents; (2) they should take care of them when they are sick; (3) they should give them financial help if needed; (4) if children live nearby, they should visit their parents at least once a week; (5) if they live at a distance, they should write to them; and (6) they should feel responsible for them.

Expectations assume tangible form in daily activities such as shopping for groceries, preparing hot meals, cleaning house, doing laundry, accompanying a parent when paying bills or cashing checks, paying the rent or mortgage for them, doing heavy work around the house, going with them to the movies or other social functions, and helping them climb up and down stairs.

As might be anticipated, as parents grew older, they were found to expect more from their children. Although while they still had their spouse, parents expected less of their children; as they became widowed or divorced, they expected more. Understandably, the higher the income of the parents, the less concrete help they needed; the sicker they grew, the more help they wanted. All in all, while they were still in the "young old" age group, the aging parents did fairly well by themselves and rarely turned to their children. However, once parents entered the "old old" category, they tended to become less self-reliant.

A typical situation in which aging parents' attempts to remain independent falter in the face of illness and a deteriorating neighborhood is reflected in the following example:

Abe Heller impatiently waited on the front porch of the Sunset Golden Age Center, alternately watching the front driveway and the checkers board in front of him. He apologized to his friend, Sol Perlman, if he seemed distracted. He was waiting for his daughter, Betty Eisman, to pick him up; they were going to the hospital to visit his wife who had slipped on the stairs last month and broke her hip. "Such a woman!" he exclaimed with a shake of his head. "You'd think that by now she'd know how many front steps we have—we've only lived in this apartment for thirty-six years. But then, she's eighty-one years old, so maybe she's entitled to forget a little."

Usually he went to visit Momma every day by himself, even if it meant taking two buses. But today Betty was coming to tell them what happened when she went to see their landlord. That *goniff* had written to tell them that he was going to tear down their building soon because it doesn't pay to keep it in repair.

With a sigh, he said they should have listened to the children when they wanted them to move out to the suburbs where they all lived. But their apartment was comfortable, on a bus line, and near the neighborhood where he had had his own little tailor shop for fifty-two years. Even though he gave up the store six years ago, he still liked to stroll down to the corner each morning to buy the paper and have coffee with his old friends. But now they're planning to tear down the whole row of stores to build a fancy shopping mall; the entire neighborhood is going to be fixed up, they were told. And not many of the old friends are left, anyway.

Not that he's complaining, he hurried on to say. He and Momma have had a very good life in Minneapolis, since they moved here from Brooklyn fifty-eight years ago. He's always made a good living; they have three fine children, eight wonderful grandchildren, and even three great grandchildren—may God bless them! And they both have their health—or at least they did, until Momma's accident. Of course, Dr. Fishman tells him he has a little high blood pressure and the veins of his legs aren't so good. But what can you expect at eighty-four? And Momma has had sugar in her blood for a long time, and lately she's having trouble reading the newspaper. The new doctor at the clinic said she needs an eye operation; maybe that's why she fell. But she knows how to cook just the right meals for him and for her, too, and they get along just fine, the two of them. They've always been proud to be independent, never having to ask for help from anyone—even from the children.

But now, added Mr. Heller with another sign, "Everything is changing. Momma still isn't so steady on her feet; she'll have to use a walker. Betty and her husband want us to move in with them. Harry is a fine man; we get along very well. He looks on us like his own parents. But who wants to live with children? It's not like having your own place, with no one else telling you what to do.

"Wait!" he interrupted himself. "There's the horn. Sorry, Perlman, we'll have to finish this game next week. Can't keep my daughter waiting. . . ."

What Children Give

Shifting from the aging parents' viewpoint to that of their middle-aged children, we find that parent-caring is becoming a major concern for this "sandwich" generation and a major source of life stress. Observation has shown that a large number of people in mid-life express preoccupation with some aspect of care for their elderly parents. However, they seem less concerned about strained financial resources than strained personal relations, fatigue in fulfilling the demands of too many roles, inadequacy of community support, and lack of accurate information by which to judge their parents' changing behavior.

In her survey, Shanas found that the kinds of help children gave their parents were similar to the kinds of help that parents had once given them: help with home repairs and housework, care in illness, and various kinds of gifts. One form of help not usually mentioned is having the older people and their children share a home. Family members also help the elderly negotiate the complex bureaucracy. They become sources of information so that parents can understand and use the full range of options and resources available and help them secure that to which they are entitled. During times of crisis, such as illness or death, children are usually the first to step in.

One study on Jewish families in Los Angeles, in which the mid-life children were interviewed, found that almost all of the aging parents still living in the community had physical problems that assumed first priority. Bertha Simos noted that the children became preoccupied with finding adequate medical care, driving their parents to medical appointments, and making sure that prescriptions were filled and medication taken. They also had to transport physically ailing parents to social and recreational activities, find them suitable living facilities, provide general protective services, and give them physical and emotional support.

Their parents' overall unhappiness and depression were most discomforting to the children, observed Simos, followed by their stubbornness and emotional coldness, which were considered long-standing personality traits rather than related to the aging process. The children also reported such psychological difficulties as complaints against others, fears and anxieties, loneliness, complaints about physical symptoms, and feelings of hopelessness. And they often overlooked their parents' grief and mourning reactions to loss of persons, familiar objects, and previous abilities.

A variety of familial problems emerged in this study, including increased friction between the two parents (which often increased with age and tended at times to be deflected onto the children), children's inability to interact with their parents, and parents' reluctance to socialize with others because of limited physical mobility and self-consciousness over the overt signs of disability. Death of one of the parents often seriously affected the other's ability to function, resulting in depression or efforts to manipulate the child into taking the role of the deceased partner.

Increased medical expenses sometimes exhausted parental savings and embittered the children, who felt deprived of what they considered to be their rightful inheritance. Often they began to dread the prospect of their parents' future illness and the accompanying medical expenses. Most of the children did not regard their parents as responsible for their financial plight, while others felt angry at those parents who either had money and refused to use it or who refused to apply for financial aid out of a false sense of pride or independence. The children did not feel guilty about their parents' financial problems in the same way as they did about their psychological ones. They regarded their parents as having worked hard in the past and felt that it was now society's responsibility to care for them.

Class Differences

One generalization frequently made is that middle-class children give money while lower-class children give services. This was substantiated, by and large, in one recent study that divided help-giving into two categories: care-managing and care-providing. Patricia Archbold found that care-managers usually came from a higher socioeconomic background, as measured by income, education, and occupation, than did care-providers. They were also employed full-time in socially valued career positions and felt little overt conflict over delegating parent-caring activities to others. Care-providers, on the other hand, were not career-oriented and, in the few instances where they did work, felt torn between their jobs and their feelings of obligation to the parent, resigning in some cases to provide full-time care.

Care-managers used a wide range of social supports, devoting a major share of their time to obtaining and retaining appropriate persons, such as physicians, lawyers, social workers, and nurses, to provide services. They also paid more attention to the psychological and social needs of their parents: taking them on drives, accompanying them to the hairdresser, church, or out for dinner, buying them TV sets, and bringing visitors to see them. Care-providers had few such social supports. They were preoccupied with performing the heavy physical tasks of providing nursing care and personal services to the parent by themselves. Their lives became rigidly scheduled around such daily routines as meals, bowel habits, bathing, exercises, and rest periods.

The cost-benefit balance of providing care varied. Care-managers felt they gained satisfaction, increased knowledge about themselves and about aging, improved relations with their parents, and a sense of personal meaning. They measured the major costs in terms of time limitations, loss of mobility, career interruption, financial difficulties, and feelings of guilt. They said that care interfered first with their personal and family time, then with time with friends, and finally their work time. For the care-providers, the costs were much more severe. Decreased freedom—both on a daily and on a long-range basis—lack of privacy, constant irritation, and guilt were major items. Moves, retirement plans, and vacations were all affected. Loss of privacy and intrusion into their personal space were especially hard on their families. Resentment, anger, and frustration resulted, particularly on the part of spouses.

In general, exhaustion, both physical and emotional, in caring for aging parents, emerges as one of the most debilitating consequences felt by children at this stage. When combined with other mid-life stresses, the effect could become the proverbial last straw:

Helen Bennett looked down at the letter that she had just pulled out of the mailbox. "Oh, no. . . . This is just too much!" She kept repeating the words as she skimmed the seven pages filled with her mother-in-law's cramped, neatly formed handwriting. Bob's father was beginning to show signs of senility and the doctor thought he might have Alzheimer's disease. Could she come down and investigate nursing home possibilities? It was getting impossible to take care of him at home, with his recent colostomy and other physical problems. Their current nurse says she can't manage him and wants to leave.

Helen's mind went back over the long years she had put into parent-caring. Ever since she was young, she had taken on responsibility for both of her parents. They had lived on a farm in central Pennsylvania and, as an only child, she always had to help them make big decisions. Then, when her father was hurt in a tractor accident eighteen years ago, which left him semiparalyzed, she had to take over, helping them move into the small town nearby, arranging for disability payments and for extra money to be sent to them, and organizing nursing care and physical therapy for him.

When her father died seven years ago, all of her mother's loneliness and dependence was transferred to her. She still calls her at least twice a week, pouring out her troubles and disappointments by the hour. Helen has been trying for years to have her come to live with them or, when she refused, to move into a Golden Age home run by her Lutheran denomination, but Mrs. Schirmer has always clung to her own house. Now, at age eighty-six, the arthritis in her hands has grown so bad, she can no longer do much, and Helen has to drive down every few weeks to check up on her.

And Bob's parents—they're in even worse shape. They're down in New Haven and their other two sons live quite a distance away: Fred owns a car dealership in Cincinnati and Donald is an engineer in Denver. So Bob and she have always felt responsible for them; after all, he's the oldest son. Both parents are now in their eighties and have had numerous health problems. Mr. Bennett always had a bad heart and over the years his health become even more complicated by nephritis. Recently he underwent a colostomy, which requires continuous nursing care and supervision.

Mrs. Bennett herself has chronic asthma and bronchial difficulties and really can't handle him. Since she doesn't get along with her other daughters-in-law, she always turns to Helen when they have to arrange nursing care or hospitalization for either of them. She can't recall the number of times she's had to drop everything to rush down to New Haven when a medical emergency came up. Bob was always far too busy, so it was left to her to consult with doctors about the care they needed and to make arrangements.

But now, of all times! Bob probably hasn't told them of his plans to give up his practice and move down to Boston *and* to divorce her. Will this change the picture? She feels too exhausted, too wiped out to go down there for another round of medical consultations and interviews with nurses. . . . And besides, why should it be *her* responsibility now? Let Bob take over—or his girlfriend, Laura!

Filial Maturity

As already mentioned, the term "filial maturity" was coined as a protest against the use of such terms as "role reversal" and "parenting one's parents" and refers to the development of a sense of personal maturity on the part of the mid-life child in that he/she accepts his/her parent's dependence and is able to provide physical and emotional support in a nonthreatening, mutually helpful way. Most middle-aged children find that, as their parents age, regardless of past conflicts and unresolved developmental issues, they need to take over the decision reins. Moreover, they must implement these decisions, even though the nature and extent of their parents' needs may involve real deprivation and sacrifice, both on their part and on that of their children. For some, this involves a serious struggle over priorities.

Ideally, says Elaine Brody (1974) the filial issue should occur and be resolved as a normal developmental phase rather than in the crucible of an acute crisis, such as the need to institutionalize a parent. In order for the adult child to become filially mature, the aging parent must have the capacity to become dependent. This is not easy. While parents can understand the need and, in most cases, do agree to give up their independence and head-of-the-family roles, they may hesitate or postpone the final admission. Ambivalence and indecision on both sides may ensue.

This ambivalence is felt in a number of areas. On the part of the parents, they may fear that, if they become demanding, they will alienate their children and cause them to distance themselves. At the same time they want their children to recognize them as individuals with their own rights, needs, and limitations and with independent life histories that predate their children's birth. Usually, what they want, basically, is continued contact with continued independence.

In an essay in which she analyzes aging King Lear's relations with his adult daughters, Zena Blau points out another core dilemma. A family's (or society's) continuity requires that its elder members give up their key roles to the next generation. But the younger members are often eager to take on the roles before their parents are willing to yield them. Lear's tragedy is caused not by his old age or the decline of his powers, but by his decision to retire and invest the powers of his office in his daughters, which leads to a reversal of their roles.

While cultural norms demand that adult children honor their filial obligations to parents in their time of need, both time and energy are scarce resources, observes Blau. When an individual has several competing role obligations, he or she must set priorities. Ties to spouse and child tend to be felt as having greater immediacy and urgency since children, at least, have a future, whereas obligations to parents are retroactive and their current love and emotional involvement are usually far less intense.

Personal strains and negative feelings are more strongly related to *perceived* parental dependency than to the actual amount of help provided, notes Victor Cicirelli, who uses the term "filial anxiety" to refer to the feelings generated in adult children when contemplating and anticipating the possibility of providing help to parents.

Children may feel the need to monitor their parents' well-being more carefully and often become worried, anxious, and stressed about their own capacity to deal with the impending burdens. Another source of this anxiety may be rooted in the middle-aged children's efforts to set an example for their own children by caring for the needs of the aged parent in the hope that such care will, in turn, ensure their own future care when their time comes. They may recall the intolerance of their own parents toward their grandparents and remember the pain of seeing a helpless aged person cast off.

Sometimes parents' aging and their failing powers awaken in middle-aged children intense negative feelings about their own decreasing abilities and the aging process. They may also be at the point of recognizing the gap between their own earlier dreams and the reality of what they themselves have accomplished. Instinctively they may try to turn to their parents for protection and nurturance, as in their childhood days. Instead, they find that it is the parents who now crave nurture, care, and support. Their health has deteriorated, their finances are strained, their locomotion is hindered, their access to places and people is limited, and their opportunities have decreased just at the time when their needs and wants have increased. Few people and places now want them. They may have been signaling to their children for some time that now they are the ones who need to be looked after.

The Dying Process

Sometimes separation through institutionalization and loss of an aging parent through death can be perceived as one more crippling object loss to the middle-aged child. This is often met with mixed emotions. If the dying process is prolonged and painful, the family also suffers. As aging parents become physically and emotionally incapacitated, they sometimes require huge sums simply to be maintained at the minimal level of dignity and comfort that their children feel they owe them. Financial pressures may be compounded by their inner feelings of guilt and anguish and their sincere wish that the helpless parent, who may no longer resembles their earlier memories, would die quickly and painlessly.

At times, the parent's deterioration may reawake earlier feelings in the child of not having been loved and now stimulates him/her to overreact, to exert frantic, time-pressured efforts to obtain some loving response from a depleted, helpless parent through inappropriate, oversolicitous behavior. Or, at the other extreme, they may revenge themselves for having felt emotionally deprived by their own absence, neglect, and even abuse.

Old people today are more likely to die in public places, such as hospitals or nursing homes, than at home behind the veil of domestic privacy. And since it often takes so long to die, middle-aged children frequently become involved in negotiating and supervising their parents' extended terminal illness and ultimate death. In addition to the practical issues involved, they become obsessed with the mounting psychic costs and with such ethical questions as "the right to pull the plug" and "death with dignity." Sometimes the dying process can lead to renewed closeness and intimacy between children and the surviving parent, but at other times it can be very divisive and destructive. Still, the death of a parent, reminds Eda LeShan, can open up new avenues of insight and perception about dependency, mortality, the value of love and acceptance, and the meaning of "family."

Such introspection can add to the mid-life child's feelings of maturation or, as is seen in the following vignette, of despair:

Frank Donnelli sighed heavily as he stared out of the airplane window. He felt deeply depressed. He was returning from Scranton where he had spent a week at his father's bedside. Mario Donnelli had suffered a massive stroke at age seventy-nine. Yesterday they had taken him by ambulance to his daughter Rosa's home in New London, but it was obvious that he hadn't much longer to live.

Since Momma died four years ago, Poppa had just let things slide. Frank had spent most of the past week sorting through papers that had accumulated in the old rolltop desk in the corner of the bedroom—unpaid bills, old snapshots and letters from long-forgotten relatives, outdated business correspondence still addressed to "Donnelli and Sons, Fine Foods." They had closed the store years ago, but Poppa still refused to move out of the old neighborhood where, he insisted, the name "Donnelli" still stood for something.

And now, it would be up to him, as the oldest son, to take over the family reins. It was easier back in Poppa's day, he thought bitterly. Though his parents always struggled—it wasn't easy raising nine children during the Depression—his father always insisted that the family do things together. He remembered how, as kids, they'd rush home to work in the store after school and on weekends, delivering orders and stocking shelves. They used to have wonderful family picnics out at the Grove on the Fourth of July, terrific football games between him and his brothers and cousins before they'd sit down to enormous meals of pasta, grilled lamb, and rich Italian spumoni. Even after he and Marie had settled down in Southern California, they'd always go back to Scranton for the Fourth of July.

But what did tradition mean now to his own family? Oh, he and Marie had a fine life; since he met her at a USO party when he was stationed at the San Diego Marine base, he never looked at another girl. On his return from the Pacific and a quick run through college on the G.I. bill, he settled for a job at the D.A.'s office and he's been there ever since. They bought their own home in a good Catholic neighborhood and all five of their children went to parochial schools.

But their children—look at them now! Tom, their first born, the one who was supposed to carry on the torch—they haven't even heard from him for the past nine years, ever since he got mixed up in the anti-Vietnam war movement and slipped over the border into Canada to escape the draft. Their second son, Paul, is "artistic"; he works as a stage designer in San Francisco and Frank doesn't even like to think about the sort of life he leads. And the kid, Joey, is headed for trouble for sure. He's supposed to be still in high school, but he's out of classes more often than he's in. Lately, he heard he's been running around with a pretty dangerous gang over in Gainesville. . . .

Even the girls haven't given him that much pleasure. Oh, he's proud of Lainey, who, of all the kids, made it through law school. But instead of joining a respectable law firm, she's down in San Diego trying to help undocumented aliens—wetbacks from Mexico—evade the law. And Sharon, their older daughter—she couldn't wait to get married and leave a good job as a nurse to marry a crazy s.o.b. who beat her and chased after every skirt in sight. Now, after three kids and God knows how many black eyes, she's come home and wants her sick mother to care for the babies while she goes back to work. He can't bear watching Marie look at the kids with tears in her eyes. . . .

So where's the name of Donnelli now? Their whole family seems to be falling apart. Lucky his father isn't around to see what's happened to them. Tradition means nothing to his sons; they don't give a damn for the family name. He closed his eyes and whispered, "Poppa, where did I go wrong?"

Involvement of Significant Others

Unless the person in mid-life is an only child, unmarried, and without children of his/her own, care of an aging parent also involves
others in the family network. Sometimes they reach tacit or expressed agreement as to what can or should be done. More often, as
stress increases, tempers erupt over the issues of both filial responsibility and filial maturity.

Siblings

By the time they have reached the middle years, brothers and sisters
usually manage to settle their sibling differences and to establish a
working relationship, ranging from close and positive to distant and
intensely negative. But the needs of elderly parents often serve to ex-
acerbate and reawaken old sibling rivalries. Rita Rogers notes:

> This is the time when one sensitively recalls how the mother and older
> sister shared secrets, how it hurt when the older sister was given cov-
> eted special clothes [such as] the first fur coat, the first trip, a special
> birthday party. The younger sister remembers the alliance that seemed
> to exist between the mother and older sister, which had provoked a
> sense of being small, insignificant, below the status of adult women.
> Now, years later, when the elderly parent is in need of parenting, the
> younger sister often yields responsibility to the older sister, as though to
> say, "You are the older one, therefore you take care of mother or fa-
> ther." . . . The resentment experienced throughout her life as the little
> sister is converted into a refuge role through which she can retaliate to
> the "big sister." [1981:192].

This rivalry may persist to the parent's deathbed. At times, one
sister or brother may be doing most of the work while another appears to be getting most of the credit. Often the put-upon sibling
does not give the others a chance to do their fair share because the
purpose is to show how unworthy the rival is. And often, of course,
the parent instinctively grasps the benefits to be derived and fans the
competition. Sometimes the bickering and quarrels that arise at
such pressure points may be passed on to others in the system, to in-
laws and to adult children, each of whom takes their own position
and either foments or tries to quell the disruption and tugs-of-war.

Frequently the divisiveness among children over parent-caring
splits along gender lines. Even without reopening the Pandora's box

of who gave and got more over the years, daughters usually tend to take on or share the role of active kin-keeper, providing both concrete help and emotional support while sons often limit themselves to financial assistance and occasional visits. A daughter, in recognition of the special bond with her mother, as discussed in Chapter 7, may carve out the time and effort from her crowded life to help her mother and/or father, while a son, who has made a more complete separation from his parents and has taken on different obligations within his own family, may not. Moreover, his wife, the daughter-in-law, often feels little filial obligation; on the contrary, she may still harbor grudges over past slights and either neglects or actively opposes such attention to her husband's parents.

In the following vignette, we see another aspect of the situation depicted in the earlier part of this chapter that illustrates this point:

Betty Eisman, fifty-one, sat with her two brothers in the breakfast room, drinking coffee. She had asked Herbert, fifty-six, who manages a large supermarket in a new shopping center on the west side of the city, and Franklin, fifty-four, who teaches history at the state university in St. Paul, to take time out from their precious Sunday mornings to discuss the latest crisis in their parents' lives.

"I know you're both very busy, boys," she started, "but Mama and Papa are in trouble and need help." She went on to tell them that Mama is ready now to leave the hospital; her broken hip, which took a long time to knit because of her diabetes, has finally healed enough for her to be discharged, even though she'll probably have to use a walker for some time. The hospital social worker, who came in yesterday, warned her that since Mama's cataracts have reached the point where she can only see things dimly; it's dangerous for her to try to keep on doing her own housework. And besides their apartment building is slated to be torn down as part of the big urban renewal project that's being started in that area. The worker thinks they ought to think about other living arrangements.

"Yeah, I know about the building," interrupted Herb. "I spoke to Diamond, the landlord, just yesterday and he tells me they want all the tenants out by next month. The whole neighborhood will be gutted. Pa's still talking about sharing bagels and cream cheese with the other old guys down at the corner cafe, but in a few weeks, it'll all be wiped out. I better talk to Lillian again about their coming to stay with us in Benton Bay."

"Well, you know," interjected Frankie defensively, "Doris and I have been asking them to come and live with us, out near the university. But we're both working full time and there's no public transportation out there."

"Come on, boys," answered Betty wearily, "I know both of you want to help. Mama and Papa have always been good to us and we all feel we owe them. For that matter, Harry and I have been pushing them for years to come and stay with us, now that the girls are gone. But that's no longer good enough. They're getting to the pont where they need more intensive care."

With a decisive gesture, Herb pulled out his checkbook. "Is it a question of money? Maybe we could find round-the-clock nursing care, at least until Mama gets better. You know, Betty, all you have to do is ask."

"Of course," she replied, patting Herb's hand affectionately. "I know you'd give the shirt off your back for Mama and Papa. But that's not all. Now I've got a problem myself. You know Harry has always felt very close to Papa and Mama, since his own parents were wiped out in Germany. But we had a big blowup yesterday. I never felt he resented my running over to take Mama shopping all these years and Papa to the doctor's. Lately I've been spending a lot more time at the apartment, cleaning up and cooking meals for Papa and then running out to the hospital. Now Harry wants me to go away with him on a business trip and . . ."

"Wait a minute," Frankie broke in. "You make it sound as if you're the only one who does anything! And Herb, the big shot, sits back and pays the bills. What about me? You've always tried to push me out, even when we were kids. But don't forget, they're my parents, too. Both Doris and I recognize our responsibilities; we just don't know what *we* can do that will help. But, if it's not possible for them to live alone anymore and they don't want to come to stay with any of us, what are we talking about? You know how Papa feels about going into an old people's home."

"I honestly don't know *what* the alternatives are," Betty answered. "Maybe I better call Jewish Family Service and ask for some advice, find out what's available. But boys, this is something I can't do alone. I want you both to come along with me when I talk to them. You know the old family motto, 'All for one and one for all!' Well, this certainly concerns all of us, so we better decide together. And then we'll need to stand together to talk to Mama and Papa."

Spouses

Throughout a marriage, parents-in-law often act, knowingly or not, to drive further wedges of dissension between bickering husbands and wives. During the transition to late mid-life, this dynamic becomes particularly evident. Although the topic will be discussed further in Chapter 9, it should be mentioned here that, if the mid-life husband and wife enjoy satisfactory relationships, then their bonds with either's aging parents are, for the most part, manageable or do not pose a serious threat. However, when the spousal relations are tense and disagreements occur, the strain of involvement with an aging parent may serve to escalate the conflict and act as the precipitating factor to upset the precarious balance between them. Moreover, if one spouse gets along better with either set of parents than the other, a family coalition can be set up to defeat the other. Or, if one spouse has, over the years, adapted to meeting the dependency needs of the mate, the extra drain of responding at this time to the additional needs of the aging parent—again, either his or hers— may simply become too threatening or too taxing to bear.

Children

Through several projects with three generations of women at the Philadelphia Geriatric Center, Brody (1981) observed that the youngest generation felt more strongly than either their mothers or their grandmothers that grandparents should expect help from their grandchildren and their children. The "women in the middle" lacked consensus: some could not define the responsibilities of their daughters toward their mothers; others seemed to want to protect them from excessive responsibilities; still others expressed values favoring strong family cohesion. Their indecision appeared to reflect their own feelings of being pressured from both above and below.

While parents are still relatively self-sufficient, most mid-life women, as already mentioned, tend to assign their young adult children's needs higher priority than those of their parents. However, when aging, ailing parents require extensive—and expensive— medical treatment or long-term institutionalization, they may have no choice but to drop other commitments and respond as well as they can. And their children may have to develop their own version of "grandfilial maturity" by postponing their own demands until their parents can respond freely once again.

References

ALDOUS, JOAN. *Family Careers*. New York: John Wiley & Sons, 1978:285–301.

ARCHBOLD, PATRICIA G. "Impact of Parent-Caring on Women." *Family Relations* 32, 1 (January 1983):39–45.

BLAU, ZENA S. *Aging in a Changing Society*, 2nd ed. New York: Franklin Watts, 1981:40–57.

BLENKNER, MARGARET. "Social Work and Family Relationships, with Some Thoughts on Filial Maturity." In Ethel M. Shanas and Gordon F. Streib, eds. *Social Structure and the Family*. Englewood Cliffs, N.J.: Prentice-Hall, 1965:46–59.

BRODY, ELAINE M. "Aging and Family Personality: A Developmental View." *Family Process* 13, 1 (March 1974):23–37.

_____. "Women in the Middle and Family Help to Older People." *Gerontologist* 21, 5 (1981):471–480.

CICIRELLI, VICTOR G. "Adult Childrens' Attachment and Helping Behavior to Elderly Parents: A Path Model." *Journal of Marriage and the Family* 45, 4 (November 1983):815–825.

_____. "Adult Children and Their Elderly Parents." In Timothy H. Brubaker, ed. *Family Relationships in Later Life*. Beverly Hills: Sage, 1983:31–46.

COHEN, STEPHEN Z., and BRUCE M. GANS. *The Other Generation Gap: The Middle-Aged and Their Aging Parents*. Chicago: Follett, 1978.

HESS, BETH B., and ELIZABETH W. MARKSON . *Aging and Old Age*. New York: Macmillan, 1980:251–260.

HESS, BETH B. and JOAN M. WARING . "Parent and Child in Later Life: Rethinking the Relationship." In Richard Lerner and Graham B. Spanier, eds. *Child Influences on Marital and Family Interactions: A Life-Span Perspective*. New York: Academic Press, 1978:241–273.

JANZEN, CURTIS, and OLIVER HARRIS . *Family Treatment in Social Work Practice*. Itasca, Ill.: Peacock, 1980:116–140.

JOHNSON, ELIZABETH S., and BARBARA J. BURSK "Relationship Between the Elderly and Their Adult Children." *Gerontologist* 17 (1977):90–96.

LeSHAN, EDA J. *The Wonderful Crisis of Middle Age*. New York: McKay, 1973.

MALDONADO, DAVID, JR. "Aging in the Chicano Context." In Donald E. Gelfand and Alfred J. Kutzik, eds. *Ethnicity and Aging: Theory, Research, and Policy*. New York: Springer, 1979:175–183.

MILLER, DOROTHY A. "The 'Sandwich' Generation: Adult Children of the Aging." *Social Work* 26, 5 (September 1981):419–423.

NEUGARTEN, BERNICE L. "The Future and the Young-Old." *Gerontologist* 15 (1975):4–9.

———. "The Middle Generation." In P. K. Ragan. *Aging Parents.* Los Angeles: University of Southern California Press, 1970:258–266.

PARENT, MARY K. "The Losses of Middle Age and Related Developmental Tasks." In Elizabeth Prichard, et al. eds. *Social Work with the Dying Patient and the Family.* New York: Columbia University Press, 1977:146–153.

ROGERS, RITA R. "On Parenting One's Elderly Parents." In John G. Howells, ed. *Modern Perspectives in the Psychiatry of Middle Age.* New York: Brunner/Mazel, 1981:187–197.

SCHARLACH, ANDREW E. "Relief of Filial Distress Among Women with Aging Mothers." Paper Presented at Annual Meeting of the Gerontological Society of America, San Francisco, November 1983. Reproduced.

SCHMIDT, MARY G. "Failing Parents, Aging Children." *Journal of Gerontological Social Work* 2 (1980):259–268.

SCHORR, ALVIN. *Filial Responsibility in the Modern American Family.* Washington, D.C.: Department of Health, Education and Welfare, Social Security Administration, Division of Program Research, 1960.

SCHWARTZ, ARTHUR N. *Survival Handbook for Children of Aging Parents.* Chicago: Follett, 1977.

SEELBACH, WAYNE C. "Correlates of Aged Parents' Filial Responsibility: Expectations and Realizations." *Family Coordinator* 27, 4 (October 1978):341–350.

SHANAS, ETHEL M. "The Family as a Social Support System in Old Age." *Gerontologist* 19 (April 1979):169–175.

———. "Older People and Their Families: The New Pioneers." *Journal of Marriage and the Family* 42, 1 (February 1980):9–15.

SIMOS, BERTHA G. "Adult Children and Their Aging Parents." *Social Work* 18, 3 (May 1973):78–85.

STREIB, GORDON F., and RUBYE W. BECK. "Older Families: A Decade Review." *Journal of Marriage and the Family* 42, 4 (November 1980): 937–956.

TROLL, LILLIAN, SHEILA J. MILLER, and ROBERT C. ATCHLEY. *Families in Later Life.* Belmont, Calif.: Wadsworth, 1979.

TURNER, JOSEPH G. "Patterns of Intergenerational Exchange: A Developmental Approach." *International Journal of Aging and Human Development* 6 (1975):111–115.

CHAPTER 9

Bonds with One's Mate

Whenever changes and disruptions occur during the passage to late mid-life, they inevitably affect the primary interpersonal relationship at this time, the husband-wife tie.* Some of this upset is inherent in the changing nature of the marriage itself and the conflicts that arise during these years; other tensions are reactive to or the consequences of changes in other aspects of the mid-life situation, as discussed in the previous five chapters, or to unforeseen external pressures. Whatever the source of the disturbance, it frequently becomes played out in the marital area.

The married couple's primary task at this stage, according to Sonya Rhodes, is that of *rediscovery versus despair*. The durability of the marriage depends on the adaptations made to reestablish a satisfactory balance between the spouses. Whatever part the couple's children previously played in sustaining the marriage, now the

---

*In this chapter I shall be speaking of "marriage," "marital relations," and "spouses," although I do not mean to imply that a long-term, committed relationship between two people of opposite sexes or of the same sex cannot exist without the formal, socially sanctioned contractual arrangement that we call "marriage." The important criteria are the role commitments, the sharing of living and financial responsibilities over time, and the interweaving of personal life-styles into a common unit with a joint history.

parents have only each other with whom to negotiate their new relationship.

The Nature of Marriage at This Time

Overall Tone

Some mid-life marriages appear calm and placid, on an even keel much of the time. Both spouses seem content with a relatively low emotional tone; they like being where they are in their own growth and development. They do not seem to hunger for great excitement and show little ambition or drive. They can be described, says LeShan, as "terribly good, decent, kindly people who want to live simply and without a good deal of turmoil." On the other hand, some of the most difficult, rocky marriages turn out to be stable and strong at this stage; although the partners have lived through a great deal of turmoil in the past with each other, they eventually find a deep and solid foundation on which to anchor their relationships. Nevertheless, partners are often unprepared, not only for the ways in which their own roles change, but for the need to adjust to the "new look" of the spouse.

Many couples regard this stage in their marriage as better than earlier ones, a time of freedom from financial worries, lessened housework and other chores, offering new possibilities for their becoming mobile and expressing themselves. Partners who engage in mutual activities have been found to view their marriage more favorably than those who do not, although even those who do not share common interests can compensate by developing a sense of mutual understanding.

When the mid-life participants in the San Francisco Transition Study were asked how they expected their marriages to change once the children left home, both men and women expressed the hope that there would be greater closeness between them, notes Majda Thurnher. About 80 percent described their spouses primarily in positive terms, although the women proved dramatically more outspoken than the men. While the men appreciated their wives' virtues and readily admitted that they themselves did not meet their wives' expectations, the women tended to be more openly critical of their husbands and more confident of their own role performance.

In another longitudinal project, Arlene Skolnick found that satisfied husbands and wives seem to have similar personalities; the greater the degree of likeness, the higher the level of satisfaction. Overall, she found that individual marriages change more in a positive direction than in a negative one, with such external influences as having more money available and children's leaving home playing an important part. It should be noted, however, when looking at such marriages over time, that by this stage we are dealing with a self-selected population; those whose marriages have failed earlier are no longer available.

Areas of Change

Style of Life.   During the transition to late mid-life, many husbands and wives use their first opportunity in about twenty-five years to make significant changes in their life-styles. They may take advantage of their greater financial security to improve the quality of their physical living arrangements, either redecorating or remodeling their present homes to meet their own rather than their childrens' needs or opting for the greater convenience of a centrally located service apartment. Some begin to indulge in long-deferred plans to travel, to start hobbies and collections, to purchase personal comforts and luxuries, to entertain and go out to plays and concerts, to lay the groundwork for long-term retirement plans, or simply to "relax and be themselves."

Other persons, however, report a real inability—in themselves or in their spouse—to "live it up," to change long-entrenched habits of thrift and deferment of gratification, although they no longer need to do so. Some find it hard to reorder their priorities, even when children no longer depend on their help or aging parents can still fend for themselves.

The incident below reflects this conflict:

Harry Eisman burst through the door, clutching a large bouquet of roses, and rushed into the kitchen where his wife, Betty, was taking a casserole out of the oven. As she turned, he put both arms around her waist and gave her a resounding kiss. Excitedly he told her his big news: As part of his recent promotion to State Director of Sales for Welbilt Electric, he has been given three weeks to visit all of their sales outlets in the region. This afternoon he decided to combine it with a vacation for two.

As they sat down to dinner he poured out his plans. They'll drive leisurely from one town to another and, while he sees his dealers, she can go sightseeing or shopping. If they find a good spot on a lake or along the Mississippi, they can stop off for a few days. They'll make a second honeymoon of it—actually their first, since they never had a real one before. When they were married thirty years ago, all they could afford was a weekend in Atlantic City. Now they can relax, take their time, really get to know each other again. With this new job, he no longer has to hussle so hard, can take things easier. . . .

Excitedly, Betty chimed in. Maybe later on, they can go even farther—to England, to visit the cousins who raised him during the war; or even to Israel, where she has relatives. . . . She stopped suddenly. In all her delight at Harry's announcement, she had forgotten her own news. Hesitantly, she told him about her visit that morning to the hospital where her mother was recuperating from a broken hip. The social worker had told her father and her that Mama could be discharged as soon as they could find a suitable place to live. Since she'll still be using a walker, their third-floor apartment won't do; anyways, they have to vacate it by the end of the month.

"So?" asked Harry, ominously.

"So, I thought that maybe we could bring them here for a while until we can arrange something more permanent. . . . After all, we have plenty of room with both the girls gone. And it might be easier for Mama and Papa; you know you like them, Harry."

At this point, he blew up. "Like them, of course I like them! But what has that to do with us? Here I'm inviting you to come on a second honeymoon and you drag in your parents! The next thing you'll tell me is that you want to take the grandchildren along with us, so you can give Marilyn a rest. Or maybe you need to baby-sit for Carole again."

Betty stopped, her mouth half open. She had just been about to mention that she had promised to take care of the boys while Marilyn went with her husband to St. Louis next week. Meanwhile, her husband was working himself up into a rage.

"Everyone else is important to you; you have to mix into everything and try to solve everyone's troubles—the girls, your parents, the neighbors . . . even the cleaning woman! Little Miss Fixit, that's who you are! But your own husband, he's the last one that counts with you!" Angrily, he shoved back his untasted dessert and stamped into the other room.

Slowly, Betty cleared off the table and stacked the dishes. She realized guiltily that she *had* been taking Harry for granted for a long time. He had always been so easygoing about her family. He himself no longer had any relatives, since his parents had been destroyed in the furnaces. What always endeared Harry to her was that he just fitted into the family; when they would go to her parents for the holidays, he used to say they were *his* Mama and Papa, too. All these years, when she had been busy with them or with the girls, she never dreamed that he was feeling neglected.

Now she went into the living room where Harry sat in his armchair, pretending to read the newspaper. In a voice thickened with tears, she agreed that he was right; she hadn't considered how much this trip meant to him. He put his arms around her and they kissed, and then they sat down to figure out how they could manage to get away. In the morning she would call both girls and tell them that they'd have to get along without her for the rest of the month, that the two of them were going on a trip. As for her parents, she'll ask her brothers to come over and see if they can work out some living arrangements for Mama and Papa at least for the next few weeks and maybe for a longer time.

Later that evening, after they had gone to bed and made love in a far more arousing and satisfying way than they had for a long time, Betty snuggled down in her husband's arms and sleepily thought: That psychologist on TV the other morning was right. Couples should learn how to fight more. It adds spice to their marriage.

Sexual Performance. "Sex? It's gotten better and better. . . . Right now, I'm enjoying sex more than I ever did in my life—maybe even more than I ever though I could." This answer from one fifty-two-year-old participant in Rubin's study on mid-life women appears to be characteristic of many women at this time of life. Freed from the fears of possible pregnancy and the self-consciousness of the children's presence in the home, many women experience a heightening of sexual drive. Other researchers agree that healthy, well-adjusted middle-aged women who are happily married may experience little or no change in their sexual activity patterns at this time; in fact they often find that their sex life has improved substantially.

For other couples, the picture is far less rosy. Those men and women who had uninteresting or unsatisfactory patterns of sexual relations in earlier stages of their marriage or who report previous problems of impotence or frigidity may now use menopause as a welcome opportunity to terminate sexual relations entirely and to rid their lives permanently of the embarrassment and frustration that sex has come to represent to them. For those who view bearing children as the primary—sometimes the only—reason to engage in coital activity, the cessation of fertility obviates its further need.

A surprising number of men and women seem to equate physical attractiveness and youthfulness with sexual appeal. Here we find disparate standards. Men in their middle and late forties are considered mature and powerful; their status is defined in terms of personality, intelligence, career achievement, and earning power; their sexuality becomes part of their "machismo." Women, however, as mentioned in Chapter 4, are measured in terms of their physical youthfulness; thus, as they grow older, they see themselves and are seen by others as less attractive and sexy.

Sometimes, the difficulty lies in the imbalance between the husband's and wife's sexual performance. The wife at this stage may experience a heightening of sexual drive, particularly if menopause has removed her concern over impregnation. She feels free now to enjoy sex without worry. Unfortunately for her, the adequacy of her husband's sexual activity may decline rather noticeably at this stage. Even though he remains interested and under proper circumstances capable, his impotence may upset his self-image and lead him to avoid further sexual encounters.

Masters and Johnson found that sexual inadequacies in men take a sharp upward turn at about fifty years of age, although they attribute such difficulties as much to psychological as to biological causes. Fear of impotence often becomes a self-fulfilling prophecy. As mentioned earlier, though the normal male at this age may take double or triple the time to gain an erection, ejaculate with about half the force, and require up to twenty-four hours before experiencing another erection, he can still perform well sexually, given the proper stimulation and encouragement.

As for women, Helen Kaplan points out that their sexual functioning is extremely variable and depends on their overall emotional state and on their ongoing relationship with their husbands. Many women report an increase in erotic appetite during the menopausal years. However, if their husbands are avoiding sex and these women attribute it to their own declining physical attractiveness, they, too, may choose to refrain in order to spare themselves the pain of sexual frustration or rejection. Other women may be angered by having to curb their own rising sexual needs in line with their husbands' decreasing capacities. On the other hand, some women tend to be extremely protective of their husbands' anxieties and will moderate their own demands to avoid posing a threat to his sense of manhood.

Marital and sex therapists have been urging couples during these years to broaden their sexual interactions to include sensual as well as sexual pleasuring. They point out that sex for older couples does not have to be performance- or orgasm-oriented, that its objective should be to achieve intimacy and fulfillment through a broad spectrum of sensate and feeling interactions. One key element in enjoyment at this stage is to cultivate open and honest communication and mutual sensitization to each others' needs and desires.

Complementarity Bonds. Couples often use this transitional period to rework their complementarity bonds into a closer, more mutually satisfying pattern. For the first time since the children were born, they now feel free to "let down their hair and be themselves." Clearly, spouses each bring their own personality patterns and past life experiences into their interactions with each other. Still, the ways in which the stresses and challenges of mid-life affect the marriage depend, not only on their personal histories, but on the couple's capacity to deal with these stresses together and on the effectiveness of their joint problem-solving patterns.

At this stage it may become necessary for spouses to recognize, redefine, and reintegrate the successes and failures in their marriage. They may find their priorities shifting from earlier needs for security, performance, and role fulfillment toward a desire for greater companionship and understanding. Unfortunately, Carol Nadelson notes, in situations where mates may define success or failure in different ways or experience the change in complementarity at different points in time, the spousal balance may waver and tilt—leading to either a new reequilibrium or to further strain and disruption.

As already mentioned, when marital partners experience difficulties in reassigning roles and redefining rules, open communication between the two becomes critical. Unless channels are clear in both directions and not overloaded with conflicting messages, complications become inevitable. Women, particularly, tend to view this two-way communication as vital during this stage because of the numerous changes in role content and continuity that they undergo.

Some marriages at this stage, warns Richard Kerckhoff, may be considered "good" when they are, in fact, simply unpainful, unexamined rather than stimulating or challenging. He questions whether the reduced pressures at this time may lead not to marital bliss but to the marital "blahs" and points out what marriage counselors have long noted: when trouble arises in mid-life marriages, it is often related more to the *boredom* of the union than to its traumatic qualities. Husband and wife, absorbed in their own commitments over the years, may have grown distant and uninterested in what the other is doing and feeling.

For some partners, the emptiness of the relationship becomes too much to bear. The purpose of having lived together, now that the children are gone, seems to have disappeared. Some wives admit, "It was all for the children. I only put up with my husband because of them." Similarly, husbands claim, "I supported my family until they were grown; now I feel free to go." Both may feel a marked sense of loss yet express a lack of interest in having the bond continue. Unless vitality is injected into the relationship, the marriage itself stands endangered.

Extramarital Affairs. One answer to the emptiness of such a marriage is to seek fulfillment elsewhere. Mid-life men in particular seem to feel the need for a final fling before the "gates close." Sometimes they embark on an affair—with a younger woman. One study of extramarital sexual relations during the middle years found that men whose children had left home seemed more open to such involvement than those whose children were about to leave or than women either before or after the children have left home. These men also had lower marital adjustment scores and said they received less sexual satisfaction within their marriages than other husbands, reports Ralph Johnson.

An example of an attempt to enjoy such a fling is evident in the following incident. It is part of one man's efforts to demonstrate that he is not yet "over the hill":

As the car sped along the expressway, Paul Alberts began to whistle under his breath. He had spent a strenuous week up in Green Bay going over the specifications for the new upstate shopping center on which he was submitting a bid. It was his first step into the "big time" and, if it was accepted by Kramer Builders, would mean the start of a whole new line of work. Who said that, at age fifty-four, he was sliding down hill, coasting along until retirement?

Of course, that wasn't the only reason he was feeling so good. He chuckled reminiscently as he thought of his young secretary, Donna, still sleeping soundly back at the motel when he left an hour ago. They had spent the last four days together, working during the day and playing at night. Mornings he had been busy lining up subcontractors and building suppliers; afternoons he and she worked together, figuring out specifications and competitive prices. And evenings . . . he began to grin as he remembered last night.

Yeah, that was the smartest move he had ever made, hiring Donna six months ago when it became clear that Ethel, "fat, fussy, and forty," who manned his one-girl office, wasn't able to keep up with the flood of work. Donna was only twenty-eight, but she had worked seven years for his competitors, Hansen Brothers, ever since her divorce. She was quiet but smart as a whip; there had been a current of electric tension between them ever since she started. But nothing had actually happened until this week, when he asked her to come along with him to take notes and keep track of figures.

That first day she handled herself like a pro, keeping in the background while he argued with those dumb Swedes over lumber and delivery schedules. Every now and then she'd send him a note about some item that had slipped his mind. That night, back at the motel, they had dinner and drinks and both had gotten high—as much on excitement as on liquor. Later, when he knocked on the door connecting their rooms, she was waiting for him. And what a night it was! Donna was seductive and full of ideas; she really knew how to turn him on and taught him tricks he had only heard about.

In the morning he returned to his room and they became boss and discreet secretary again. That's the way it had been all week: business partners during the day, lovers at night. What a flip it had given to the negotiations; he really felt strong and in control. As a team they were unbeatable. The old power was really back; it had been years since he felt so much of a man.

Briefly, his thoughts made a guilty jump back to his wife, Jessie. No, it had never been that good with her, even in the beginning when he had come back from Korea. She was sweet, but so passive in bed. She never refused him but never took the lead, never wanted to try anything new. And then, by the time the four children were born, she had become entirely absorbed in them and in her aches and pains. She made it clear that she had little time or interest in him and his needs.

Matters grew worse between them after Junior was killed celebrating his high school graduation; she blamed him for the boy's wanting to join the Marines like his father. Anyways, she just drew inside her shell; every time he tried to reach out to her, like asking her to work with him when he started his own business, she said she was too tired or had a bellyache or God knows what else. They just grew farther apart as the years kept slipping by. He'd bury himself in his work and she in her doctoring and her soap operas . . . it must have been at least four years since he even touched her. He had thought that part of his life was over; he had never been one to sleep around, except maybe at Shrine conventions. But now . . . he sighed with satisfaction . . . now life had taken on a new shine.

Briefly, Paul Alberts looked at the dashboard clock. He was already on the outskirts of the city. He'd just stop at home to check on the mail and find out how Jessie was feeling after her last doctor's visit; then he'd go down to pick up the blueprints he needed before driving back to Green Bay for the big meeting with the Kramer people and where Donna was waiting. The car swung off the freeway and into the street leading home.

Loewenstein feels that sexual monogamy at this stage of marriage may actually be more difficult for women than for men. In her study of women's lives over time, she found that almost half of those over forty had had intense love experiences; one-third of these were sexually consumated "passions." Many of these women did not want to jeopardize their marriages for the sake of another passion but felt conflicted over it.

Effect on Marriage.   The specter of the infidelity of one's mate may be one of the points of greatest anxiety in mid-life marriages, says LeShan. One key aspect is whether it is possible to be intimate with more than one partner at a time. She wonders whether intimacy implies exclusivity and concludes that, in some situations, the affection and understanding that exists between spouses, despite the limitations of the marriage, enables them to withstand the strain of one of them having an affair. The critical element in such a situation may be the maturity of the partner having the affair and his/her ability to carry the burden of guilt without having to confess to the other. A limited marriage may even improve when increased psychological fulfillment, even if externally generated, brings new dimensions to the relationship.

Of course, disclosure of an affair does not necessarily imply that the marriage is over. The tears and agonies of the showdown often serve to clear the air and even improve the spousal ties. When faced with an ultimatum, the straying partner may decide he or she prefers the shared comfort and habits of a long-term marriage to the immediate gratification and taxing expectations of a new relationship. Unfortunately, others often get into the act. Children, relatives, and/or friends all line up behind one spouse or the other to encourage or castigate, forcing them into positions from which they cannot retreat. Sometimes the injured partner may decide to retaliate, to "show" the other. Thus the situation escalates and eventually becomes untenable.

But even when a couple decides to continue the marriage after an affair, it can rarely be resumed unscathed. They may remain bound in the legal sense; but enduring scars usually remain. It may take years of living a marriage of form without substance before husband and wife regain their mutual bonds of trust and commitment.*

A sense of betrayal may be the special fate of the traditional woman, whether she faces life alone or with a marital partner, concludes Loewenstein. Bitterness becomes especially acute for those women who become single, not through their own choice but because they feel abandoned through death or discarded by divorce. This becomes very evident in the following vignette in which a husband suddenly tells his wife that he wants a divorce:

"You want to *what?*"

Helen Bennett stared at her husband blankly. She had been leaning back in the lounger, only half listening, as they sat on the patio having a predinner drink. Bob had been talking about his new research project at the Medical Center down in Boston. Her mind had been busy with the end-of-season sale that Mimi LePage and she were planning at their boutique.

---

*This is the stuff of which soap operas are made. A chicken-or-egg speculation is whether real-life marriages tend to echo the high drama of such daytime and evening television programs or whether they merely report artistically that which is occurring in the real world.

Patiently, Bob Bennett repeated his last words. He hadn't told her before because it wasn't settled, but now he has been offered a full-time position as clinical professor at the Pilgrim Medical School down in Boston and has the chance of receiving an important research grant. He had been cutting down on his practice here in Meadowlake ever since his heart attack last year; now he wants to give up his practice altogether and move down there.

"But Bob . . . your commitments to the hospital, to your patients, to the Medical Association . . . how can you give those up?" Helen stammered. "And what about us? All of our friends are here. And Meg and her family live in Concord . . . What about my work at the boutique?"

Bob carefully put down his glass. Not looking at her, he said, "That's why I thought you'd prefer to stay here with all your ties, and I'd go by myself. Our lives are taking different directions now and there's no reason for you to tag along with me. Maybe the best solution is for us to divorce. You can have the house and the big car and I'll see you have an adequate income. . . ."

Helen shook her head dazedly. Only one word had penetrated. "Divorce? You want a divorce? Are you out of your mind? What will everyone say? We, the Bennetts, the ideal couple? Why divorce now, after thirty-one years? Because of a *job*?"

He stood up and leaned against the railing. "Well, that's not the only reason. Remember Laura Morgan, that research assistant I introduced you to last year when I brought you down to see where I was working? Well, she and I . . . I mean, we've been having an affair for the last nine months. It just sort of grew out of our interest in the research seminar and I've been staying at her place when I go down to Boston each week. So I thought . . ."

"Oh, stop it; just keep quiet!" She rose abruptly, her glass shattering on the stone floor. Without looking back, she rushed into the house and into their bedroom, slamming the door shut. She threw herself on the bed and lay, one arm over her eyes, her mind filled with a jumble of disconnected thoughts.

After all these years . . . after thirty-one years of nursing him and taking care of his needs and supporting him when he was going to school . . . after bearing his three children and raising them and being a model wife and mother . . .

Again her thoughts veered. Bob . . . Bob having an affair? That was so unlike him; he was *never* that highly sexed, always seemed to care more for his patients or his work than in sleeping around. If anything, *she* was the one who was more interested in . . . anyways, who had more opportunity to have an extramarital fling. Men had always admired her looks, would make passes at her. Her mind slid to Herbie Sommers, their former insurance agent who for a while "stopped by" several times a week. . . . And that good-looking tennis pro at the club a couple of years ago. And, of course, there was George Harrison, their neighbor, who would get high at parties and start propositioning her.

But Bob . . . how could he do this to her? She'll become the laughing stock of the neighborhood. . . . How will she tell the children? And what about her mother; what will she say? She'll probably blame her for not holding onto him. How could she explain—tell them that she's outlived her usefulness to Bob and he's throwing her away?

"But it's true," she said aloud. "After all these years, after all I did for him, he's kicking me out. So where do I go from here? What do I do now?"

Alternatives

Marital Breakup*

Divorce. We have noted that, during the transition to late midlife, strains and stresses are usually played out within the marital relationship. Sometimes, however, the marriage itself cannot stand the pressure and the bond is broken through separation or divorce.

Actually, as partners grow older, many of their earlier incompatibilities brought about by differences in religion, race, social class, levels of education, family backgrounds, and personality patterns have either been ironed out and adjusted to or have contributed to the breakup of the marriage before the couple becomes middle-aged. Moreover, by the time the spouses have reached their late forties and early fifties, previous barriers, such as financial strictures and the need to care for children, have been resolved. As already discussed, many women by this time have returned to school or to professional settings for further training and/or have reentered the work world on a full-time basis.

*The extensive subjects of divorce, widowhood, living alone after a marriage breaks up, and remarriage can only be touched on briefly here. Readers are referred to Golan, 1981:142–189, for more detailed treatment of these topics, although not specifically within the context of the entry to late mid-life.

For mature persons, the perils and problems of divorce may be fewer and less complicated than they are for younger persons. They have more resources, they tend to disagree less over possessions simply because they have more of them, and they can use this time as an opportunity to simplify their lives by disposing of possessions like large homes that they no longer need. Their children are adults and can handle the divorce of their parents more easily than when they were younger. Each partner may have reached a better understanding of himself/herself and may be searching for changes that could include the breakup of a poor marriage.

On the other hand, the emotional and social investment in a marriage after so many years is not lightly given up. Many mid-life individuals see this as the failure or repudiation of, literally, the "best years of their lives." While the divorcer, the spouse who takes the initiative, may consider this as an escape from an untenable or unfortunate situation, the divorced partner often sees this as a betrayal, the breaking up of a contractual promise of a dual arrangement in which uncounted bonds have been built over the years and to which they are deeply committed.

Yet, with all this, one recent Census Bureau analysis finds that the divorce rate for persons in this country between the ages of forty-five and sixty-four has increased 83 percent from 1960 to 1978. It may be true, of course, that this rising divorce rate reflects, not so much increased marital unhappiness at mid-life as the relative ease with which such bonds can now be broken. Livson notes that divorce laws have become more liberal and religious views sanctifying monogamy "till death do us part" are changing. A new morality that urges people to change is prevalent, one that places individual fulfillment above obligations to others and urges both women and men to free themselves of traditional commitments and to adopt new life-styles, both in and out of marriage. She sees recent development, such as the sexual revolution, the personal growth movement, and the women's movement, as adding to this ethic. *

Some family sociologists attribute the increase in the divorce rate to the increase in no-fault divorce laws that have liberalized and reformed the process. Donna Berardo views the growing acceptance of divorce as a reasonable and even desirable alternative to an unhappy marriage. Changes in the traditional roles of women and an increasing emphasis on individualism add to the trend. Adjustments

---

*The most recent trend to a more conservative stance is too new be evaluated at this time.

to the breakup are complicated by the additional losses of former in-laws, couple friends, and financial standing through the division of property and other resources. The loss of personal identification with the mate's status position, the need for many women to develop new labor market skills, and the need for both men and women to increase their financial resources all add to the actual costs of the divorce and the loss of the partner's income.

Separately, these losses and adjustments may be traumatic, but, cumulatively, their effect can be devastating. In addition, they are often accompanied by the need to adjust psychologically to such aspects as coping with a sense of failure, dealing with the development of an individual identity after being part of a longtime couple unit, and reentering the dating game only to discover that the mores have changed. Successful readjustment after the mid-life crisis of divorce may be easier for those with sizeable personal and financial resources, a strong kin network, higher educational levels, and single friends or friends with whom one can interact on personal basis.

From the clinical perspective, mid-life persons who are considering divorce usually have had a long joint history marked by definite patterns of living together and numerous shared sets of experiences. The divorce itself activates profound emotional dislocations. While many of the issues underlying the breakup may have been present since the start of the marriage, only now are they brought out into the open.

Yet, despite the statistics on mid-life divorce, Henry Friedman found that far more nonadaptive marriages survive and continue into old age than are dissolved during this period. Many individuals who appear to be mature in other spheres may not feel free to question the nature of their marital relationships. Fears of being left alone and basic dependencies often augment the practical problems of living alone after so many years of living together.

Persons at this stage usually give up their marital relationships with great reluctance, particularly if they have not been the one to instigate the breakup. Both men and women struggle with the dread that they will not be able to find another relationship offering the security of their previous marriage. To them, *any* marriage, no matter how stressed, may be better than no marriage. Even when they are faced with a fait accompli, the divorce casts a dark shadow over their subsequent years.

Widowhood.   Marital breakup of a very different kind occurs when one of the spouses dies during this stage and the survivor is left with his/her life in shambles just at the point when the partners had freed themselves of previous responsibilities and were looking forward to enjoying their lives together in relative comfort and freedom.

Widowhood differs sharply from divorce because the death of the spouse at this stage in the life cycle occurs when the relationship was presumably positive and the marriage had been functioning at an optimal level. The trauma thus becomes doubled: first, because the loss—whether due to an auto accident, a sudden heart attack, or a swiftly spreading cancer—plunges the spouse into the morass of bereavement; second, because the bonds of the marriage, which could have sustained the mate during and after such a loss, are themselves ruptured and the person is left to deal with the situation alone.

Sudden death, observes Kalish, particularly when it is also unanticipated, leaves the surviving partner unprepared. It often precludes the dying person's making appropriate arrangements for his/her family. Such persons may not have had the time or opportunity to get their financial affairs in order, to explain to their spouses how the household operates or where important documents are, to bid family members good-bye or to offer (or receive) absolution for past deeds or family schisms.

Even when the death is not unexpected—when the person has had a lingering terminal illness, a history of previous heart disease, or has made prior suicide attempts—it is still experienced as untimely and shocking. Those widowed invariably report that, no matter how much anticipatory grieving had taken place and regardless of how they had braced themselves for the inevitable, the actual death found them unprepared and bereft.

Unlike younger widowed spouses who have had no earlier experience with death, the person in mid-life has probably already passed through a similar event: One or both parents or a child or sibling may have died. So, even though the spouse's death occurs prematurely and "out of sync," once the first shock is over, the surviving mate should, theoretically, be able to call on his life experience to cope with the situation. Nevertheless, widows and widowers find that the loss of one's spouse is unique, a deeply stressful event that one never gets used to but can only learn to live with (Golan, 1975). Moreover, the bereavement process is a long and lonely one.

Men and women react, on the whole, somewhat differently to the loss of their mate. Men often feel they have lost part of themselves; women tend to feel deserted and abandoned. While men may find it more difficult to express their grief, they also tend to recover somewhat more quickly than women and tend to remarry fairly soon after the death. Women, on the other hand, seem to feel more isolated once the support offered by family and friends during the first few weeks following the death dissipates. They may also have to prepare for widowhood as a lifelong role, since realistically, relatively few women over age fifty are given the chance to remarry.

The surviving spouse's adjustment and identity changes may be related, to a large extent, to the nature and quality of the previous marital relationship, notes Linda George. In cases where there had been a strong couple orientation, where friends, leisure-time activities, and household tasks were all shared, death brings a serious dislocation to the person's daily functioning. Conversely, if the marriage had been characterized by separate activities, different friends, and divided household duties, disruption tends to be less severe.

Once the first trauma is over, employed widowed persons may find that returning to work is a godsend. Not only does it give them a familiar structure and continuing framework unconnected with their loss (unless they had also worked with their husband or wife), but it eases the effect of lowered income, which death of a spouse usually brings, particularly to women. Since by this time active parenting and housekeeping activities are reduced, surviving spouses can concentrate on, or expand, their occupational or professional role.

If, however, they have never worked before or have worked only intermittently, widows may now find themselves unable to find work or can obtain only poorly paying, part-time jobs that offer them little chance to augment the meager social security (OASI) benefits and other sources of income that may have accrued by this time. Those with little or no labor experience, many of whom may not have completed high school, are not likely to find work in their later years. This in turn often sharply reduces the style of living to which they had become accustomed during their married years and, in many cases, makes them dependent on their adult children or other relatives.

Nonwhites and those in close-knit ethnic communities appear to adjust to widowhood with fewer problems than do whites or "mainstream" Americans. These subcultures seem to offer more structured guidelines for appropriate behavior during widowhood, with extensive informal social support networks to help them pass through the adjustment period. In many extended families, the older widowed mother becomes a person of considerable power and status.

Singlehood. Many persons in mid-life, whose marriages have disintegrated as the outcome of death or divorce, may decide not to marry again. Some of the reasons given are purely pragmatic: They have not found a suitable candidate, they are not inclined to reenter the mating game to search for one, or they may no longer understand the operating rules. Some may not feel the need; their former spouses have provided for them sufficiently or they do not need to seek a substitute father for their grown children. Some are so engrossed in their work role that they are simply not interested. Still others become absorbed in their adult children's families and find the role of grandparent sufficiently gratifying. They may prefer to devote themselves to their own aging parents or to take on other family responsibilities. Or, as has already been mentioned, they may simply not have the opportunity. As one fifty-year-old widow said wryly, "Who wants a tired, worn-out middle-ager when they can get a young slick chick?"

While these rationalizations may well be true, they often overlay other, more subjective reasons. Here the difference between widowed and divorced persons becomes apparent. The widow/er usually gives reasons for not remarrying in terms of the positive aspects of the previous marriage: the deceased spouse was so wonderful, no one could replace him/her. The mate may have been so well known or socially respected that he/she prefers to retain the status as the surviving spouse and perhaps even continue his/her activities. Or the partner's final illness and death may have been so difficult or traumatic that widow/er is determined not to go through such a harrowing experience again.

Many divorced persons couch their reasons for not remarrying in terms of what that "bastard" or "bitch" once did to them; they prefer not to become vulnerable again. So many negative residuals may remain from the marriage itself and from the corrosive divorce litigations that they remain submerged in reactions of bitterness, anger, hurt, and guilt. Others may relish their new freedom and liberation from a bad or empty marriage so much that they resolve not to be "hooked" again. They may prefer, at least for a time, to engage in less binding, more time-limited relationships.

It should also be kept in mind that widowed or divorced persons, at this age, are not always autonomous. Adult children may oppose a second marriage, feeling their parent is too old or too gullible; they may also worry that their inheritance may be dissipated. Other family members or friends may see a new union as socially undesirable or inappropriate. Religious or cultural strictures may prohibit or limit remarriage; in some subcultures an original marriage is seen as a lifetime commitment even though the mate is no longer present.

For some who have never married, being single in middle age is a continuation of a decision made at an earlier stage when pursuing a career was given precedence or a style of life was chosen that precluded the long-term, formal framework of marriage. For others, sexual preference involved them in same-sex partnerships, many of which have continued for many years, with the same commitments and losses as are involved in heterosexual marriage. For these persons, the same difficulties arise when the relationship is broken in mid-life, plus the additional complication of experiencing a lack of social and familial supports that might have made the transition easier.

Remarriage. With all this, the majority of persons in their late forties and early fifties do seem to marry again, although figures are elusive and contradictory. Some are so accustomed to the framework of married life that they may decide to remarry even though they no longer retain illusions of its being for love or a replay of their first marriage. Reasons often given include the need for companionship, as a remedy for their own loneliness and as a way to find a partner for social engagements. They may see this as the best (or only) way out of their financial difficulties or may want someone to look after, or someone to care for them in their later years. Often well-meaning friends and relatives may push the person prematurely into remarriage, sometimes with unfortunate results.

Surprisingly, despite popular misconceptions, when middle-aged persons remarry, they frequently choose partners very close to their own age and, in many cases, very similar to their previous spouses in interests and background. However, for those who have had unfortunate first marriages but felt so committed or entrapped that they continued to stay in the relationship until this stage, the new marriage is viewed as the opportunity for new beginnings, a restitutive second chance to engage in a positive, rewarding marital experience.

According to George, some characteristics of successful remarriages in later life include the following attributes: They take place between persons who have known each other for a long time, the individuals share similar interests, they appear to have been well-adjusted prior to their remarriage, they have adequate financial assets, they have the approval of their children and friends, and they give top priority to each other over their children.

The decision to remarry is certainly a difficult one, laced with ambivalence. The following incident reveals the inability to take this step, despite its material advantages:

Charlene Farwell sat silently at the linen-covered table, her head in its neat blue hat bent, her worn hands smoothing the heavy silverware. Muted music played softly in the dimly lit restaurant. Homer Jefferson, bald and portly, smelling of expensive cigars, looked at her anxiously from across the flower centerpiece.

"Charlene, you've got to make up your mind. This is the third time I'm asking you to marry me and I'm waiting for your answer." His voice was persuasive. "You know I have to go back to Nashville. I've already closed down my real estate operations up here and my brother Harris is waiting for me to join him in his factoring business. Not that I expect to work much; it'll be mostly retirement and taking it easy for me, just letting Harris use my money to make me more. I still have my house down there, from when I was married to Flora, my first wife. But she's been gone more than six years, you know, and I really need someone, someone like you."

Charlene's eyes still did not meet his. "I just don't know how to answer you, Homer. You're a very nice man and we've been getting along fine, the two of us, these past four years. You've been very good to me, always giving me gifts and taking me out to fine places like this. But . . . how can I explain? Chicago is my home. I've lived here almost all my life. My family, what's left of it, is mostly here. I was married here and we lived here all those years when George was in the service. My roots are here and so is my job. The Campbells have been really nice to me, you know."

"Wait a minute," interrupted Homer. "Didn't you tell me that ol' Mrs. Campbell is moving to Palm Beach and wants you to go along? You'd be uprooting yourself if you did that. So why can't you uproot yourself and come down to Tennessee with me?" He put his pudgy hand over hers. "I'll be awfully good to you, Charlene. You know, whatever you want you can have. You won't have to work anymore, just be the lady of the house. And if you don't like the house I have, well, we can sell it and buy another in whichever neighborhood you want. And I'll always take care of you, even after I'm gone."

"But that's another thing, Homer. I've only just turned fifty, you know. And you . . . well, let's face it, you're almost sixty-five. Your emphysema is getting bad and you've had two kidney stone attacks this past year. The doctors tell you that you've got to take things easy, stop smoking, and get out of the damp weather. You really need someone to take care of you, and I . . ."

Homer drew back his hand and glared at her angrily. "Wait a minute! Are you telling me that I'm getting old, that I can't take care of you enough, that I'm not enough of a man for you?"

"Oh, Homer, stop your foolishness! Of course, you're enough for me; we've been doing just fine in bed and you know it. But I still want to keep active; I still want to keep on working, maybe do something new. I just don't feel ready to retire like you. Being the lady of the house just isn't right for me, even if it is your house, Homer."

He sighed heavily and reached for the check on the small silver tray. "Well, I guess I've got my answer, even though it's not what I wanted to hear. Four years together and we fit each other like a pair of old shoes. And now you're throwing me over and I can't even figure out why!"

Charlene leaned forward, one hand on Homer's arm. "I'm not even sure I know why, Homer. It just doesn't feel right for me, marrying you and going down to Nashville. Maybe I'll be sorry about losing this chance; I know I'll miss you. But it wouldn't be good for you, either, when I can't give you what I don't have in me to give."

She looked down at the pale lavender orchid he had pinned on her suit at the start of the evening, her eyes blurring with tears.

With this we end our examination of the theoretical aspects of the transition to late mid-life and how they are perceived in real-life situations. We now shift our perspective to what happens when persons in difficulties during this period turn to professionals for help.

References

ALDOUS, JOAN. "The Return to the Couple Relationship." In Aldous. *Family Careers*. New York: John Wiley & Sons, 1978: 185–195.

BERARDO, DONNA H. "Divorce and Remarriage at Middle Age and Beyond." In Felix M. Berardo, ed. *Middle and Late Life Transitions*. Annals, AAPSS 464 (November 1982): 132–139.

BLOCK, MARILYN R., JANICE L. DAVIDSON, and JEAN D. GRAMBS. *Women Over Forty: Visions and Realities.* New York: Springer, 1981.

CLEVELAND, MARTHA. "Sex in Marriage: At 40 and Beyond." *Family Coordinator* 25, 3 (July 1976): 233–240.

COHEN, JESSICA F. "Male Roles in Midlife." *Family Coordinator* 28, 4 (October 1979): 465–471.

DEUTSCHER, IRWIN. "The Quality of Postparental Life." In Bernice L. Neugarten, ed. *Middle Age and Aging.* Chicago: University of Chicago Press, 1968: 263–268.

DONOHUGH, DONALD L. *The Middle Years.* Philadelphia: Saunders Press, 1981: 282–295.

FRIEDMAN, HENRY J. "The Divorced in Middle Age." In John G. Howells, ed. *Modern Perspectives in the Psychiatry of Middle Age.* New York: Brunner/Mazel, 1981: 103–115.

FUCHS, ESTELLE. *The Second Season: Life, Love, and Sex for Women in the Middle Years.* Garden City, N.Y.: Anchor/Doubleday, 1978.

GEORGE, LINDA K. *Role Transitions in Later Life.* Monterey, Calif.: Brooks/Cole, 1980: 88–98.

GLICK, IRA O., ROBERT S. WEISS, and C. MURRAY PARKES. *The First Year of Bereavement.* New York: John Wiley & Sons, 1974.

GOIN, MARCIA K., and RODNEY W. BURGOYNE. "Psychology of the Widow and Widower." In John G. Howells, ed. *Modern Perspectives in the Psychiatry of Middle Age.* New York: Brunner/Mazel, 1981: 26–35.

GOLAN, NAOMI. "Wife to Widow to Woman." *Social Work* 20, 5 (September 1975):369–374.

_____. *Passing Through Transitions: A Guide for Practitioners.* New York: Free Press, 1981: 142–189.

_____. "Transition to Postparenthood: A Challenge for Family Therapists." Paper Presented at the Fourth International Congress on Family Therapy, Tel Aviv, July 5, 1983. Reproduced.

HUNT, MORTON. *Sexual Behavior in the 1970's.* New York: Dell, 1974.

JOHNSON, RALPH E. "Marital Patterns During the Middle Years." Doctoral Dissertation. Minneapolis: University of Minnesota, 1968. Reported in Aldous, 1978: 191.

KALISH, RICHARD A. "Death and Survivorship: The Final Transition." In Felix M. Berardo, ed. *Middle and Late Life Transitions.* Annals, AAPSS 464 (November 1982): 163–173.

KAPLAN, HELEN S. *The New Sex Therapy.* New York: Brunner/Mazel, 1974.

KERCKHOFF, RICHARD L. "Marriage and Middle Age." *Family Coordinator* 25,1 (January 1976):5–11.

LeSHAN, EDA J. *The Wonderful Crisis of Middle Age.* New York: McKay, 1973.

LIDZ, THEODORE. *The Person: His and Her Development Throughout The Life Cycle*, rev. ed. New York: Basic Books, 1976: 501–510.

LIVSON, FLORINE B. "Coming Out of the Closet: Marriage and Other Crises of Middle Age." In Lillian Troll, Joan Israel, and Kenneth Israel, eds. *Looking Ahead.* Englewood Cliffs, N.J.: Prentice-Hall, 1977: 81–92.

LOEWENSTEIN, SOPHIE F. "Toward Choice and Differentiation in the Midlife Crises of Women." In Carol L. Heckerman, ed. *The Evolving Female: Women in a Psychosocial Context.* New York: Human Science Press, 1980: 158–188.

————. "Passion as a Mental Health Hazard." In Carol L. Heckerman, ed. *The Evolving Female: Women in a Psychological Context.* New York: Human Science Press, 1980: 45–73.

LOPATA, HELENA Z. *Women as Widows: Support Systems.* New York: Elsevier, 1979.

MASTERS, WILLIAM H., and VIRGINIA E. JOHNSON. *Human Sexual Inadequacy.* Boston: Little, Brown, 1970.

McCONNELL, ADELINE, and BEVERLY ANDERSON. *Single After Fifty.* New York: McGraw-Hill, 1978.

McGILL, MICHAEL E. *The 40-to-60-Year-Old Male.* New York: Simon & Schuster, 1980: 137–168.

MUSSEN, PAUL, JOHN J. CONGER, JEROME KAGAN, and JAMES GEIWITZ. *Psychological Development: A Life Span Approach.* New York: Harper & Row, 1979: 410–445.

NADELSON, CAROL C. "Marriage and Midlife: The Impact of Social Change." In Carol C. Nadelson and Malkah T. Notman, eds. *The Woman Patient.* Vol. 2. New York: Plenum Press, 1981: 145–158.

————, DEREK C. POLONSKY, and MARY ALICE MATHEWS. "Marriage Problems and Marital Therapy in the Middle-Aged." In John G. Howells, ed. *Modern Perspectives in the Psychiatry of Middle Age.* New York: Brunner/Mazel, 1981: 337–352.

PFEIFFER, ERIC, ADRIAAN VERWOERDT, and GLENN C. DAVID. "Sexual Behavior in Middle Life." *American Journal of Psychiatry* 129 (April 1972): 1962–1967.

RHODES, SONYA L. "A Developmental Approach to the Life Cycle of the Family." *Social Casework* 58, 5 (May 1977): 301–311.

RUBIN, LILLIAN B. *Women of a Certain Age: The Midlife Search for Self.* Harper & Row, 1979.

SIMON, ANNE W. *The New Years: A New Middle Age.* New York: Knopf, 1968.

SIMOS, BERTHA C. *A Time to Grieve: Loss as a Universal Human Experience.* New York: Family Service Association of America, 1979.

SKOLNICK, ARLENE. "Married Lives: Longitudinal Perspective on Marriage." In Dorothy H. Eichorn, et al., eds. *Present and Past in Middle Life.* New York: Academic Press, 1981: 269–298.

SPENCE, DONALD L., and THOMAS B. LONNER. "Career Set: A Resource Through Transitions and Crisis." *International Journal of Aging and Human Development* 9, 1 (1978–1979): 51–65.

STARTZ, MORTON R., and CLAIRE W. EVANS. "Developmental Phases of Marriage and Marital Therapy." *Social Casework* 62, 6 (June 1981): 343–351.

THOMPSON, GAYLE B. "Economic Status of Late Middle-Aged Widows." In Nancy Datan and Nancy Lohmann, eds. *Transitions of Aging.* New York: Academic Press, 1980: 133–149.

THURNHER, MAJDA. "Midlife Marriage: Sex Differences in Evaluation and Perspectives." *International Journal of Aging and Human Development* 7, 2 (1976): 129–135.

TROLL, LILLIAN E., SHEILA J. MILLER, and ROBERT C. ATCHLEY. *Families in Later Life.* Belmont, Calif.: Wadsworth, 1979.

WASSERMAN, SIDNEY. "The Middle-Age Separation Crisis and Ego-Supportive Casework Treatment." *Clinical Social Work Journal* 1 (September 1973): 38–47.

WILLIAMS, JUANITA H. *Psychology of Woman: Behavior in a Biosocial Context*, 2nd ed. New York: W. W. Norton, 1977.

ZUBE, MARGARET. "Changing Behavior and the Outlook of Aging Men and Women." *Family Relations* 31, 1 (January 1982): 147–156.

PART III

Answering the Call for Help

W‍E NOW SHIFT our interest from the potential complications that may arise during the transition to late mid-life to what can actually occur in real-life situations. The vignettes from the lives of our six individuals and couples, which were used in Part II to illustrate areas of stress, have now been reassembled and presented as six "master case situations" in which someone is asking for help with some facet of the situation. The salient questions now are: To whom do these persons turn at this time? If they turn to professional helpers, what do they ask for and what are they given?

In Chapters 10 through 15, each of the case situations is presented separately.* First, a summary of the initial interview in which the person asks for help is given, detailing the presenting difficulty and giving some background information. (The practitioner in each of these cases is a professional social worker, and many of the treatment considerations are placed within the settings in which these social workers operate: family service agencies, mental or physical health services, or private practice. However, many of the

---

*These cases have all been masked and edited to remove irrelevant details and to maintain conciseness. In some instances, several cases have been combined to make the treatment issues stand out more clearly. None represent identifiable life situations or persons.

decisions taken and directions indicated would apply equally well to clinical psychologists, marriage counselors, and other clinicians who make up what we euphemistically call the "helping professions.")

Next, since no two professionals would treat a situation in exactly the same way, the opinions of a panel of experts were solicited. To obtain these opinions, some forty-eight practitioners and teachers of practice from all over the United States and Canada were each asked to read three of the six initial interviews quoted in these six chapters and give their views as to how they themselves would assess the situation and plan to treat it. They were asked how they saw the presenting problem, their interpretation of the underlying core issue with which the client(s) seemed to be struggling, their choice of the most useful "problem for work" with which they would start, their proposed treatment strategy and arrangements, the central themes on which they would concentrate, at which point they would terminate, and their predictions as to the outcome of the case.

In explanation, it should be noted that these questions are in keeping with standard teaching of social work practice, regardless of one's theoretical orientation. Practitioners usually "start where the client is," with the problem he* brings in for help. During the initial interview, as the practitioner listens, asks questions, and discusses the situation, she is also making a preliminary diagnostic assessment of what is going on in the client's situation, what are the core issues with which he seem to be struggling.

As they talk further about the situation, the social worker tries to makes a judgment as to what would be the feasible starting point for intervention, the "problem for work," to use Helen Perlman's term (which is not necessarily synonymous with the initial request), and usually discusses it with the client. Then, the practitioner formulates in her mind, what helping strategies might be most effective: to provide a supportive relationship to help the client pass through a difficult period, to offer the client the opportunity to scrutinize intensively the dynamics of his past and present relationships in order to help him understand the current impasse, to help him change his behavior patterns through cognitive means, to provide concrete assistance through material help or by intercession with others, etc. As a logical follow-up, the worker considers the treatment arrange-

---

*To avoid the awkward "he/she" designation, the feminine form of the pronoun will be used in this section for the professional and the masculine form for the client. This does not imply any sexist connotations. Readers are asked to switch the gender of the terms as applicable.

ments: whether it would be preferable to see the client individually or with someone else, and how often to do so.

Even in the first interview, the experienced practitioner is already mapping out in her mind, on the basis of what she has heard and what has taken place in cases similar to this, the central themes that she would probably want to go into, to varying degrees, during the course of treatment. While this is usually subject to change, depending on how the situation develops, it serves as a guideline "in the back of her head" to keep treatment moving and focused on the client's difficulties and dilemmas for which he wants help.

Again subject to change, the experienced practitioner usually has some "endpoint" in mind, some change in the current situation that will, if not "solve" the problem completely, at least make the client feel more in control of his life and able to continue on his own, without further assistance. While this is speculative and often shifts as the case progresses, again it serves as a gauge to measure the positive changes taking place.

Finally, a practitioner often makes another prediction in her mind: What are the prospects for success in reaching the goals that have been set? Will significant others involved also be able to change? Does the prognosis look bright or, at the most, guarded? This is, of course, a subjective evaluation, but it's often a useful one in keeping the worker's and the client's expectations in line with the realities of the situation.

Once we have established the range of possible lines of assessment and treatment planning, we present, in the third section of each chapter, the way in which the case was actually treated, as taken from recorded notes and verbal discussions with the workers who handled the cases. As will be noted, sometimes this was in keeping with the experts' views; sometimes, a different course was taken. What was evident was that the worker in each case appeared to be aware of the transitional aspects of the situation and used this perspective in the helping process.

Finally, my own comments and discussion of the helping process are presented.

CHAPTER 10

"They'll Be Better Off Without Me!"

Case Situation #1: First Interview with Jessie Alberts

Jessie Alberts, fifty-three, was referred to the medical social worker by her family physician, Dr. Harold Manton, on an emergency basis. Last Thursday she had swallowed twelve sleeping pills, leaving a suicide note which said that no one seemed to need her anymore and that her family would be better off without her. Her husband, who returned home from a business trip unexpectedly, found her and rushed her to the Emergency Room of Lowell Hospital. There her stomach was pumped out and she was given emergency treatment, then referred back to her family doctor. She had been under his care for a number of years, primarily for tachycardia (uneven heartbeat), low blood pressure, and recently for menopausal symptoms. He put her on tranquilizers and a mild antidepressant. He hesitates to prescribe stronger medications and attributes many of her symptoms to "family troubles"; she has done a lot of weeping in his office over the past years.

Mrs. Alberts, a thin, pale woman with faded blond hair pulled back in a bun, kept her head bent and her hands tightly clutching her purse as she talked. She knows it was very foolish of her to take the pills; her husband, who brought her down here, is very angry with her. But she'd had a hard time sleeping lately and just wanted to be rid of it all. Now he missed an important business meeting because of her, and Diane, their daughter, had to come home from school, right before midterm exams, to look after her. She knows even Dr. Manton is fed up with her; all she does is cause trouble for everyone!

With just a little encouragement, her story came out in short, tear-punctuated fragments. She was born on a farm in central Wisconsin but, during the Depression, had been sent at age four to be raised by her grandparents in Milwaukee. They were good to her, she guesses, but they were old and didn't speak much English. Mostly she did the housework and shopping for them.

She met *Paul* in high school and they had gone together for three years until he left school to join the Marines. He served in Korea for two years while she went on to teachers' college. He returned home just after she got her teaching certificate, but she never started to work because they were married immediately. He took a job in his uncle's construction firm, they bought a small house in a new housing development, and she became pregnant almost at once. Over the next ten years, they had four children—a "perfect family," she said with a glimmer of pride. Paul, by that time, had started his own construction firm and she devoted her life to raising the children and keeping house.

Thirteen years ago, their life began to fall apart. *Paul Jr.*, their oldest son, was killed in a car crash on graduation night, after he and his friends had gone out to celebrate before he went to enlist in the Marines the next day. After the tragedy, her husband became very morose, buried himself in his work, and, when home, would just shut himself up in the den with six-packs of beer and the football game. All the warm feelings between them began to "shrivel up"; often he'd spend the night sleeping on the couch and would leave without waking her.

The children were all affected by the atmosphere at home. *Frank*, their second son, dropped out of high school and started hitchhiking around the country. In one of his infrequent calls home, he told them he had met a girl and settled down in Eugene, Oregon. Later they heard he married her and now, at twenty-nine, manages a supermarket for his father-in-law; they almost never hear from him. *Jim*, their third son, who always used to follow Junior around, had a lot of trouble in school, so they transferred him to a parochial school where classes were smaller. When he finished high school, he informed them that he was joining the Catholic church. Now, at twenty-six, he is studying for the priesthood in a seminary on the East Coast; his father becomes furious when his name is mentioned. *Diane*, their youngest, is twenty-one; she has always been closest to her mother. She started attending college in town but this year met a young man, Carl, who attended the state university in Madison, so she transferred there to be with him. Last week she called to say that she was moving into his apartment and probably won't be coming home much on weekends. Next year, when Carl graduates, they plan to move down to West Texas, where he's from.

Mrs. Alberts had grown increasingly upset as she talked. Now, between sobs, she said Paul had driven her down here but left immediately to return upstate where he is bidding on a new shopping center that will keep him up there for most of the next few years. He's already mentioned that it might be a good idea for them to move there. But she hates to meet new people and doesn't want to give up the few friends she's made in the neighborhood over the years, the stores she is accustomed to, and Dr. Manton, who has tended to her health problems and is so very understanding. Besides, two of her sisters live in that area and they're always talking about how successful their children and grandchildren are; she hates visiting them.

Dr. Manton had told her years ago that her heart wasn't strong and that she had to watch herself. That's why she never went back to work, even though Paul once suggested, when he started his own business, that she learn bookkeeping and run the office for him. Now he has a smart young secretary who knows all about his business and often travels with him. She wouldn't be surprised if she was more than his secretary; ever since her hot flashes started three years ago, she and Paul haven't had any sex together.

At this point, Mrs. Alberts put her head down on the desk and began to cry in earnest. Almost inaudibly she said that she has lost everything else, she'll probably be losing Paul next. They no longer have anything in common and all he does is shout at her. It might have been the best thing if he had not found her until it was too late, then he'd be rid of her for good.

Professionals' Opinions

Most of the twenty-five clinicians who reviewed this case situation agreed that Mrs. Alberts was in a precarious state, as typified by her feelings of depression, isolation, and sense of "hopelessness and helplessness." Her suicide attempt was seen as a cry for help. The majority felt that she had experienced multiple losses over the past years and was now in a crisis of exhaustion, with little to look forward to.

Mrs. Alberts was viewed as being too fragile to be offered more at the outset than a supportive, understanding relationship in individual treatment. The majority of experts felt she should be seen twice a week until she became more stabilized. The central issues of her current losses and lack of self-worth should be examined, with termination coming when she showed some capacity to engage in work, develop new interests, and when her depression lifted. Only a few mentioned her as being in a mid-life transition, although this may have been taken for granted in view of her menopausal difficulties.

The probability for change was viewed as fairly positive, while a minority saw it as guarded. Only one person predicted a very positive prognosis.

How the Case Was Treated

The following intervention, reconstructed from the social worker's treatment notes and final summary, took place some time before the case was selected as an example of mid-life disruption. This information, while not shared with the respondents in the study, actually follows their recommendations fairly closely.

This case was referred to Family Service in a Midwest city by the medical social worker at the County General Hospital who saw Mrs. Alberts's situation as serious but no longer critical. Dr. Manton, who made the initial referral, did not regard her as being actively suicidal and felt her family problems should take precedence over her medical ones. (He admitted feeling uncomfortable that he had not recognized the extent of her upset until after her suicide attempt.)

Mrs. Alberts was interviewed by an experienced professional social worker, two days after her discharge from the hospital, on a high-priority basis. Her daughter had driven her to the agency and waited in the outer office since Mr. Alberts had to attend an urgent business meeting upstate.

Beginning Phase. As the worker elicited the information given above, she began to make a diagnostic assessment. She saw Mrs. Alberts as being in a state of active crisis: Her daughter was leaving her, her husband would soon follow, and she saw herself in danger of losing everything important in her life. Her predominant emotions were those of sadness and depression; she could not see any way out for herself. Her preoccupation with the series of significant losses in the family, starting with their eldest son's accidental death and culminating in Diane's announcement that she was moving out of the family circle, was paramount. She felt herself to be the victim of circumstances beyond her control, that her life had no future. It was therefore decided to use a crisis intervention framework: to see her supportively at the outset in order to help her mourn her losses and put them into some perspective; then, when she would feel more in control, to help her consider the possible changes in her future life direction.

The practitioner proposed that Mrs. Alberts return the next morning to continue their discussion. She wanted to see her several times more until Mrs. Alberts felt less upset; then they would make further plans. With her consent, Diane was called in and the treatment plan outlined: Her mother would be seen twice more this week on a high-priority basis. Meanwhile, Diane would remain at home until her father returned; she said she had already called the university and had her midterm exams postponed. When they left, Mrs. Alberts had ceased crying and even smiled tremulously as she thanked the social worker for letting her "spill out her troubles."

Middle Phase.   When Mrs. Alberts came in the next day, her affect was still somber, but she had an air of suppressed excitement about her. When Diane and she had returned home, they had a heart-to-heart talk about her plans to live with Carl at school and to go to Texas with him without getting married. Mrs. Alberts was able to tell her how much this upset her, even if "all the girls did it." Diane hadn't realized how deeply her mother felt about it; since she never expressed her feelings openly, she had assumed she didn't care much. Ever since Paulie was killed, when Diane was only eight, she and her brothers knew that any family upset would make Dad angry and give Mom a sick headache, so they always tried to work out their problems without involving them. One of the reasons she wanted to be with Carl was that he made her feel safe and cared for, something she hadn't felt at home in a long time. At this point, said Mrs. Alberts, she and Diane had cried together.

When the clinician commented that Paulie's death hit the whole family hard, Mrs. Alberts agreed it was a real turning point. Almost inaudibly she said that, in all of the "good years," she couldn't believe that she deserved Paul's having chosen her, so she tried to do everything he wanted in order to make their family life "perfect." But she always felt certain that some day she would have to pay for her happiness. She saw her son's death as a personal retribution, confirming her fears. Each new blow that followed was further proof that she was unworthy; after all, her grandmother used to warn her that it was a sin to want anything too much. That's why she tried not to get too close to Frankie and Jim, so her own needs shouldn't hurt them; in some ways she saw their departure as an escape from her fate. But with Diane, who was all the good things she herself wasn't . . . if she left, it would be too much to be borne. She really would be alone then.

At this point the practitioner asked about her husband; surely he hadn't left her also? No, sobbed Mrs. Alberts, but he was about to. She felt it was only a matter of time before he became disgusted with her and moved out. She hadn't been a proper wife for a long time and, after all, he was only fifty-four and still in the prime of life. She knew she had lost her looks, with all the doctoring she had these past years. Now, with her change of life, she was sure she was no longer sexually attractive to him. She hadn't been surprised when a neighbor told her that she had seen Paul and his new secretary having lunch over in Northridge.

For the rest of this interview and throughout the next one, they concentrated on Mrs. Alberts's feelings of loss and unworthiness. Using techniques of support and some clarification of reality, the practitioner tried to help her understand that Paulie's death was a tragedy but not their fault; neither she nor her husband could blame themselves that a trailer truck had run a red light and hit their son's car. Effort was made, again and again, to check Mrs. Alberts's perception of events: Frank, their second son, may have run away and become a "hippie" (her term) for a while, but he had eventually settled down, married, and now appeared to be doing well. Even Jim, whom she saw as sensitive, like herself, seemed to be trying to find some sort of meaning that would help him deal with his own world. As for Diane, she also appeared to be looking for some meaningful relationship within the context of her generation. Mrs. Alberts agreed that a number of the mothers she knew were also struggling with their children's different values and behavior. "At least," she said with a glimmer of a smile, "Diane hasn't become pregnant yet."

Her ties with Dr. Manton were also discussed in terms of his possible "desertion": His nurse had called to cancel her weekly appointment with him, saying that he would be out of town. They reviewed the years that she had been his patient and how he had helped her heart condition, her low blood pressure, and the hot flashes that had bothered her the last few years. Actually, it had turned out that he usually saw her for only a few moments each time; it was his nurse who checked her blood pressure and monitored her current medication. Often, the highlight of her visits were her talks with the other women in the waiting room, with whom she had become friendly over the years.

Some medical information, phrased in simple terms that she could understand, was given to her, particularly about her menopausal symptoms and about sexual functioning during and after the climacteric. Mrs. Alberts was surprised to hear that postmenopausal intercourse could be even more rewarding than before; she had felt sure that the loss of fertility meant loss of sexual interest and gratification.

The highpoint in this case occurred during the fourth interview when Mr. and Mrs. Alberts were seen together on Saturday morning at the worker's suggestion. He was dumbfounded to hear that his wife was sure he was going to leave her, that she felt he was disgusted with her and wanted to break up their marriage. He had been severely shaken when he discovered her a week ago, unconscious, on the living-room sofa, he said; since then he has been filled with guilt and remorse. Defensively, he admitted he had neglected her these past years, but he had become completely absorbed in his growing business demands. Jessie was always so quiet and withdrawn, she never seemed interested in what was happening to him and never asked how the business was going. Bitterly, Mrs. Alberts replied that he never shared anything with her and always seemed anxious to leave the house. But when she asked him directly, "Do you want to leave me?" his immediate response was to take her hand and say, "No, Jessie, I don't."

The social worker commented at this point that if such was the case, they had better learn to improve their ways of communicating with each other—they had a lot of catching up to do. With Mrs. Alberts's permission, she mentioned a few of the family concerns they had been discussing the past week. When Mr. Alberts learned how she felt about their son's death, he also began to talk about it. He said he had blamed himself for Paulie's decision to join the Marines, which he saw as a contributing factor to the accident. But his way of handling his guilt was to bury himself in his work. He tried to cut himself off from the rest of the family and became, instead, a workaholic. The younger boys' leaving home proved to him what a failure he had been as a father.

Whatever happened in the past, said the clinician, they now had only each other left; what did they want to do about it? Mrs. Alberts mentioned hesitatingly that once Paul had suggested she go to work in his office. Did he still want her to do that? He replied that the business had become too complex by now; if he won this new bid on the shopping center, he probably would move the office to Green Bay and begin to computerize the operation. Anyway, this week he had been offered the chance to go into partnership with a contracting firm up there, so he would no longer have to run the firm single-handedly. But he did think they ought to move up there so they could spend more time together and "keep an eye on each other more." Mrs. Alberts, with unexpected spirit, said she didn't know why they couldn't move; she was getting pretty tired of keeping up a four-bedroom house just for the two of them, especially with Diane's leaving home and his being gone all week. Maybe they could find a smaller place that would suit just the two of them. And meanwhile she could start to sort out their outgrown "bits and pieces" that she'd hung onto all these years.

Ending Phase. A final interview was held with Mrs. Alberts three days later. She reported that Paul and she had talked the whole weekend. They spent a lot of time recalling the good years at the start of their marriage, before they began to drift apart. He even took her out for dinner Saturday evening for the first time in years. Before he left yesterday, she had definitely promised to go up to Green Bay with him next week to look for an apartment in the new area north of the city.

The rest of the hour was spent in tying up loose ends. Mrs. Alberts talked briefly about her own family, but she felt her sisters could no longer hurt her, now that she was sure of Paul. They also discussed what she would do after they moved. Mrs. Alberts thought that, once they were settled, she'd like to go back to school—not to get a degree but maybe to take some courses in home decorating or craft work; she has always been good with her hands. When she left, she thanked the worker fervently for "saving her life" and promised to let her know how things worked out.

Follow-Up. Nothing further was heard from the Alberts for two months. Then Mrs. Alberts called to say they had sold their home and moved to Green Bay. She and Paul were getting along fine, better than they had for many years. She still got "down in the dumps" occasionally and had to push herself to meet new people, but Paul was coming home every night, which helped. Both of them agreed to try to tell each other how they feel about things, no matter what.

Her most exciting news, however, was that both sons had come home to help them celebrate their wedding anniversary last week. Diane had called her brothers to let them know what had happened and they arranged to pay a surprise visit. Frank has a lovely wife "who knows just how to handle him" and two smart little boys. Paul spent much of the weekend playing ball in the yard with his grandsons. He also talked with Frank for hours about business. With the shadow of Paulie no longer between them, they found they had a lot of common interests.

She felt very nervous when she first saw Jim; after all, they had had very little to do with Catholics, much less priests. But she needn't have worried. Last year he had decided that the priesthood was not his vocation and had become interested in teaching instead. Now he teaches history in a high school in South Boston and is studying for his doctor's degree at Boston College. He was still pretty much of a loner but seemed more content than he used to be.

Diane had brought Carl home with her and they announced that they planned to get married in June, after he graduates. They decided to have the wedding at home and she and Diane were starting to plan it already, even though it would be just a small family affair. Mrs. Alberts admitted it would be hard having her move down to El Paso, but Diane has already made her promise that, when their first baby is born, she'll come down to stay with her for the first weeks. After all, that's what grandmothers are for!

This case is a good example of treatment during the transition to later mid-life. We see a number of significant changes taking place concurrently: the physiological changes brought about by Mrs. Alberts's menopause, the ending of her active parental role, the possible loss of her home, and the growing estrangement between herself and her husband. While the series of losses started some years ago, now, while she is in this period of developmental change, Diane's announcement acts as the final straw pushing her into serious depression, despair, and a suicide attempt.

Treatment was cast, appropriately, in a crisis intervention framework which focused in the first three interviews on helping her mourn her multiple losses. Then, instead of remaining at that supportive level and helping her to learn to live with her grief, the focus broadened, in view of her past history of adequacy and the temporary nature of the transitional period. Concern was shifted to those areas in her life which still could be changed. The last two interviews concentrated, not on the past (although a number of issues, such as her early emotional deprivation could have been explored further), but on the present and near future, on her relations with her husband and what could be changed in their marriage. At the same time that the worker helped Mrs. Alberts to say goodbye to her daughter, she was also encouraging her to open new doors into the future when she and her husband would be living once more as a couple and their mutual needs, including their ability to communicate better, would take priority.

Although Mrs. Alberts at the outset appeared totally depressed and diminished, with her earlier coping capacities buried under the weight of her grief and guilt, she emerged, after only five interviews of sensitive, focused treatment, as able to gather new hope to face her future—a more optimistic outlook than many of our experts predicted.

CHAPTER 11

"He's Kicking Me Out—Where Now?"

Case Situation #2: First Interview with Helen Bennett

Helen Bennett, fifty, elegantly dressed and carefully made up, arrived promptly at the private therapist's office after phoning for an early appointment. When asked what the difficulty was, she leaned back and said, "Well, I seem to be having a hard time making up my mind and I need some advice." She went on to explain that her husband told her last weekend that he has been having an affair with a younger woman for the past year. Now, after thirty-one years of marriage, he is asking for a divorce so that he can marry her.

Mrs. Bennett insisted that she had absolutely no inkling of what had been going on. She thought they had a perfect marriage and the request "absolutely stunned" her. She told Bob she needed time to think about it, but he moved out that evening and said she could reach him at his office or his hotel.

The Bennetts have long been considered an ideal couple by their friends; in fact, she said, they are the only couple in their set who have remained married to each other all these years. *Dr. Robert Bennett* is a well-known cardiologist with a large private practice; he also heads the Cardiology Department at the local teaching hospital and is a consultant to several insurance companies. They have a beautiful home in the northern suburb of Meadowlake, a summer cottage on Cape Cod, and three wonderful children. Their oldest, *Meg*, twenty-six, is married to a stockbroker and lives nearby; *Phyllis*, twenty-four, is a fashion designer in New York; and *Mark*, twenty-two, has just been accepted into Harvard Medical School, his father's alma mater.

Mrs. Bennett said she had started going together with Bob while they were still undergraduates. They both came from rather modest backgrounds but Bob was very ambitious and determined to make it. She had been a fine arts major but dropped out of school in her senior year and took a secretarial course instead. They were married right after his graduation and she worked as a legal secretary to help put him through medical school. The first years were very hard on both of them; she remembers the series of crummy, one-room apartments they lived in while he struggled through medical school, internship, residency, and finally his cardiology specialization. He was always either studying or working extra hours at the hospital. They never had any money or time to spend on themselves, but both felt very invested in his career and were sure it would be worth it in time.

Even after Bob opened his first practice in Granville and they started having children, their life continued to be full of pressures. She had to be both mother and father to the kids because Bob was either on call, attending medical meetings, or taking special courses to keep up with the latest developments in his field. Mrs. Bennett had to manage not only their own household but their parents' as well. Her mother is a widow and very lonely; she calls her only daughter frequently. Particularly since her father died seven years ago, Mrs. Bennett has felt that her mother has become very dependent on her. Bob's parents both have health problems. His father recently had a colostomy and is scheduled to have further surgery soon. His mother has chronic asthma and frequently has to be put on oxygen. They live in New Haven but think nothing of calling her long distance to have her arrange nursing care or hospitalization for one or the other, and then to keep visiting them.

Not that she minded helping. Over the years she has become very active in the volunteer program at the hospital, run by a group of doctors' wives. She has always seen herself as part of her husband's professional life, giving dinners for visiting celebrities or for important persons in the community who could add to the prestige programs at the hospital. As the children grew more independent, she traveled with Bob to medical meetings and tried to share all his interests. Their friends would hold them up as a model couple who did everything together; each year she'd talk to the young residents' wives on how to help their husbands' careers.

The ordered pattern of their life began to change last year when Bob had his first heart attack at age fifty-two. It was a mild one, but he decided to take the advice he always gave his middle-aged patients. He began to cut down on his private practice and to give up most of his administrative duties at the hospital. Instead, he started playing more tennis and golf and, for two days each week, he would drive down to Boston to take part in a research seminar on problems in heart transplantation. Of course that gave her more free time so, since the children were now all out of the house, she joined a friend of hers in starting a high-fashion boutique at the new shopping center nearby. However, she made a point of always being home by the time Bob returned.

Last Sunday, when he "dropped his bombshell," Bob revealed that he and one of the younger women in his research group have become interested in each other; he has been staying at her apartment on the nights he spends in Boston. He feels she has revitalized his intellectual interests and they have decided to embark on a new research project together. Dr. Bennett also told his wife for the first time that he has been offered a full-time appointment on the research faculty of Pilgrim General Hospital's medical school. Once the divorce goes through, he plans to marry Laura, sell his practice, and move to Boston.

Bitterly, Mrs. Bennett summed up the situation: "He's giving me a clear message: I've outlived my usefulness to him. He's starting a new life with a new partner. After all these years, after all I did for him, he's kicking me out. But what about me? I've built my whole life around him and his career. So where do I go from here?"

Professionals' Opinions

The twenty-four professional social workers who examined this case situation agreed that the presenting problem was Mrs. Bennett's shock over her husband's announcement that he was leaving her and wanted a divorce. The marital breakdown was seen as the precipitating factor, but differences of opinion were expressed as to the underlying core issue. Some saw it as the threat to her identity and self-esteem, others as the loss of her status as a physician's wife and the life-style connected with it, still others felt it to be her feelings of being rejected and having outlived her usefulness.

The majority would start working with her on her reactions to her husband's treatment of her, some advocating an intensive crisis approach aimed at restoring her equilibrium. Others would concentrate on helping her focus on her plans for the future, where she would go "from here." Some would, initially, offer her support and understanding until she was ready to deal more intensively with the underlying dynamics; others would reverse the process and start seeing her intensively and then taper off as she gained control over her current situation. Almost all preferred to see her in individual treatment with some suggesting additional conjoint therapy with her husband—if he was still in the picture.

Central themes to be covered would be dealing with her feelings of grief and loss over her marriage, examining her own part in its development, evaluating her own capabilities and helping her actualize them, and aiding her in considering the options by which she could build a new life-style. Opinion was divided as to the possibility of her benefiting from intensive, insight-oriented treatment: Some viewed her as a woman of considerable ego strength, who could profit from this, while others preferred a more practical orientation geared to her interpersonal achievement and to the building of a more satisfying future for herself. One-third rated the prognosis as very good while the rest saw it as fairly good.

How the Case Was Treated

This case was taken from the files of a clinical social worker in private practice who has specialized in marital and divorce problems and is reported in her own words.

Mrs. Bennett was seen for a total of ten interviews over a three-month period. Although she ostensibly came in for help in making a decision about her husband's request for a divorce after thirty-one years of marriage, it became apparent almost at once that he had already started the separation process some months before and had sealed his decision by moving out of their home two days ago. What Mrs. Bennett faced was the need to adjust to this fait accompli, to deal with the severe blow to her self-image and self-esteem, and to begin to make her own plans for the immediate future.

Beginning Phase. The first part of our initial interview was taken up with a sparring match with Mrs. Bennett. In discussing "this little problem," which turned out to be her husband's announcement that he was leaving her, giving up his practice and the complicated life structure erected around his position as a prominent cardiologist, and moving away to start a new career with a new partner, she was at first carefully guarded and uncommunicative, insisting that she had absolutely no warning of any break. What she wanted was a little direction in how to "turn him around." I, in turn, became increasingly obtuse and kept challenging her lack of awareness. Finally I stood up and said I didn't see how I could help her. Obviously her husband had made up his mind; what she wanted was so unrealistic that it would be a waste of both of our times to try to reverse the process. With this Mrs. Bennett's facade collapsed. After a long silence, she said in a muted voice that she realized she had been kidding herself. What she really wanted was help in dealing with Bob's message that she'd outlived her usefulness. Her whole life had collapsed and she had to figure out where she could go from here.

Once she acknowledged this, we really began to work. We agreed to concentrate, not on bringing Bob back, but on reshaping her own life pattern on a sounder foundation.

Middle Phase. We began to meet on a twice-weekly basis. She started to examine her past life intensively, going back to her childhood as a skinny kid, determined to climb out of the rut of her immigrant parents' marginal farm and to make something of herself, regardless of the cost. Once she met Bob at the state university where she was working her way through as a waitress, she hitched her wagon to his, giving up her own plans to be a fashion designer to join his dream. After they were married—against his parents' wishes—she dropped out of school, took a secretarial course, and supported them both as a legal secretary while he went on to medical school. For the next thirty years they divided their roles: He concentrated on building his professional career while she smoothed his way. It was she who ran the home, raised the children, took care of both their parents' needs, arranged their social life, even hired his office staff and handled his correspondence.

Rarely could they count on time for themselves or with the children. She recalled one family camping trip to Yellowstone that they had planned for almost a year. Just as they finished packing the camper and were ready to take off, a crisis arose at the hospital: The

X-ray technicians were threatening to strike. For three days, the children and she sat around while he, as hospital administrator, became involved in labor negotiations. Finally, in disgust, they drove up to Lake Champlain for a week without him. Phyllis, who was around fourteen at the time, vowed then she'd rather marry a janitor than a doctor; at least he could keep regular hours and spend time with his family!

Throughout our sessions, Mrs. Bennett made a determined effort to examine her own thoughts and feelings, although it was difficult for her to acknowledge anger, loss, or guilt. When I raised the issue of her own part in the shape their marriage had taken, she admitted she had gained a great deal from the role of doctor's wife, that she enjoyed being "Mrs. Doctor Bennett." As they became more affluent, she learned to handle herself in complex social situations; she and Bob built up this image of the "model professional couple," even though they had little to say to each other in private and rarely shared their feelings. Certain topics were simply taboo.

Oddly enough, it was only after his heart attack last year that she saw Bob as vulnerable and afraid. She, too, became frightened; the structure of their life seemed to be crumbling. But she pulled herself together, saw that he followed the medical regime laid down, that he kept to his diet, and that he exercised. With the children all out of the house, she had much more time for herself, especially since Bob had cut down on their professional and social obligations and had begun to spend two days a week in Boston. So she joined a friend in starting a high-fashion boutique at the Meadowlake Shopping Center. She really enjoyed this and took on the buying and selling end while Mimi handled the financial and office part. With a flash of insight, she said, "I must have been preparing myself for the day when I could no longer count on Bob. . . ."

Mrs. Bennett came in for her fifth interview furious. Last night their neighbor, George Harrison, had come over to see her. The word had evidently spread that Bob had left and George offered to service her "as if I were a cow!" This opened up the topic she had been trying to avoid for some time, how she saw herself as a sexual woman. For the first time she admitted her doubts as to her own "sexiness." Bob, by nature, was always cool and methodical, even in their sexual relations. He rarely varied his routine or techniques in bed. Once he'd come to a climax, he'd quickly turn over and fall asleep, often leaving her still aroused and unsatisfied. She had long been worried that she was frigid—as George had accused her of being last night. She would read articles in women's magazines and listen to sex therapists on daytime TV, but she never had the nerve to experiment or even talk to anyone about it. At this point, I gave her some appropriate sexual information and some material to read at home on ways of gratification; despite her apparent sophistication, she was actually quite naive in this area.

At the end of our sixth session, Mrs. Bennett asked to cut down our interviews to once a week. By this time she had agreed to start divorce proceedings and consulted a lawyer who was working out a property agreement with Bob's attorney. Meanwhile, her friend, Mimi, wanted to pull out of the boutique since the family was moving to California. Mrs. Bennett decided to try to run the shop on her own, which meant working full time.

She also informed me that she had let the children know last weekend about the divorce. She was astonished that neither Meg nor Phyllis was surprised; evidently they had come to the conclusion some time ago that their parents' marriage was largely one of convenience. Phyllis advised her frankly to "get out while she was still young enough to find another man." Mark seemed most upset, but he agreed with his sisters that it was their parents' affair. His last comment was that divorce must be an occupational hazard for doctors; he better watch out for that.

At this point I made a strategic decision. We had reached the point in therapy where we could either start a more intensive phase of introspection or taper off. Since Mrs. Bennett was in the midst of making a number of significant life changes, it seemed unwise at this time to challenge further her defenses of denial and rationalization. She agreed to this shift with some relief. For the next three sessions we concentrated on her present reality situation. She planned, once the property division was made, to move out of the big house and into a small apartment near her shop. And, in the fall, she wanted to take some courses in merchandising and business methods.

But first, she had decided that, instead of going to Cape Cod for the month of August, as they had done every year for the past eighteen years, she would take a cruise alone, maybe down to the Caribbean or to the Greek Islands—somewhere where no one knew her and where she could be herself, completely. Her mother, Bob's parents, the children, the shop—even the ladies' auxiliary at the hospital—could all take care of themselves for a month. "This is on me, for me, by myself!"

Ending Phase.   Since I myself was gone for the month of August, I did not see Mrs. Bennett again until early September, although I found two postcards, one from Majorca and one from Crete, on my return. When she finally came in, I was struck by the change in her appearance. She was casually dressed, deeply tanned, and far more relaxed than I had ever seen her. She had taken a four-week luxury cruise to the Mediterranean and Greece and had a wonderful time. She met a number of new acquaintances and even had two short, "unserious" affairs. Now she felt much better about herself and ready to start a new chapter in her life.

She reopened the boutique and planned to redecorate it completely, maybe even giving it a new name, like "Athene." Her lawyer had informed her that arrangements were almost complete and they expected to have the divorce hearing next month. She even met Bob yesterday as she was leaving the hospital just after handing over the gavel of president of the auxiliary. They were pleasant to each other but didn't have much to say. He had already moved to Boston and would be returning to Meadowlake only once a week. Most of what she felt was relief that that part of her life was over.

Since it seemed obvious that Mrs. Bennett was completing the transition to a new stage in her development, we agreed to terminate our work together at this time although she promised that, if things got rough in the future, she would again be in touch.

This case is far different in form and content from the previous one, but the issues it deals with are equally characteristic of this transitional stage. The precipitating factor of Dr. Bennett's request for a divorce became the opening wedge to enable Mrs. Bennett to examine her whole life structure and to make some middleweight and heavyweight changes, to borrow Goodman's terms. Once the clinician helped her establish an appropriate focus, she was able to return selectively to her past, find some key patterns in how her marriage developed, mourn the way of living she was leaving, and then change her direction and start to develop a new identity and self-image. She answered the existential questions, "What am I now?" and "Where do I want to go?" in what was a very positive way for her.

The clinician's decision to concentrate on her mid-life changes would certainly be open to challenge by some professionals. However, in view of Mrs. Bennett's limited ability to view herself introspectively and the fact that she was facing a serious turning point in her life and had to make a number of adaptations in her life structure, the judgment appears sound to me. To "take her apart" at this point seemed to be contraindicated.

This case can be seen as a prime example of how disruptions of change can be handled in an intensive but focused way to help the denying client cross the perilous bridge.

CHAPTER 12

"I'm Redundant: No One Wants Me!"

Case Situation #3: First Interview with Roy Carter

Roy Carter, fifty-four, a once-handsome but now rather shabby-looking man, with shaking hands and bloodshot eyes, arrived late for his appointment with a counselor at Family Service. Nervously fingering his hat, he said that his wife, *Martha*, is suing him for divorce after sixteen years of marriage because of his drinking. Taking a deep breath, he said it was a complicated story and he better start at the beginning.

This is his second marriage. His first wife, Blanche, died twenty years ago of complications following pneumonia. He was away at the time; as an aeronautical engineer, his job entailed a good deal of travel. They were living in Seattle, but after Blanche died, there was nothing much to hold him there, so a few months later he and their two children, *Mildred*, nine, and *Kendall*, seven, moved down to California. They managed with a string of so-called housekeepers who looked after the kids until he married, four years later, his secretary, Martha Owens. By that time he had moved out of actual engineering work and into administration at Norton Aircraft.

Martha and he weren't "crazy kids in love"; it was never the way it had been with Blanche. But they suited each other and she was a whiz at work, so it seemed natural to ask her to take over at home, too. She was a divorcée at the time; she had two boys of her own, whom she had raised alone ever since her first husband, a jazz musician, had run out on her. She seemed very good with his kids; as a matter of fact, she got along better with them than he did.

After they married, they bought a home in Pasadena and settled down, all six of them. Martha, who decided to give up her office job, ran the household with her usual efficiency and no-nonsense attitude. They lived a very comfortable life, except for the usual hassles as the kids grew up. She saw to it that they all married well and, by now, all four are out on their own. His own two aren't even in the area; Mildred moved back to Seattle with her husband and Kendall is working as a petroleum engineer in Texas.

Most of their home life was very involved with the company's operations. With a "push here and there" from Martha, he rose up through the hierarchy until he became vice–president in charge of new sales. Somewhere along the line, he said, he had begun to drink seriously. Sure, he had always drunk to some extent; at the beginning it was mostly social drinking, nothing he couldn't handle. The "three-martini lunch" became part of the routine; it certainly helped him handle difficult customers.

Three years ago the balloon burst and "everything blew sky-high." The aircraft industry was experiencing a particularly serious recession and suddenly, without warning, their company was raided by a competitor who was looking for a tax write-off. Within a week, half of the jobs in administration were simply wiped out. Some of the junior executives were able to scramble and find places for themselves with other companies but, because of his age—"fifty-one is *old* in this business!"—and high rank, he was simply let go, with a fairly decent severance settlement but with no prospects or promises. Even his stock options turned out to be worthless.

At first he couldn't take it in; he looked on his situation as sort of an extended vacation. For a while he took it easy, then he began to "call around" to let it be known that he was available. But despite all the guys who "owed him" for giving them a leg up the ladder, nothing worked out. After a few months he began to feel really uneasy and registered with several employment services that specialized in relocating executives. When nothing came of that, he figured he had grown out of touch with his engineering background, so he took a couple of quick refresher courses. This only made him realize how new developments in aerospace had changed the entire field since he had been active in it. He kept sending out résumés and either getting no answer or receiving polite but firm turndowns. A

year ago he had to face the grim fact that he was expendable—
"Redundant, the British call it."

Since then he has tried a few times to find other kinds of work,
but the answer is always the same: He is either too old, too over-
qualified, or without the needed experience. So mostly he's been sitting around at home, watching TV and drinking. He used to stick to
vodka and gin, but lately he's been settling for cheap white wine. He
never gets roaring drunk; mostly he gets more and more quiet, with
just a "haze" to keep himself from thinking.

What's been happening with Martha is the real nub of the matter. At first she was very understanding and helpful; she helped him
work up his résumé and sent out letters for him, even tried to use her
own connections. But as the noes kept coming in, she became more
and more fed up; she's a "fighter" who can't understand why he
feels so shamed and humiliated when men whom he trained turn
him down. A year ago, when their funds began to dry up because
they always lived up to the edge of their income, she decided to go
back to work herself. She took a real estate operator's course, passed
her licensing exam easily, and has blossomed as an independent realtor. She's very successful, even though it means she's out of the house
every day and most evenings, sometimes weekends as well.

At this point, Mr. Carter broke down completely. He said Martha has totally changed and avoids him as much as she can. She
refuses to cook his meals and has moved into another bedroom,
claiming he "stinks" and is of no use to her. Their joint bank account
has been used up, as have their other convertible funds, including
his severance pay. She's opened a separate bank account for her
earnings and refuses to give him even pocket money. A week ago,
without warning, she had divorce papers served on him. He's tried
to talk to her about it, but she refuses to discuss it with him; even the
children all side with her. He's still living at home, but now she's
talking about putting the house on the market. He feels his whole
world is crumbling and there's nowhere to turn. Sure, drinking is
part of the problem, but it's also the crutch that keeps him going. So
what can he do now?

Professionals' Opinions

Many of the twenty-four professionals who reviewed this case situation recognized it as a very prevalent condition among couples at

this stage of life. Most viewed it either as a case of marital conflict with excessive drinking as one aspect of it, or as a case of mid-life alcoholism marked by marital conflict and impending divorce. The majority felt the underlying issue was Mr. Carter's depression, lowered self-image, and sense of inadequacy triggered by the loss of his executive job three years ago, while others viewed his underlying dependency as the core issue. Operationally, more than half would start intervention by dealing with his alcohol dependency, either by themselves or through referral to A.A. or some similar treatment program. Others would begin with the disturbed marital relationship provided his wife would agree to cooperate.

The appropriate treatment strategy would be to center on providing material and arrangemental help, coupled with offering him a supportive relationship; few recommended intensive therapy. Central themes to be covered would be his depression, poor self-image, and fears for the future and include how to increase his ability to take care of himself, to improve his self-esteem, and, of course, to master his alcohol abuse. Goals for treatment would be for him to function better, to stop drinking, and to find employment. Only a few experts saw continuation of the marriage as a viable goal. None saw the prognosis for Mr. Carter as very positive, but the majority thought it might be fairly positive if he would cooperate. One-third felt there was little or no hope for improvement.

How the Case Was Treated

Treatment in this situation was compiled from reports of several similar cases and followed the same overall guidelines recommended by our panel of experts. It took place in a family agency in the Los Angeles area.

Beginning Phase. Initially, Mr. Carter was seen for individual treatment by a professional social worker on a fairly supportive level. She diagnosed his condition as depression in a rather dependent mid-life man who had developed a pattern of responding to pressure with excessive drinking. Since he had been functioning at a high level until fairly recently, it was decided to try to help him reverse the downward slide into serious depression by intervention on several levels, with emphasis on the reality factors in his life situation.

After the intake interview, his wife was invited in (with his consent) to see whether she would be interested in conjoint therapy with her husband. Mrs. Carter refused; she made it clear that she was through with her husband and was washing her hands completely of the situation. Divorce proceedings had been started and, as soon as she could, she would be leaving for Santa Barbara to join a prestigious real estate management firm. She said firmly that she had done what she could for Roy but now had her own future to consider and did not want to be further involved. When Mr. Carter was informed of this, he said he was not surprised; Martha only liked to back winners.

Middle Phase.   Although initially Mr. Carter felt quite uncomfortable talking about himself, he became intrigued when the clinician commented that he seemed to have experienced a number of losses over the years and they could try to find some "common thread." Over the next few interviews they went selectively over his past. He could scarcely recall his father, who joined the Canadian air force and was killed in the early years of World War II; his embittered schoolteacher mother always blamed her husband for deserting her.

After growing up in Buffalo as an only child of a working mother, he studied aeronautical engineering and went to work for Norton Aircraft in their Seattle plant. He loved his work and began to build his professional career; he also married Blanche, whom he described as "the best thing that ever happened" to him. But after ten years of personal and professional happiness, during which their two children were born, Blanche contracted pneumonia one damp winter while he was away testing the prototype of a new aircraft his group was developing. Her family blamed him for neglecting her; in fact, she died before they could contact him. Until today his children hold him responsible for their mother's death; this lay at the root of their never being close after that. Now, for the first time, he could mourn her death.

Mr. Carter said he himself never got over the loss; even after they came down to Southern California, he just withdrew within himself and his job. That's why he allowed Martha, his secretary, to gradually take over his life. She was very much like his own mother and very unlike Blanche; she always knew what was best. After they married, it became easier not to argue and to do as she said. She was the one who pushed him into administration, to which he felt he had never really been suited. She ran both her own kids' lives and his, too; they all learned to go along and not to fight her. But at least his kids got out as soon as they could.

Not that they didn't have a comfortable life over the next fifteen years, particularly since he became close to his old school buddy, Franklin Holden, president of Norton. He really trusted Holden; that was why, when the axe fell, it was his betrayal that hurt the most. These same themes of dependence, desertion, and loss were predominant as he recounted his downward path after losing his job. It rankled that men whom he had trained and regarded as his protégés refused to help him, even though many owed their positions to his advice and earlier recommendations.

When the practitioner commented that, realistically, he was now fifty-four, not twenty-four, that the field had changed, and that he might have to face the fact that he probably could no longer work as an aeronautical engineer or as a vice president again, Mr. Carter broke down and asked, "So what will become of me? Am I just a basket case? Is this the end of the line?"

It was at this point that the social worker suggested that he join a recently formed support group of middle-aged, middle-class men, several of whom were in the same executive class as he, who were all unemployed or who had been given early retirement. The group was led by an agency volunteer, himself a retired business executive. In their meetings they discussed such practical matters as retraining, possible job prospects, filling out applications, and writing appropriate job résumés. Mr. Carter became an active participant, finding that he had much in common with the other men, most of whom were victims of the fluctuating economic recession and/or recent technological changes. He made a preliminary application for disability payments but canceled it when a job lead he had found on his own came through. He began to teach high school dropouts computer programming in a specially funded state program on a part-time basis.

The theme of Mr. Carter's drinking came up frequently during treatment. He insisted he was not an alcoholic, that he used it merely to "keep himself going," and that he could stop if he had sufficient incentive. But when, in discussing his wife's leaving him, he began to talk about his sexual impotence and was challenged directly as to the part excessive drinking played in this, he became very upset. Holding his hands over his eyes, he said, "Yes, I am a drunk, a stinking stumblebum headed for skid row. That's what Martha called me and she was certainly right."

At this point, Mr. Carter was referred to a special alcohol and substance-abuse program that the agency frequently used for its clients. He began to attend semiweekly sessions there and at one point, shortly after he started to work, when he began to experience withdrawal symptoms, was briefly hospitalized.

Ending Phase.   After six weeks, in view of Mr. Carter's tendency to become dependent upon women and because he was once more in a relatively stable condition, attending the mid-life men's group at the agency and receiving considerable support there, as well as participating in the alcohol treatment program, it was decided to terminate individual sessions. However, he continued to call the social worker periodically when things would "gang up" on him.

Follow-Up.   Six months later, Mr. Carter was seen for a follow-up session. At this time he was neatly dressed and had lost his withdrawn, gaunt look. He reported that he now lived alone in a two-room apartment in Burbank and was working full time as a teacher in the vocational retraining program at a local community college. He still attended the mid-life men's group but had become a model of "one who had been there" for others to follow. He had not touched alcohol for the past four months and served as a peer counselor for others in the treatment program. He still felt quite lonely and did not go out much, but recently he had become interested in a woman teacher at school; they would stop for coffee after late classes and found they had much in common.

Mr. Carter said he had not heard from Martha since their preliminary divorce hearing but, when his daughter called last week on his birthday, she told him that Martha is now an executive in her property-management firm and frequently appears on TV talk shows as an expert on women in business. On the whole, he liked his new life, which was less pressured and more low-keyed than when he was at Norton, though he missed some aspects of it. He wasn't earning much money now but his needs were modest and he felt that "At least I'm finally my own man."

This case, so characteristic of men in their fifties who use drinking to mask their underlying depression, as discussed in Chapter 5, illustrates the combination of individual treatment, participation in support groups, and referral to appropriate community resources that can be used in a "broad push" approach to change the direction of a person's life during the transition to late mid-life. No effort was made to treat Mr. Carter intensively or to attempt a far-reaching reconstruction of his personality. Rather, intervention was reality-oriented, designed to help him bridge the turbulent period from his high performance (at a price) in his forties to a more realistically modest level of functioning in his fifties.

It is too soon to predict whether he will be able to maintain this new life over time and develop more satisfying personal relationships in the future. But at least he has shifted his expectations and taken control of his own life, so that a fairly optimistic forecast can be made.

CHAPTER 13

"What's Happened to Our Family?"

Case Situation #4: First Interview with Frank and Marie Donnelli

Frank and Marie Donnelli were waiting nervously for the doors of the Community Mental Health Center to open when the social worker arrived. Rather shamefacedly Mr. Donnelli explained that they had a "little flare-up" at home last night and the neighbors called the cops. When the Crisis Squad arrived, they recognized him because he works in the district attorney's office. Anyway, by that time things had quieted down and his wife was in the bedroom crying. So instead of making out a report, the officer in charge suggested they come over here to talk to someone about their family troubles.

Mr. Donnelli, fifty-two, is a tall, heavy-set man with close-cropped black hair and red-rimmed eyes. He has worked for the past twenty-six years in the district attorney's office, where he is now in charge of cases involving financial and corporate fraud. Mrs. Donnelli, forty-nine, small and thin, wore a scarf wrapped around her head, shading her pale, lined face. Mr. Donnelli related their story, although his wife would lean over from time to time to whisper to him.

Sheepishly, he said that this was the first time anyone had to call the cops on them; they were a respectable Catholic family and always prided themselves on their good name in the parish. They raised their five kids and gave them good educations. He's built a fine record at work and now is at the "top of the ladder" in his office; in fact, he expects to apply for early retirement in three or four years.

But things have been piling up on them for the last few months, one on top of the other. Marie has been having "women's troubles" for some time and, three months ago, the doctors discovered a tumor, so she had to have a hysterectomy; even now, they aren't sure they got it all out and she's getting chemotherapy. Then Mr. Donnelli's father had a stroke back East and he had to go out there for a week to try to straighten out his tangled legal affairs, which still are in a real mess. And then, just last month, Sharon, their eldest daughter, came home for a visit with her three little kids. She's been having trouble with her husband—a real skirt-chaser—and he just walked out on her. It looks as though she's here to stay for a long time, at least till things get straightened out.

The climax came yesterday when he got a call from the police chief over in Gainesville. Their youngest boy, Joey, not yet eighteen and supposedly studying for final exams, was picked up with a couple of young hoods for stealing two cars and staging a drag race down Main Street. They're holding them without bail, since they knocked down an old man who is still unconscious in the hospital.

Mr. Donnelli said he was so upset after hearing this, that he couldn't concentrate on his work, so he just shut up his office, stopped off at the corner bar for a couple of shots to steady himself, and then came home. He wanted to tell Marie about Joey before she heard it on the radio, but Sharon's kids were making such a racket, he couldn't get in a private word with her. So he stayed in the bedroom drinking beer with vodka chasers. About ten o'clock, when things quieted down, he came out to talk to Marie and he guesses he raised his voice a little; the more he spoke, the angrier he got. Finally—he doesn't know what got into him—he just picked up a kitchen chair and heaved it out of the window; that's when the neighbors called the cops. But it also sobered him up and he just sat there, with his head in his arms, until they came.

At this point, Mrs. Donnelli took over. She didn't want anyone to think they usually fight like this; as a matter of fact, it's the first time in their whole life that such a thing had happened. Frank is a fine, upstanding man whom everyone in the neighborhood looks up to. He was an all-city football star in high school and got three citations in World War II, even though he came in only at the tail end.

When he came back from the Pacific, he went to Notre Dame on a football scholarship and then came home to settle down, even though he could have gone on to become a "football bum." They were married right after he graduated and he has been a model husband ever since.

The Donnellis had four children in rapid order: *Tom*, twenty-eight, whom they haven't seen for the past nine years, ever since he slipped over the border into Canada to escape the Vietnam draft. Mrs. Donnelli half whispered, "Such a wonderful boy until we made the mistake of letting him go to Berkeley instead of Loyola!" Next came *Sharon*, twenty-six, who married early and had three kids in a row because she thought that would hold her husband to her. *Lainey*, twenty-five, is their career girl who, of all the children, carried out her father's dream and went into law. She is now working as a public defender down in San Diego. After that came *Paul*, the artistic one, who is a stage designer in San Francisco.

There was a gap then, becaues the doctor told her to slow down on becoming pregnant for a while. But six years later they had *Joey*; he was an "accident," but she was glad about it because she could name him after her father who had just died. With tears rolling down her cheeks, she said he was always her baby, someone special . . . and now look what happened to him. She guesses Frank is right when he says she spoiled him rotten; now he's messed up his life and theirs, too.

Mr. Donnelli said heavily that there is nothing they can do about Joey now. He's in the hands of the law and will have to take what's coming to him. But their whole family seems to be falling apart. They started out with such high hopes and dreams; he remembers when they got married, they felt the whole world was wide open for them. They'll be married thirty years in a couple of months, and what do they have to show for it? He's made a bigger mess of his life than his father—all *he* lost was his money; he kept his good name. But what will "Donnelli" stand for after he goes? Family tradition means nothing to his sons; all they've done is bring shame to the family.

Professionals' Opinions

This case was seen as typical of families who encounter a series of stressful life events that build up to a climactic crisis. The twenty-two professionals who assessed the situation differed in the order of importance and weight attributed to the various elements—Joey's arrest, Sharon's return home with her three small children, Mrs. Donnelli's life-threatening illness, or Mr. Donnelli's father's stroke— but all agreed that this was a basically well-functioning family whose coping patterns had broken down under the cumulative stress of these blows, resulting in Mr. Donnelli's explosive outburst.

Overall agreement seemed to be that the core issue was Mr. Donnelli's feelings of disappointment, frustration, and anger over his children's failure to live up to his expectations, as well as his father's illness and his wife's condition, with some placing this within the mid-life context of intergenerational stress. More than a third suggested starting with the family's inability to handle the current stress but chose different points of entry. Some would start with the Donnellis' role as parents, others with Mrs. Donnelli's health problems and her husband's inability to share his concern with her, while still others would start with specific problems involving the children. Most of the experts recommended an active, crisis intervention or stress-reducing strategy, using Mr. and Mrs. Donnelli as the basic client unit. The use of support and understanding was seen as preferred treatment techniques. The majority advocated weekly sessions, though some suggested seeing them more often until the immediate crisis subsided.

As major themes for treatment, over half of the clinicians advised concentrating on helping the family enhance their self-esteem and mastery, building on their innate family strengths. Others recommended centering on Mr. Donnelli's worries over his wife's illness, utilizing the strong marital bond between them. Generally, this was seen as a fairly short-term intervention that could be terminated when coping patterns had been remobilized and the couple had resolved their ambivalence over letting their children go. More than half felt the prognosis to be fairly positive and the rest, very positive; only one expressed little or no hope for change.

How the Case Was Treated

This case was treated in the Crisis Treatment Unit of an outpatient community mental health center on the West Coast by a professional social worker, with some consultation from the director, a psychiatrist. The couple was seen together for six sessions over a period of three weeks, the last time with the rest of the family. Then they were interviewed once more three months later for a follow-up. The format follows the usual one for crisis cases, although the focus was broadened in the latter part of treatment.

Beginning Phase. By the time the initial interview was completed, it became evident that the Donnellis were very anxious to work on their deteriorating family situation. However, since Mrs. Donnelli appeared exhausted, it was suggested they return the next day.

Middle Phase. By the second session, Mr. Donnelli had already heard from Joey's lawyer that, while four boys were being held, Joey's part was considered relatively minor and it was agreed at the arraignment that he be released into his father's custody. Mr. Donnelli drove over to pick up his son and they had a long man-to-man talk. He let Joey know how upset and angry they all were over what he had done but that they would back him up, no matter what happened. In turn, Joey, who was really shaken by the accident, told his father that he had been truanting because he felt they were all so preoccupied with Grandpa's stroke, Mama's illness, and Sharon's coming back home that no one was paying attention to him. But he hadn't counted on those guys being so reckless and he had already promised himself that, if he got out of this mess, it was the last time he'd have anything to do with them.

The practitioner used this to remark that the Donnelli family seemed to stick by its members. What made him feel that their family ties were dissolving? Mr. Donnelli began to talk about his eldest son's running away to Canada and how this angered him, a former Marine who risked his life in the Pacific. After he spent some time ventilating his feelings of shame and outrage, the social worker wondered how Tom felt: Wasn't it hard on him, raised with this strong sense of family solidarity, to be cut off from the rest of them? After all, the Vietnam war was over a long time ago and others had been repatriated. Mrs. Donnelli then revealed that they had received a letter from an organization of former draft-evaders who were urging families to help them arrange for their sons' return. She had been afraid to show it to Frank or even mention it. Mr. Donnelli was touched by her concern but upset that she had withheld the letter from him.

From this, he began to talk about his father's recent stroke and how he felt when they took him to the nursing home, that now the mantle of "family head" was really on his shoulders. Would his son feel the same when he, his father, grew old? For the rest of the interview, he wove back and forth between the pride his father had given him, both in being a Donnelli and in being an American, and in his son's rejection of all that when he left. Somehow he felt it was his own failure that made Tom develop such "left wing" ideas. Without being drawn into the political discussion, the worker pointed out that Tom's questioning the country's direction in the seventies sounded as though he was concerned with supporting values he could pass on to *his* sons. Mrs. Donnelli's only contribution was to say softly as they left, "After all, Frank, he *is* a Donnelli."

By the third interview four days later, a number of changes had taken place. Joey's case was heard in Juvenile Court, since he was not yet eighteen, and he was placed on informal probation in the custody of his father. Very subdued, he was now back in school, studying for his final exams and trying to make up for lost time. Meanwhile, Mr. Donnelli had contacted the organization his wife had mentioned and received an address in Vancouver where they could reach Tom. They had called him over the weekend and had a long reunion over the phone. They reported that Tom sounded much more mature and self-confident; he married a Canadian girl and was now, of all things, an accountant with a small business of his own. He was very shocked to hear about Mama's illness and wanted very much to come back to see them. Mr. Donnelli has an appointment with his congressman to see whether this can be arranged.

This opened up the subject of the extent to which parents can run their children's lives, to shield them from making the same mistakes they themselves had made. Mrs. Donnelli reminded her husband that he had defied his father's wish to go into business with him and, instead, had married and settled down on the West Coast. The worker added that, even though Sharon had married against their wishes, she had to find out for herself that it couldn't work. At least, when her marriage broke up, she had her family to come back to. Even Lainey's "stubbornness" to practice law as she saw fit and Paul's choice of a different life-style were brought up as examples of individual choice within a strong family network.

By this time, both Mr. and Mrs. Donnelli were taking active parts in the discussion. While he tended to generalize about the way things should be, she had a knack of putting her finger on the heart of the situation. She also pointed out his tendency not to listen to what others were saying.

The fifth interview had to be canceled because Mrs. Donnelli had an adverse reaction to her last chemotherapy treatment and had to stay in bed. When they came in two days later, both were shaken and the social worker brought up the issue they had been avoiding until now: Mrs. Donnelli's illness. It became apparent that it was foremost on their minds but both were afraid to talk about it. With the practitioner's encouragement, Mrs. Donnelli voiced her own fears that she was repeating her mother's last illness, that she would never live to see her next birthday. Mr. Donnelli, visibly distressed, told her of Dr. Perini's prediction that she would have, at the most, a year's time left. For the rest of the session, the worker remained virtually silent as they talked to each other about their thirty years together, going back to reminisce about how they had first met down in San Diego and how much they had shared over the years. At the close, the worker suggested they might want to talk to the children about their mother's illness and what it meant to them.

Ending Phase. The final session was held at the Donnelli home on the weekend, so that all of the family, except Tom, could participate. Mr. Donnelli started by telling them they wanted to discuss the "family secret" about which they were all worried: Mama's illness. The four children listened in silence while Mrs. Donnelli, in a low but steady voice, repeated what she had said the previous time, that she knew it would be only a short while until her time would come and how she did not dread dying so much as leaving Poppa and them. Mr. Donnelli put his arms around his wife and told her how much he would miss her but how it hurt him to see her suffer. Then, turning to the children, he said how much they wanted the children to be close to them at this time, "for both our sakes."

Each of the children took turns expressing how they felt about Mama's leaving them, how, to them, she was the heart of the family, the one to whom they could always turn. Sharon shared with the rest how she had hated to come home after Ken shoved her out, but how both Pop and Mama took her in without question. Lainey spoke of her need to live up to her father's aspirations but how Mama always stood as a buffer when he would become angry over her insistence on practicing law in her own way. Paul, silent until now, said he knew he had disappointed both of them but Mama's unquestioning belief in him supported him while he struggled to figure out who and why he was. Turning to his father, he asked him directly whether, even if he could not agree with him, he would share

Mama's trust in him? Finally Joey, sitting hunched in his chair with his eyes on the floor, mumbled that he guessed he was the biggest disappointment of all to Pop and Mama. But it was hard being the youngest; everyone was always telling him what to do and no one took him seriously. The rest were all grown up but he . . . he still needed Mama, he added in a choked voice.

By this time everyone was emotionally exhausted. In a calculated change of mood, the worker wondered if they might begin to plan practically what they could do over the next months to make their mother's life easier. Everyone began to make suggestions. Both Lainey and Paul offered to come home weekends to spend more time with the family. Sharon announced she would postpone going back to work and would keep a close eye on Mama to keep her from overdoing it. Mr. Donnelli reported that his boss had already agreed to limit his investigative responsibilities so he could spend more time at home. He also told the rest of the family about their contacts with Tom and their efforts to expedite his coming home.

When the two-hour session ended, there was a real feeling of unity in the Donnelli home; once more they were a close-knit, caring family. As the worker left, it was agreed that they would try to handle their situation without outside help, although they understood that the practitioner and the Crisis Center stood by, ready to assist whenever they were needed.

Follow-Up. Nothing further was heard from the Donnellis, although a local newspaper ran a feature story several months later about Mr. and Mrs. Thomas Donnelli who were visiting their family with their two children. Shortly thereafter a follow-up session was held with Mr. and Mrs. Donnelli, at home.

Mrs. Donnelli appeared thinner and frailer than ever but had a new spark in her eyes as they talked about their eldest son's visit. Mr. Donnelli admitted that both Tom and he had grown up in the years they were separated and they no longer felt the need to battle each other. Since Tom's draft number had never come up, technically he was not considered a draft evader and it had been a relatively simple matter to have his status clarified in the eyes of the government. They had talked about his returning here to live but Tom felt he had finally been granted Canadian citizenship and was reluctant to give up the business he had struggled so hard to establish. But at least they promised to return often so Mama could get to know her two new grandchildren.

The whole Donnelli family was going through a difficult period as Mama's health fluctuated. When it was in remission, as now, things would go smoothly, although twice she had to be hospitalized for further surgery. Then the anxiety level would rise and the situation would grow tense. But at least they were trying hard to support each other; Sharon was turning out to be the real "rock" on whom the rest of them now leaned.

Mr. Donnelli reported that his father passed away two months ago and he took Marie back to Scranton with him—at her insistence—to attend the funeral. For both of them, it was a moving experience just seeing the whole community turn out to honor his father. Even the mayor spoke at the ceremony, recounting the part that the Donnellis and the rest of the Italian community had played in the city's development. Mr. Donnelli brought back with him his father's box of medals from World War I and mementos from his childhood in Palermo, which he had left to his oldest son. They had already mounted them in a case on the living-room wall, next to his own medals and insignias from World War II. The children would tease him about his "hundred and ten percent Americanism" but the grandchildren loved to hear stories about how the medals were won.

Treatment in this case closely followed the crisis intervention model, with the focus on the present active disequilibrium, then the selective reaching back into the past to the original hazardous event (Tom's defection), and then returning to the present and immediate future. What distinguishes it, however, are the transitional issues which were raised: helping the Donnellis restore their faith in their family solidarity and their ability to support each other and do some anticipatory grieving during Mrs. Donnelli's terminal illness.

As the experts predicted would happen, this family was able to utilize their innate strengths and trust in each other to foster constructive coping during a critical interval in their personal and familial development.

In discussing this case, the practitioner admitted her own reluctance to step out of this case, in view of her empathy with the Donnellis' distress, but felt it would diminish their strength and violate their privacy not to allow them to pass through the transition at their own pace. This is a difficult issue with which many professionals wrestle: How much is enough?

While this is an issue in treatment in general and is argued end-lessly by professionals in discussing case outcome, it assumes particular importance in dealing with transitional situations where the intervention is geared to helping the family mobilize their own strengths to cope with the complications and necessary adjustments. My own view, while allowing for particular variations in responses to stress, tends to favor maximizing clients' abilities to function autonomously.

CHAPTER 14

"How Much Do I Owe My Parents?"

Case Situation #5: First Interview with Betty Eisman

Betty Eisman, fifty-one, a short, plump woman with fluffy gray-brown hair and a dimpled smile, asked to see a worker in the Aged Department of the family agency to discuss what should be done about her parents who are no longer able to manage at home. *Mr. Heller*, eighty-four, suffers from chronic hypertension and other cardiovascular complications but otherwise is still alert and active. *Mrs. Heller*, eighty-one, is a long-term diabetic and the cataracts in both her eyes have been growing worse. They were doing fine, however, in their small apartment, with "Poppa" doing the shopping and "Momma" most of the cooking and cleaning, that is, until last month when Momma slipped on the front stairs and broke her hip. She's now ready for discharge from the hospital, but yesterday the social worker suggested that they begin to think of other living arrangements, particularly since their neighborhood is deteriorating and their apartment building is scheduled to be torn down shortly.

Mrs. Eisman feels very responsible for her parents; in their family they always had the motto, "All for one and one for all!" She and her two brothers agree that they had a wonderful childhood and they owe it to their parents to take care of them now. As the only daughter and the one who lives closest, she has always taken her parents shopping and to their doctors' appointments, since Poppa no longer drives. She's the one they call when the landlord refuses to fix the boiler or the refrigerator acts up. Rather wryly she said, "My brothers have always been very generous with their money, but their wives only let them visit Momma and Poppa once a month—for no more than an hour." She herself spends at least two mornings a week with them.

If she had her way, she'd bring Momma and Poppa home with her without any question; they have a large house and both of the girls are married. She is very close to her daughters and baby-sits regularly for *Marilyn*'s two boys when she wants to go shopping and for *Carole*'s baby while she attends her morning art classes. In fact, she has "half promised" Carole to take care of little Cindy so that she can accompany her husband when he goes to Chicago next month for a computer update course.

At this point, Mrs. Eisman paused and took a deep breath. The real problem, she guesses, is her husband. *Harry* has always been very easygoing about her close ties with her family. As a matter of fact, he has always envied them; he himself had been smuggled out of Germany just before the last world war; his parents never made it and he's the sole survivor in his family. He was raised by some cousins in England and then came to the United States by himself after the war. He started with nothing and worked his way up by sheer willpower; when she met him five years later, he already owned his own business selling stoves and refrigerators. Since they were married, he's worked day and night for her and the girls; for the last eight years he has been the area distributor for a well-known line of electrical appliances.

Just last week he told her that he was being promoted to director of sales for the whole state. He brought her a bouquet of flowers and told her that, starting next week, he has to make a three-week tour of all their outlets in the region and wants her to come along. They can take their time driving and make it a second honeymoon—a first, really, since they never had a real one. He feels they need to get away a little, "to get to know each other again." So when she broke the news about her parents, he really blew up.

Tearfully, Mrs. Eisman said she knows she has neglected Harry these past years; she's always been so caught up in their girls' lives since they were babies. And lately, she's been rushing to drive her father to visit her mother each day in the hospital and back to prepare his meals before she came home. Harry never complained until now, but last night they had a real fight. He says she sees herself as "Little Miss Fixit" who has to move in and take over everyone else's troubles—except their own.

When he calmed down, they tried to consider how they could manage. The girls will have to get along without her, even though she has always urged them to share their troubles with her. Both daughters married early and have had their share of adjusting to do: Marilyn's husband ruptured a disk at work last year and spent half a year in a wheelchair. And Carole and her husband have had a hard time getting used to being parents, just a year after they were married. But Harry is right; they're grown up now and have to live their own lives.

But this still doesn't solve the problem of her parents. She can't let Momma go back to their third-floor apartment, with her eyes growing worse and her still using a walker. Poppa won't be able to help her much; he doesn't even know how to boil water by himself. She spent all night, after Harry finally fell asleep, trying to figure out what to do. No matter which way she turns, another obstacle comes up. Most of all she feels that, even if they could work out some practical solution for her parents to manage at home for the next few weeks, the questions still keep popping up in her mind: How much does she owe her parents? How much does she owe the girls? And Harry . . . how much does she owe him?

Her neighbors keep telling her she is much too "traditional." Mrs. Kane, on the one side, has been working ever since her last child started kindergarten. Now she's head buyer at an exclusive women's shop. Mrs. Barnard, on the other side, doesn't work, but she's always out playing tennis or running or playing bridge; she's also on her fourth husband. She, herself, doesn't begrudge spending her time on her family. But the question remains: Which family comes first?

Professionals' Opinions

The Eismans' situation was considered fairly typical of family agency cases. Several respondents reported that a considerable part of their caseload dealt with similar requests to arrange care for ailing parents. Here, the timing was causing a problem because the need occurred just at the time when Mr. Eisman wanted his wife to travel with him in order to reestablish the primary importance of their marital bonds. The majority of the twenty-five experts who reviewed this case saw it as a "squeeze situation" with Mrs. Eisman caught in between the conflicting loyalties to her parents, her children, and her husband. In addition, a good number saw her as struggling with the issues of her own mid-life identity and sense of self.

The majority of practitioners would start by helping Mrs. Eisman deal with the concrete problem of her parents' immediate needs, although some would also try to help her disengage herself to some extent so that she could attend to her husband's needs, redefine her priorities, and/or deal with her own confusion and fragile self-esteem. Virtually all said they would provide material and arrangemental help for her parents and, at the same time, use a supportive, educative approach; a few, however, suggested trying for more intensive, insight-oriented treatment. The preferred arrangement would be to see her alone and, in addition, to see her together with her husband, her parents, and, for some of the time, with her children or siblings.

Central themes to be covered would include the issue of her responsibility to others and the extent of her loyalties to the three generations of her family. Almost half advised concentrating on her feelings of guilt, anger, and/or dependency, while others preferred to help her examine her ties with her husband and their mutual expectations. Termination would be attempted when practical arrangements for her parents had been completed, when the marriage had been strengthened, and when she was able to set more appropriate priorities. Almost two-thirds predicted a very positive prognosis, while the rest saw it as fairly positive.

How the Case Was Treated

The case was seen by a professional social worker at a private sectarian family agency in the Midwest. It started out as a fairly routine request for agency assistance in arranging care for elderly parents who were no longer able to manage on their own. The fact that it occurred just at the time when Mrs. Eisman and her husband were crossing their own bridge to later mid-life resulted in several complications that called for a shift in focus from the provision of arrangemental service to helping Mrs. Eisman deal with the issues of her conflicting loyalties and her priorities.

Beginning Phase. In the initial interview Mrs. Eisman recounted the difficulties her parents were having and also her own conflicts, in view of her husband's request that she travel with him over the next few weeks. The social worker suggested that they proceed at several levels.

First, in regard to her parents, they might differentiate between immediate and long-term needs. In terms of housing, which seemed to have first priority since her mother was ready to be discharged and could not climb stairs, Mrs. Eisman could investigate a list of furnished apartments that the agency used for temporary needs. Several of these were on the first floor, in the same general neighborhood where her parents had lived for so many years, and close to the religious, social, and shopping facilities with which they were familiar.

As soon as her parents were settled, she advised that Mrs. Eisman and her brothers sit down with their parents to consider a more long-term solution: independent housing in a project for the elderly, several new retirement homes that had just been erected in the city, established convalescent homes and institutions where health care was available on a round-the-clock basis, or sectarian facilities, such as the Jewish Home for the Aged. Since all of these facilities had waiting lists, the family needed to weigh the parents' present and future needs, financial resources, and preferences and then register well in advance.

The worker recommended that Mrs. Eisman contact the Visiting Nurses' Association for a professional to supervise her parents' medical regimen and administer her mother's daily insulin injections. She also advised talking to the supervisor of their home care program to apply for part-time home help to ease the housekeeping burden on her parents, to do the shopping, cleaning, and cooking that she had handled while her mother was hospitalized and which her father could not do.

The practitioner also suggested that, when the Eismans returned from their trip around the state, they might want to discuss the whole issue she had raised about "whose family comes first?" Doubtfully, Mrs. Eisman said she'd ask her husband but he didn't like outsiders interfering in their private affairs. They really were managing fine; she had just gotten a little upset and had wanted some advice "to settle things in her mind." But now she'll wait and see; it might be that, with her parents' situation more settled, she'll feel less pressured. If need be, she'll get in touch.

Nothing further was heard from Mrs. Eisman for almost three weeks. Then one day she tapped on the social worker's door and apologized for not having called in advance. She had come to the office to fill out some forms for her parents' home care service and thought she'd fill her in on developments.

Mrs. Eisman said her parents were getting along fine. She had found them a pleasant ground-floor apartment just three blocks from their old place, with an enclosed porch where her mother could sit and recuperate. The homemaker arrangements were working out well and they had already applied for admission into the Jewish Home for the Aged, although their turn probably wouldn't come up for at least nine months.

However—and here Mrs. Eisman took a deep breath—things were not going at all well in her own family. Just three days after she had come in, Harry, who had been working very hard to arrange things for his successor at work, came home complaining of shortness of breath and chest pains. Although he insisted it was just indigestion, she called their family doctor who advised her to take him by ambulance to the Emergency Room of the nearby hospital where he would meet them. Within two hours he was rushed first to the Emergency Room and then to the Intensive Coronary Care Unit. Two consultants had been called in and agreed that it was a heart attack, a coronary occlusion.

For three days he had remained in intensive care, related Mrs. Eisman, then they moved him to the regular ward. She had been spending all her days and most of her nights at the hospital. At first she wouldn't leave his side, but the girls were wonderful; they took turns staying with their father so that she could get out for a few hours each day. But now the doctors say he can be released in two more days and he'll be coming home to recuperate. Dr. Kantor insisted that, with proper care, he can live to be a hundred.

Wanly Mrs. Eisman smiled and said her question was answered now; there was no longer any doubt about which family came first. Both Harry and she had been very shaken up; they realized how much they needed each other. They had talked a lot together, there in the hospital, and she made it very clear to him that his health was the most important consideration. Fortunately, his company had been wonderful. One of the "big bosses" at Welbilt had made a special trip to visit Harry in the hospital and to assure him they were continuing him on full salary while he took medical leave. The present state director of sales would postpone his retirement until Harry felt ready to take his place.

But—here Mrs. Eisman hesitated. Something was bothering Harry outside of his health and business worries. He spent hours just staring into space, but whenever she asked him, he just patted her hand and said everything was fine. Perhaps she (the worker) could stop in to talk to him? Maybe, with her experience, she could figure out what was troubling him. With some misgivings, the social worker agreed to visit their home the following week.

Middle Phase.   When the clinician arrived, she found the Eismans in their plant-filled sunroom. Mr. Eisman was lying propped up on the sofa, his thin, graying hair neatly combed, his gray sweater buttoned up to his collar, his legs covered with a knitted afghan. His face was pale and lined. After a few minutes spent chatting about the warm spring weather and his stay in the hospital, the social worker decided to take the initiative. She told Mr. Eisman that, when she had seen his wife the previous week, she had mentioned that she was worried about him, that he seemed to have something on his mind that he didn't want to talk about.

At first Mr. Eisman denied it; with a forced smile, he asked how could anything bother him when he had been so miraculously cured? Just a few weeks ago he had been fighting for his life and now the doctors tell him he's almost as good as new. He still has a good job, a lovely wife who waits on him hand and foot, two beautiful daughters, both married successfully, and three wonderful grandchildren. What more could anyone want?

Shrewdly, the worker remarked that sometimes such a wonderful family can be a little *too* much of a good thing. At this, Mr. Eisman turned his face toward the wall, lay silent for a few minutes, and then flung his arm over his eyes and said in a bitter tone, "Yes, they are a wonderful family, but what about my own?"

As his wife listened in shocked silence, he went on to say in a muffled voice that for years he had put the thought of his own parents and his three sisters out of his mind. When his parents had scraped together enough money to bribe a gentile neighbor to smuggle him out of Germany, he was only nine. But all those years living with his mother's cousins in England, he dreamed that some day he would go back to rescue them. Instead, when the war ended, they learned that the whole family had perished in Dachau. That's when he decided that never again would such a thing happen to him. Using all his hoarded savings, he came alone to the United States when he was only sixteen, determined to build a new life, never looking back at what he had lost.

The years had been good to him, he went on. Here he turned to his wife, who was sitting next to him, tears pouring down her cheeks, and took her hand. Gradually the painful memories had faded and he had learned to "shut down his mind." He would even pretend that Betty's parents were his own as well. Whenever a familiar German phrase or the smell of certain foods started his thoughts down a path of old memories, he could usually "close the lid" pretty quickly.

But when he had this heart attack, it was as though the lock on his mind no longer worked. As he lay there in the intensive care unit, he kept having these "flashes" back to his childhood: visiting the Tiergarten in Berlin with his sisters, going with his father to his watch repair shop and listening to the clocks all ticking in harmony. He began to wonder again about his family; had *any* of them survived? They had tried to trace them right after the war through the Red Cross and official Jewish records in Geneva and Jerusalem. He knew they were officially listed as dead, but maybe he hadn't done enough to try to trace other family members. Maybe someone had escaped—to Belgium, to Sweden, maybe to Israel. . . .

Gently, the social worker told Mr. Eisman that many Holocaust survivors feel guilty over having lived while the rest of their families had died. At this he sat up and said fiercely, "But you see, I'm *not* a survivor, at least not in the way those who lived through the concentration camps themselves were. *I* was never starved or beaten; I was living safe in England when my family was taken. I was the only son; I should have rescued them!" Silently he began to cry and his wife put her arms around him tightly.

Then the worker said, even more quietly, "But you were only a nine-year-old boy. And Europe was at war. What could you have done?" Mr. Eisman pursed his lips, then slumped back and shook his head. "No, no . . . I guess there really wasn't much I could do. And my father's last words to me, when they sent me away, were, 'Heinzele, don't forget; you have to live for the rest of us.'" Turning to his wife he asked, "Betty, you know I've never wanted to talk about my family. But did I ever tell you about Liesl, my sister. . . ."

For the next hour, he talked steadily. As though a dam had broken, he brought out a flood of memories: of his gentle father, who still limped from a wound he received in World War I; of his warm, buxom mother, who made the best potato dumplings in the world; of Liesl, who used to entice him into trouble and then have him take the blame; of Theresa and Bertha, his teenage sisters, who spent hours primping before the mirror and who would wait, giggling, for their young men to take them for strolls in the evening under the linden trees. He recalled the years in Britain, when he and the elderly couple who were his only links to the past would sit behind tightly drawn curtains in the dark, listening while the big bombers flew over Brighton to the east, praying for the destruction of the Third Reich yet filled with foreboding over the fate of their family still in Deutschland. . . .

Finally, Mr. Eisman sank back on the pillows, exhausted, while Betty brought him his pills with some cold water. "That's the first time since I left England that I allowed myself to talk about those days," he murmured, with his eyes closed. "But I feel a thousand pounds lighter; I must have been carrying a heavy load."

The social worker leaned over and clasped his hands, then stood and slipped out of the room with Mrs. Eisman. Quietly she told her that it probably would take her husband a while to get over the emotional effects of reliving those memories. If they wanted to meet with her further, she would; on the other hand, if he'd feel more comfortable with some alternative plan, they should let her know. Meanwhile, she would send them the addresses of several organizations that specialized in tracing survivors of families who perished in the Holocaust, whom they could contact.

Ending Phase.   Mrs. Eisman came in to see the worker alone a week later. She said Mr. Eisman decided he didn't want to talk further about his family; it was simply too difficult. But they had told their daughters about what had happened when they came to visit on the weekend. Both had wondered over the years about their father's family, about whom he had never talked; now it was as if they discovered a whole new world. Carole, who had a flair for art, offered to draw up a family tree, and she and her father spent much of the afternoon sketching it out and putting in names and dates. Mr. Eisman opened the little japanned box of papers and photos that he had carried with him unopened all these years and they decided to reproduce the faces of his family members and put them in, next to their names, to make it more "alive."

Hank, Marilyn's husband, had a good idea. Next month there would be a worldwide convention of Holocaust survivors in Jerusalem. Why didn't the two of them plan to attend? They could also examine the records at the Yad v'Shem Center, the central Holocaust archives that were now far more complete than when Mr. Eisman wrote to them thirty years ago. The Eismans talked it over and decided to go. With a troubled smile, Mrs. Eisman said it wasn't exactly the honeymoon they had planned but it was important for Harry. He had already contacted the organizing committee in New York and they were waiting for details to book their trip. As she said good-bye, Mrs. Eisman promised to let the worker know what happened and thanked her for helping them at a turning point in their lives.

Follow-Up. Two months later, Mrs. Eisman again stopped in. They had just returned from their six-week pilgrimage. They started off in Jerusalem, attending the conference, where they met two of Harry's school friends from Berlin. One lived in a kibbutz in northern Israel and they spent a weekend there while the men reminisced about "Herr Steinmetz" and "Frau Kochleffel." Since all of the kibbutz members were survivors, Harry felt at ease. He spent hours in their museum, poring over the models of Dachau and listening to recordings of what had probably happened to his family there.

After three weeks in Israel, during which they received a list of "leads" from the Yad v'Shem archives, they went to Europe where Harry began to search for signs of his roots. They spent three days in West Germany. Harry found that his old home in Berlin had been leveled, although his father's shop still stood, crowded between a fast-food store and a supermarket. They even took the trip out to Dachau, but at the last moment Harry couldn't go through the crematoria with their neat piles of clothes and tagged luggage.

From Germany they crossed over to England and spent a week in the Sussex village where Harry had lived for six years. His elderly cousins had died in 1950, but the postmistress still remembered him after all these years and recalled how the Sterns would treasure his rare cards and letters. From there they went on to Montreal, where they discovered a distant cousin of his father's who had succeeded in escaping to Holland and from there to Canada. This cousin now owns a large plastics factory but his sons had migrated to Israel. They spent hours trying to "fill in the holes" in his childhood memories.

And now they were back. She had worried about Harry's exerting himself too much, but his heart attack seemed to give him new strength and the trip, painful though it was, was also a healing act. Harry and she felt closer than ever before. Just as she used to say he was part of her family, now she felt she was part of his.

Part of the intriguing interest in working with persons in transition lies in the vitality of the changes and adaptation to new conditions that occur, sometimes unpredictably. The Eisman case illustrates how a supposedly simple request for help in arranging care for aging parents can be transformed into a different type of situation when a new element—in this case, Mr. Eisman's heart attack—is introduced.

The experienced, skilled clinician was able to relate to the family's need on two levels, one dealing with the practical material-arrangemental tasks which had to be carried out regarding Mrs. Eisman's parents' needs for housing and home care and then, on a deeper, psychosocial level, responding to the internalized feelings and repressed memories which surfaced after the later developments in this case.

Treatment in this situation, as often occurs during transitions, did not follow the formal pattern of office interviews scheduled well in advance. Yet, with all the erratic intervals between sessions, with the shifts in direction and the unpredictable tangents, the social worker's genuine interest and empathy was undoubtedly the catalyst that helped this couple heal some hidden wounds and emerge from the transition more settled and closer than before.

CHAPTER 15

"What Can I Do for My Loneliness?"

Case Situation #6: First Interview with Charlene Farwell

Charlene Farwell, fifty, sat quietly in the Neighborhood Center's waiting room, her dark skin in sharp contrast to her crisp white nurse's uniform. When the worker invited Mrs. Farwell into her office, she said she passed by every day on the way to work, but it never occurred to her that the invitation on the window, "Come in and share your troubles," referred to her. But now she was at a crossroads and needed some advice, so she thought she would stop in.

Mrs. Farwell said she has lived in Chicago most of her life; her parents came up north from Arkansas when she was only a baby. In spite of the Depression and the "big" war, her father worked steadily in the steel industry; three years ago, when he finally retired, they gave him, not only a gold watch, but a plaque praising him for being a steady, reliable, and devoted employee. She guesses she takes after him; ever since she started to work when she was seventeen, she's had only two jobs in her whole life. She started the first one working in a "hole in the wall" folding paper boxes; when she quit twenty years later, she was supervising thirty women on the production line of one of the largest manufacturers of paper cartons in the Midwest.

That was the time, right after her husband died in Vietnam, when she felt she needed a change. So she took a six-month course in practical nursing and found a job with the Campbells, an older couple who lived out in Evanston in the northern suburbs. She's been with them thirteen years, though it's just Mrs. Campbell now, since Mr. Campbell died last year, after she nursed him through two strokes.

That's really what's bringing her in. Mrs. Campbell, who's always been "as nice and considerate as you could wish," now wants to give up her big house and move down to Florida for good; she's almost eighty and feels she can no longer move back and forth as they had every year. She has asked Charlene to come and live with her in Palm Beach. But even though she couldn't ask for a better or easier job, with as much time off as she wants, it's a hard decision to make.

Looking up from her lap, where she was carefully folding and refolding a snowy white hankerchief, Mrs. Farwell said earnestly, "My job really mens everything to me; it gives a shape and meaning to my life. Ever since George was killed, I felt I had to keep busy." It wasn't just the money; her husband's life insurance and what the government sent her as widow of a staff sergeant would have been enough, especially since their two boys were getting older. *Earl* was going through Howard University on a full scholarship and *Sherman* had already signed up to play football for Illinois. But she felt she had to get out and work with people, not boxes.

Over the years, she's somehow become the address for her whole family when trouble comes up. Not only does she watch over her parents, especially her mother who's been sickly for years, but when her sister Mattie down in Cincinnati had to go into the hospital for a month, she went out there to take care of Mattie's six children until she could take hold again. And when her cousin Ruby asked her to help care for her youngest, who had come down with hepatitis, she traveled to Harlem to nurse the child until she passed on—the third in the family. Whenever there was a birth or a burying in the family, they always turned to her. She doesn't mind; she loves the new babies especially. But she's getting tired now of helping other people live their lives.

Wistfully, Mrs. Farwell said her own boys don't seem to need her the way her other kinfolk do. Earl, who's thirty-two now and a full partner in a fancy law firm in Washington, has been married for eight years, but his wife says she is "much too busy" to settle down to raise a family. And Sherman! At twenty-nine, he runs a big truck-ing firm down on the south side and has all sorts of "big-time" con-nections, he tells her. He's had a string of girlfriends but none seem to last long with him. She's lucky if she gets to see them more than twice a year; usually it's just a quick visit at Christmas and maybe a few hours on Easter Sunday.

Last week, Mrs. Farwell had her fiftieth birthday. And she re-members looking around her little apartment—she always made a point of coming home every night, no matter how late she worked—and suddenly feeling lonely, real lonely. She's had several gentlemen friends since George died, but she always kept that corner of her life separate from the rest. Her current friend, a businessman, wants her to give up her job and marry him. He's about ready to retire and would like to return to Nashville, where he comes from. But he's al-most sixty-five and she's afraid it will become one more case of nurs-ing, since he's already had two attacks of emphysema and has chronic kidney stones.

Mrs. Farwell rose with a sigh; she has to catch her bus to get out to Evanston. She promised Mrs. Campbell she'll let her know by the end of the month if she'll go with her. All of these people needing her and reaching out for her to help them; sometimes she gets to feel so hemmed in! She's been tending to other people's needs all these years; what about her own? How can she cure her own loneliness?

Professionals' Opinions

The twenty-three practitioners who reviewed this case situation clearly recognized the scenario as a mid-life transition. Almost all agreed that the presenting problem was Mrs. Farwell's need to de-cide about moving to Florida with her employer or seeking an alter-native work arrangement. Clinicians were equally divided between those who viewed this as a turning point during which she, as a strong, capable woman, is struggling with her own identity, and those who assessed her as a depressed person with unmet depen-dency needs who has long struggled with isolation, loneliness, and unresolved loss. A third group also saw her as seeking to redefine her role with others, in view of her life changes.

One-third of the participants wanted to start by helping her de-cide about her job, but the rest preferred to deal with the larger is-sue of the switch in her life's direction, including the exploring of her needs, strengths, patterns of functioning, and future aspirations. The majority would offer her "support and understanding plus." For some, this "plus" meant intensive, dynamically oriented treatment; for others it would be short-term focused treatment; and for still others, it would be some type of experiential experience. All wanted to see her alone, with a few suggesting involving her adult sons at some point—if they would agree and be available.

While some participants would consider termination when Mrs. Farwell came to some decision about her job, the majority saw a suitable closing point to be when she feels better about herself, has started to fulfill herself in more positive ways, has gained some insight into her own needs and coping mechanisms, and/or when she has made some concrete plans for the future. Two-thirds saw the prognosis as very positive and the rest as fairly positive except for one clinician who refused to commit herself.

How the Case Was Treated

Mrs. Farwell was seen for individual treatment by a professional social worker who headed a new community outreach program that was testing a preventative approach. It was housed in a wing of the local Baptist church near Mrs. Farwell's home and used the slogan, "Keep your little troubles from becoming big ones." The worker, in later discussing the case, said that, although they were primarily a referral service, she became concerned over Mrs. Farwell's underlying depression when she spoke with her and decided to offer to see her on a time-limited basis to "help her over the hump."

Beginning Phase.   After obtaining the information given above, the practitioner suggested that, since Mrs. Farwell was having difficulty coming to a decision about work, it might be helpful to meet several times to see if she could help her "get things clearer in her mind." While plainly ambivalent over seeking help, Mrs. Farwell agreed and made an appointment for the following Monday. Subsequently they met for four intensive sessions.

Middle Phase.   When she came in rather self-consciously, Mrs. Farwell wondered whether she was being foolish. Maybe it was just that her fiftieth birthday had made her feel that the years were passing her by. The worker, herself about the same age, said matter-of-factly that many women found it to be a real crossroads, and it was a good time to look back over where she has been before deciding on which path to take. Then she asked very directly, "What was the best thing that ever happened to you?" Mrs. Farwell promptly replied, "George."

She then began to talk about her husband; she felt she had never really gotten over his death thirteen years ago. She began to recall their life together, how they had met at a USO New Year's Eve party when she was only eighteen. He was already in the army then and she had started her first job. It was real love at first sight; from the moment they set eyes on each other, they never looked at anyone else. Her parents hadn't wanted her to get married so young, but George and she were afraid he'd be reassigned and didn't want to wait. For a while she lived in a dingy, one-room apartment and he'd come home on weekends from Fort Sheridan; then his regiment was shipped to Korea and she went back to her parents' home, with one baby in her arms and pregnant with the second. When George came back two years later, they moved into their present apartment with the two little boys and she's been there ever since.

That was the happiest time for her, when George would come home every night and they lived in a safe little world of their own. He had his army career, where everyone respected him, and she had her job, which gave her satisfaction. But mostly they had each other and the children, a "just right" family. George was never one to talk much, but he was always ready to make a joke while she would take things too seriously. He'd stay at home to play ball with the boys and send her to church to "tend to their souls."

Tears rolled down her cheeks as she recalled Sunday afternoons when they would take the boys swimming off the big rocks lining the lake shore or when he'd rent a boat and they would go out on the lake. "No matter how choppy the water was, I always felt safe with George." And evenings, after the children were in bed, they'd lie on the couch listening to the radio or just talking.

After the Vietnam war started, they didn't worry for a while because he was a staff sergeant assigned to train new recruits. But, eventually, his unit was sent overseas. Things were never the same after that. George wasn't one for letter-writing and weeks would go by without a word or phone call from him. She had her hands full, what with working full time and raising the boys. Earl never gave her any trouble; he was like her, serious and determined to make something of himself. But Shermie was hard to control and always seemed to be getting into trouble. Fortunately, he made the football team in high school and then the coach kept him in line, at least during the school year.

Twice George came home for a week's leave and once she met him in Hawaii, but she kept having this sense of foreboding. When George's colonel rang the bell that day, to let her know that he had been killed in the spring offensive, she already knew he was gone before he said a word. "Part of me died there, right on the spot," she said in a muffled voice.

The worker observed softly that it must have been hard for her to have him die so far away. Mrs. Farwell nodded. "For a long while I couldn't believe it. I walked around like a zombie, not really there. I would wake up at night, sure I had heard George calling to me for help. People would talk to me and sometimes it was like I was behind a glass wall; I could see their lips moving, but couldn't hear." Looking at her damp handkerchief, she said wonderingly, "I never cried, not even when they brought his body home for burial. I felt I had to keep myself strong for the boys' sake. To think I had these tears bottled up inside all that time!"

For the rest of the interview she spoke of her determination to change her life then. She made that trip to Washington. "It was as if George and I made it together as we had promised we would some day." That's when she knew she was finished working with dead boxes; she had to be with live people. So she gave up her good, safe job and studied to become a practical nurse. "I guess I felt that, even if I couldn't help George, at least I could help others who needed me."

The next session started out on a much less emotional tone as Mrs. Farwell began to talk about her job with the Campbells. They had been very good to her, but then she gave them good value, too. She started by taking care of Mrs. Campbell when she broke her hip, and just stayed on. Both of them had their ups and downs; twice she nursed Mr. Campbell through a stroke. After the last one he was completely helpless for two years until he died last winter. It suited them to have someone reliable in the house to keep an eye on them and they knew they could count on her.

But now, the social worker observed, she couldn't make up her mind if she should continue. Mrs. Farwell struggled to clarify her own feelings. Mrs. Campbell was always gracious and kind to her; she never raised her voice or demanded too much as some employers did. On the other hand, even though they spent so many waking hours together, both of them were very conscious of the distance keeping them apart. Living here in Chicago where she could go home every night to her own place, with her own family and friends and her church was one thing; living together in Florida in Mrs. Campbell's world was something else again. As she spoke, she shook her head slowly and decided, no, it wouldn't work.

From this Mrs. Farwell went on to talk about Earl and Sherman and how she envied them their pride in their black world. They were free in a way her generation never was. Here in Chicago, after living here so many years, she still felt she had to walk carefully. In an effort to draw out her feelings about her relations with her sons, the worker remarked dryly that it sounded as though her sons were so busy with their own lives they didn't seem to have much time for her. Mrs. Farwell started to defend them, then shook her head and said she understood how busy they were, with their fancy jobs and "high-flown" friends. Maybe, she added wistfully, part of the price of feeling free was giving up old family ties. The boys didn't need her as much as they used to. "I just don't fit into their lives anymore."

For the fourth session, Mrs. Farwell came in smiling. She had already told Mrs. Campbell that she would not be going with her to Palm Beach. Mrs. Campbell was disappointed but said she could understand her not wanting to move away from her life here; on the other hand, she wanted Mrs. Farwell to keep in touch and let her know if she ever wanted to come down there. But both of them understood it was over.

She had also stopped in to talk again with that lady at the vocational service to whom she had spoken several weeks ago. She definitely decided that she wanted to work with disabled children, physically or mentally handicapped ones. She always liked children and they took easily to her. She had already put her name down for a retraining course that was opening up next week at Roosevelt University.

At this point, the worker observed that it looked as though she had made her decision about her future direction. Was there any other unfinished business she wanted to talk about? Mrs. Farwell started to shake her head, then burst out, "There is one thing . . . what's *wrong* with me?" She hurried on to explain that, since George died, she's had at least three serious relationships with men, each lasting quite a while and each of them wanting to marry her. But she always refused. Just this last week, she turned down Homer who has been courting her for four years, after he asked her to marry him and go down to Nashville to be the "lady of his house." He'd give her anything she wanted and it wasn't as though she didn't like him; she really enjoyed going to bed with him. But something held her back, kept her from saying yes. It was as if she was afraid . . . she stopped to grope for words.

"Afraid of making a commitment?" prompted the social worker. "Afraid that, if you'd say yes, you'd be disloyal to George?"

Mrs. Farwell thought for a moment, then nodded her head slowly. "Yes, maybe that's it. I keep remembering that perfect world I had with George. Even though it was so long ago, maybe I thought that if I'd say yes to Homer, George and the years we had together would just disappear." She paused, then said with a rush, "But that's just foolishness! Our world is just inside my head; it's all memories that can't disappear. And George wasn't like that. I can just hear him laugh and slap my butt and say, 'Woman, don't you be silly! You just go on and enjoy yourself, you hear? And have fun for me, too!'"

As she sat back, spent, the worker added, "Sometimes you have to remember in order to put it behind you. . . ."

Ending Phase.   Since it seemed appropriate, the practitioner and Mrs. Farwell agreed at this point that their work together had ended. She was starting her new training program on Monday, and they would leave things on an "as needed" basis; Mrs. Farwell would stop in whenever she wanted to talk things over. Two months later, the practitioner sent her a copy of a flyer announcing that the Center was starting a transition group for mid-life black women, but she called the secretary to say she was too busy with her new job to take part.

Of the six cases, this is probably the most intensive and existential in nature, dealing as it does with the client's internal doubts and indecisions as to direction. In many ways it is characteristic of the fifty-year transition, when persons put their past life behind them and begin to live "the first day of the rest of their lives."

In discussing this case, the professional pointed out that she could have limited her intervention to discussing Mrs. Farwell's current work dilemma with her and possibly referring her for vocational testing and, perhaps, retraining. Instead, she recognized the intrapsychic doubts with which she was struggling at this turning point in her life. She was able to help her confront them until, through Mrs. Farwell's own ego strengths, she was able to resolve her difficulties and proceed on her way. This case illustrates the grasping of the decisive moment which can change the direction of one's life.

PART IV

Tying Theory
and Practice Together

CHAPTER 16

Putting It in Perspective

At the start of this book we asked what it was like to be fifty. Certainly we make no claims that everyone encounters difficulties at this time. It has already been indicated that an uncounted number of individuals and their families easily pass through the years that cluster around this turning point, or do so with no more than the usual bumps and bruises that are part of the state of being alive. At the other end of the spectrum are clustered a sizeable number of persons who experience severe problems as long-term physical, psychological, and social difficulties grow more disabling with the passage of time. Such cases are well-known to physical and mental hospitals and outpatient facilities, to social service agencies, and to the legal system. But, between these two extremes, an undefined number of persons experience disruptions precisely *because* they are in the process of change and adjustment that these years bring.

It is hard to untangle which of these disruptions are related to the overall aging process, which are reactions to the climacteric and menopause, which are tied to the shifting role demands in the work, marital, and intergenerational networks, and which are responses to the realization that one has crossed the fiftieth milestone and "the road is downhill from now on." Some of the changes may be dreaded or ignored; others are welcomed and relished. Moreover, long-established personality patterns and previous experience in coping and problem-solving may differentially affect the ability to deal with the pressures of this period.

As already noted, persons passing through the transition to late mid-life may experience difficulties at any number of points along the way: some may hesitate to leave the secure past with its familiar conditions and long-held roles; others may become enmeshed in the uncertainties of the present and the difficulties in making key choices and decisions; still others stand reluctantly on the threshold, hesitant to enter a future far different from their earlier expectations.

Considerable difference has been found, as apparent in Part II, in how different theoreticians and researchers define and interpret the changes that mark this perilous bridge. Nevertheless, individuals about to enter this "danger zone" and families who have a member at this age stage, may find it helpful to understand the pitfalls that might lie ahead. Similarly, persons already struggling with problems brought about by the transition may benefit by grasping both the transitory nature of the disruption ("This too shall pass!") and the complex interactional nature of the need to change. And for those who have already passed over the bridge, it might be illuminating to understand, even as hindsight, what they have gone through, what other choices they might have made, and what they still can do to counteract maladaptive adjustments.

While knowledge of the various developmental and transitional processes throughout the life cycle is important, I find that understanding the full dimensions of the transition to late mid-life is particularly helpful to professional helpgivers. Not only do persons in their middle years account for a good percentage of clients in need of help, but their strengths, developed through past experiences in coping, and their discomfort at finding themselves in difficulties now make them rewarding persons to work with.

Moreover, since they still have so many years of active, creative functioning ahead of them, they can often recognize the interval of transitional disruption as a challenge and grasp the opportunity for help in making far-reaching changes in their life patterns.

Implications for Practice

Knowing the dimensions of the mid-life transition, on the one hand, and the potentials of mid-life clients, on the other, poses a direct challenge for professionals to sharpen their practice. As evidenced by their reactions to the case situations in Part III, practitioners find little difficulty in recognizing some, if not all, of the dimensions of this transition when clients ask for help. However, only some of them could grasp the implications of this assessment to define appropriate treatment strategies and goals. Many of them still seemed to be operating intuitively, flying by the "seat of their pants" in artistic but often nonlogical projections.

To substantiate this contention, we should go back to examine the nature of the six case situations presented in Part III. Two of these, the Alberts and the Donnellis, were in acute situational crises: Mrs. Alberts had attempted suicide and Mr. Donnelli had created a disturbance serious enough for neighbors to call the police. Here the professionals were familiar enough with crisis intervention theory to recognize the basic elements of the situation: the precipitating factor, the initial hazardous event, the state of increasing upset, and the active disequilibrium. A number of them were also able to suggest appropriate strategies for handling this acute phase. Only a few, however, were able to recognize that Mrs. Alberts was in a transitional process and that her relations with her husband was the area for intervention that offered the most hope for positive change and could thus become the focus for treatment. While the social worker, in relating how the case was actually handled, did help Mrs. Alberts mourn her various past losses, she then went on to help her and her husband work out some changes in their relationship through which they could start to build a bridge for their future life together.

In the Donnelli case, the professional panel was much more on target, since this was recognized as a crisis of exhaustion, in which the various stressful events—Mrs. Donnelli's terminal illness, Sharon's return home, Mr. Donnelli's father's stroke, and Joey's arrest—which closely followed one after the other, brought about a state of disequilibrium. The panel was also in fair agreement on the goal of enhancing the family's self-esteem and mastery but was less in accord as to how to carry this out.

The practitioner who actually treated this case chose to concentrate on the theme of building family cohesion, helping the members grapple with the degenerative changes brought about by Mrs. Donnelli's illness and the oldest son's absence to create a new sense of family solidarity.

Two of the cases, the Carters and the Eismans, were chosen because they represented role disturbances that commonly occur during this transitional period. While neither Mr. Carter, who had been unemployed for three years and whose wife had been separating from him for the past year, and Mrs. Eisman, whose family roles were intact but was faced with the need to reorder her priorities, represented active crisis situations, they nevertheless were in acute discomfort and needed help in making changes in their role functioning.

Here the professional panels were divided between the choice of handling them simply as service referrals to community resources— in Mr. Carter's case to an alcoholic treatment facility and, for Mrs. Eisman, to a home care and housing service for her parents—or to deal more comprehensively with their treatment needs. This meant reframing Mr. Carter's problem as his upset over his own future and Mrs. Eisman's as her need to resolve her conflicting loyalties among her aging parents, her adult daughters, and her husband.

In actual treatment, the worker in the first case did as the panel indicated, intervening at several levels. Mr. Carter was helped to come to terms with his wife's leaving him and with the loss of his executive position and, at the same time, encouraged to join a mutual help group (which led to his finding a new job) and to enter an alcoholism treatment program.

The Eisman case, on the other hand, demonstrates the dynamism of the transitional process and the difficulty in predicting how cases will turn out at such times. While the worker started out to attend to the practical aspects of arranging for Mrs. Eisman's parents' housing and housekeeping needs, her husband's sudden heart attack and subsequent depression opened up a whole new dimension, during which he was helped to deal with the loss of his own family during the Holocaust. Together, the Eismans symbolically moved back into his past and then, with the worker acting as a catalyst for change, were able to return to the present and start a new chapter in their marital relations.

The last two cases, the Bennett and Farwell ones, are both examples of intrapsychic problems of identity confusion and loss of direction. The professional panel showed considerable disagreement in their assessment of Mrs. Bennett's struggle and how to handle it. The majority saw this primarily as a divorce situation, but some saw her as a woman of considerable ego strength who could benefit from intensive, insight-oriented treatment, while others saw her as a reality-oriented person who could best be helped through a practical, supportive approach aimed primarily at helping her modify her environment.

The worker who actually treated the case chose to ignore almost entirely the impending divorce and to work, instead, at an intensive level, on Mrs. Bennett's intrapsychic problems of identity and individuation, on her own part in shaping the nature of her marriage, and on other aspects of her adult life. Focus was placed on helping Mrs. Bennett become her own person and choose her own future direction.

Similarly with Mrs. Farwell, while the experts' panel could recognize this clearly as a midlife transition, they differed in their assessment of her ability to handle it. Half wanted simply to help her resolve the decision about moving to Florida, while the rest preferred to broaden the framework to consider the more intrapsychic aspects of her choosing a new life's direction. While they recognized her innate strengths and intrapsychic conflicts, the experts were also divided as to whether Mrs. Farwell could benefit from intensive introspection as opposed to a supportive, reality-oriented approach. Interestingly, few of the panel seemed to take into account the limited time available and her need to make vital decisions within the next few weeks.

The worker who treated this case chose to concentrate on Mrs. Farwell's being at a crossroads. She was able to seize the opportunity inherent in the transition to help her client relive the loss of her husband, with which she had never come to terms, and her estrangement from her sons. This reworking of the bereavement process seemed to free Mrs. Farwell to make her own decisions not to accompany her employer to Florida and to start to prepare for a new career in helping disabled children. Within a short time, the clinician was able to tap into Mrs. Farwell's basic competence to help her change her direction and find a new interest in her life.

The question may certainly be raised: To what extent do these six cases represent a valid sample of typical situations involving persons in the transition to late mid-life? Certainly no claim is being made that they are characteristic of the entire population group at this stage in their life course. The permutations of problems and interactions are endless. They were chosen, however, because it was felt that they illustrated various aspects of the bridging process and, as such, represented typical "slices of life" during these decisive years.

Another objection that might be voiced in terms of treatment is that all of these cases represent "success" stories; each of the persons and couples involved seemed to have had their calls for help answered in a way that enabled them to maneuver through the heavy bridge traffic to the relatively smooth road on the other side. Candidly, this is why they were chosen. At the start it was pointed out that no attempt would be made to present a representative sampling of all practice as it takes place with all clients at this time of life. Precisely because they might all be considered successful examples, these cases illustrate the treatment potential inherent in this transitional process.

In analyzing why they were successful, we find that the practitioners in each case shared a series of commonalities in approach that undoubtedly contributed to the outcome and served to transcend differences in strategies and techniques. Out of these we may well distill certain principles of practice that are critical to intervention during periods of transition:

1. Each practitioner seems to have developed a warm, accepting, empathetic relationship with her client, which undoubtedly served as the catalyst to effect change.

2. Each practitioner had the ability to grasp that the client had undergone significant losses in the past and was able to offer considerable support while the person went selectively back into the past to mourn the loss and then came forward into the present to compare and contrast the current situation with earlier reactions.

3. Each worker seemed to grasp the potential in the transitional process, to differentiate between the immediate crisis (where one occurred) and the broader stressful pressure to adjust to new life changes. Along with this, the emphasis was not on the limitations and pathological aspects of the situation but rather on the potential for adaptation and growth.

4. Each practitioner appeared to make a rapid assessment of the total situation, both vertically in terms of where the person was in his life span development and horizontally in terms of how he was currently functioning in his various relevant life roles, and then chose one or two key areas on which to focus. In some cases, treatment emphasized the affective aspects; in others, the cognitive understanding; in still others, behavioral change. But in almost every case all three elements were present in the treatment process, even though intervention was relatively short-term.

5. Each worker was able to make good use of appropriate community resources and natural support systems to augment the client-worker relationship.

6. Finally, each worker seemed to project an aura of optimism and hope, of confidence in the client's ability to master his/her current difficulties and pass through the transition successfully, which undoubtedly served to stimulate the client's development of new coping patterns.

Conclusion

In this volume, we have concentrated on one single interval in the adult life span and have attempted to illustrate the potentials for change inherent in what can be a perilous bridge. We have indicated criteria for choice of the transitional approach and have presented some treatment guidelines for helping individuals and families deal with the complexities and interlocking difficulties that seem to form an inherent part of the transition to late mid-life.

As the panel of professionals illustrated, a range of different emphases and directions might have been chosen. Hopefully, however, in teasing out the commonalities and central issues that appear to lead to successful intervention, we can begin to develop a body of treatment approaches and strategies that can be applied to other transitional periods as well. This would certainly seem to be the direction for further investigation.

Appendix

Since this book is geared primarily to professionals, we felt it was important to examine the current "state of the art." Therefore, in preparing it, we did a study of how experienced, professional social workers would treat such calls for help—or, at least, how they would anticipate doing so, after obtaining initial information on the situation.

As noted in Chapter 1 and in the introduction to Part III, the six master case situations were divided. The first part, which represented the informational part of the initial interview with a professional social worker, was presumed to contain enough information for a clinician to make some initial decisions about the presenting problem, the first diagnostic assessment, the problem for work, the planned treatment direction and strategies, and the final goal at which to aim. After being validated,* they were presented to a sample of experienced professionals who were asked to give their professional reactions.

*These cases were validated by having three experienced teachers of practice at the University of Southern California, all with extensive direct practice experience, review them. After some changes were made, it was agreed that they did represent typical case situations among clients of this age group currently being seen by professional social workers.

We found this "preferred sample," as it is called, by asking family agency directors who their best social workers were, by seeking recommendations from deans of schools of social work and respected theoreticians, or by personal solicitation, relying on their reputations as acknowledged by colleagues or as evinced by professional publications and presentations at professional conferences. The general purpose of the study was discussed with them, directly or through the agency director, and all agreed to participate. Our final sample was forty-eight experienced, highly recommended practitioners or teachers of practice; only two of our original list of fifty did not return their completed questionnaires. *

The Sample

From their replies to a separate questionnaire on their professional background, this group was found to be highly qualified in the practice area. All participants held a Master of Social Work (M.S.W.) or similar professional degree; in addition, almost a third had earned a Ph.D. or D.S.W. in social work or in a closely allied field. Some 62 percent had obtained additional postdegree preparation in psychotherapy or psychoanalytic therapy, while 20 percent had received training in family or marital therapy. They were avid attenders of short courses, institutes, seminars, and workshops on professional topics; the median courses attended over the past five years lay in the six-to-ten bracket. They came from all parts of the country: twenty-one from the West Coast, fifteen from the East Coast, ten from the Midwest, and two from Canada. Thirty-eight were women and ten were men.

While considerable overlap was found, twenty-two participants indicated that they worked primarily or entirely in family agencies or in mental health or health settings; ten were engaged primarily or entirely in private practice; and sixteen identified themselves as primarily or entirely teachers of practice, including supervision and consultation. Of the forty-eight, thirty-three were currently prac-

*The rationale for including both direct practitioners and teachers of practice is that there is considerable overlap in these two groups. One of the criteria for teaching practice is that the person have direct practice experience; indeed, many teachers continue to "keep their hand in" after joining university faculties. Moreover, many experienced practitioners may be invited to teach courses in practice on a part-time basis while carrying on their private or agency practice.

ticing with individual clients, either entirely or to some extent; twenty-two were seeing couples entirely or primarily; and twenty-one were seeing families to some extent. Thirteen said they were primarily teaching but also seeing clients. As to the type of persons they saw, fourteen of the forty-eight were primarily seeing clients in the mid-life range (forty to sixty-four years old), and another twenty-eight saw them to some extent.

Since we were looking for experienced practitioners in order to tap their practice wisdom, our sample was heavily weighted in terms of years of experience: thirty of the forty-eight had practiced more than twenty years; of the rest, eleven more had practiced from eleven to twenty years, five had practiced from six to ten years, and only one had less than five years of experience.

In order to test the reliability of our sample, we also solicited five clinical psychologists, all with doctorates and with the same span of years of experience, and all engaged in combined direct practice and teaching. Initially we had planned on a reliability sample of ten (20 percent) but found, after the first five, that the answers showed no essential difference from our main sample, so this was not continued. Evidently clinicians,* after some years of practice, think about practice along similar lines. (Psychiatrists were not included, since their additional training in medicine and their lack of background in dealing with problems of social functioning put them in a different category of practice.)

The Instrument

The main instrument was a one-page questionnaire, labeled "Professional Reactions to Case Situations," on which eight questions were posed. An additional blank sheet was attached for further comments. Five of the questions were open-ended, while three offered a series of choices. The areas to be investigated were the following: (1) their view of the presenting problem, (2) their interpretation of the underlying "core issue" with which the client(s) was struggling, (3) their choice of the most useful "problem for work" with which to start out, (4) their proposed treatment strategy, (5) the treatment arrangements they would consider most appropriate,

---

*Analysis of the five psychologists' reactions are not included in the material presented in this book.

(6) the central themes on which they would choose to concentrate, (7) the final goals that they could see as leading to termination, and (8) their prediction as to successful resolution of the situation.

It should be emphasized that we were trying to tap into the practitioner's expertise and professional wisdom based on years of experience and skills in working with troubled persons. When I discussed this instrument with colleagues, several expressed concern about the unilateral nature of such judgments, protesting that they could not decide on such matters without joint discussion with the clients. Let me say flatly: I agree completely with this. I hope no professional social worker would carry out a case without developing a strong rapport with her client(s) and without striving for mutual agreement all along the way. At the same time, it should be kept firmly in mind that people in trouble come to professionals for help because they cannot manage or deal with their life situations by themselves. Out of years of theoretical education, practice experience, and continuous updating, a solid foundation of professional knowledge and skills is built up which the clinician draws upon to guide her professional interactions with those who turn to her for help. And it is hoped that, before arriving at a mutual course of action, the practitioner has already formulated a tentative assessment and direction for further activity.

No attempt was made to tap such subjective issues as building an effective worker-client relationship or developing empathy. Important as these aspects are, it was felt that it would be virtually impossible to foretell them with any degree of certainty at the outset of a case, although participants' views on certain types of clients and problems plainly came through in their replies.

Procedure

Each participant was asked to read three case analogs out of the total of six master case situations. (The cases were distributed so that an equal number of each was represented: twenty-five out of 150. However, their assignment was randomly made.) They were then asked to give their own professional views on how they would treat each case in the event that they were to continue to see that person.

The response was extremely high: Out of a possible 150 case situations, we received 143 replies. As already indicated, six reaction forms were not returned and one was not properly filled out. Questions were, for the most part, open-ended and participants were encouraged to add their personal reactions and interpretations. Since this study was aimed at learning from their practice experience, they willingly and generously shared their ideas, impressions, and reactions. The assumption was made that their answers were a faithful representation of how professionals would handle such case situations in their ongoing practice—to the extent that this could be predicted in advance from the limited information given. Their opinions became those of our "professional panel" or "panel of experts."

In keeping with our original agreement, individual participants' replies were not identified, nor has any attempt been made here to carry out a statistical analysis or comparison of different professionals' separate forms of practice. Since we were not interested in how different *practitioners* operate, but rather in how different types of problem situations are and can be dealt with, the focus of the findings was on the clients themselves and the difficulties they were undergoing.

A detailed analysis of the findings in the study itself will be presented in another framework.

Bibliography

ALDOUS, JOAN. *Family Careers: Developmental Change in Families*. New York: John Wiley & Sons, 1978.

ARCHBOLD, PATRICIA G. "Impact of Parent-Caring on Women," *Family Relations* 32, 1 (January 1983): 39–45.

ATCHLEY, ROBERT C. *The Social Forces in Later Life*. Belmont, Calif.: Wadsworth, 1976.

_____, and SHERRY L. CORBET. "Older Women and Jobs." In Troll, Israel, and Israel, 1977: 121–125.

BALLINGER, C. BARBARA. "The Menopause and Its Syndromes." In Howells, 1981: 279–303.

BART, PAULINE B. "Depression in Middle-Aged Women." In Vivian Gornick and Barbara K. Moran, eds. *Women in Sexist Society*. New York: Basic Books, 1971: 99–117.

_____. "The Loneliness of the Long-Distance Mother." In Hartog, Audy, and Cohen, 1980: 204–219.

_____, and MARILYN GROSSMAN. "Menopause." In Notman and Nadelson, 1978: 337–354.

BARUCH, GRACE, and ROSALIND C. BARNETT. "Adult Daughters' Relations with Their Mothers. *Journal of Marriage and the Family* 45 (1983): 601–606.

BENEDEK, THERESE. "Parenthood During the Life Cycle." In E. James Anthony and Therese Benedek, eds. *Parenthood: Its Psychology and Psychopathology*. Boston: Little, Brown 1970: 185–206.

―――. "Climacterium: A Developmental Phase." *Psychoanalytic Quarterly*, 1950: 1–7.

BENGSTON, VERN L., and JOSEPH H. KUYPERS. "Generational Difference and the Generational Stake." *Aging and Human Development* 2 (1971): 249–260.

BERARDO, DONNA H. "Divorce and Remarriage at Middle Age and Beyond." In Felix M. Berardo, 1982: 132–139.

BERARDO FELIX M., ed. *Middle and Late Life Transitions*. Annals, American Academy of Political and Social Science 464 (November 1982).

BERKUN, CLEO S. "In Behalf of Women Over 40: Toward Understanding the Effect of Menopause on Women's Affective State." Paper Presented at NASW Professional Symposium, November 1983, Washington, D.C.

BERNARD, JESSIE. "The Good Provider Role: Its Rise and Fall." *American Psychologist* 36, 1 (Janurary 1981): 1–12.

BIRREN, JAMES E. "Toward an Experimental Psychology of Aging." *American Psychologist* 25 (1970): 124–135.

BLAU, ZENA S. *Aging in a Changing Society*, 2nd ed. New York: Franklin Watts, 1981.

BLENKNER, MARGARET. "Social Work and Family Relationships, with Some Thoughts on Filial Maturity." In Ethel M. Shanas and Gordon F. Streib, eds. *Social Structure and the Family*. Englewood Cliffs, N.J.: Prentice-Hall, 1965: 46–59.

BLOCK, MARLYN R., JANICE L. DAVIDSON, and JEAN D. GRAMBS. *Women Over Forty: Visions and Realities*. New York: Springer, 1981.

BOOTH, RICHARD. "Toward an Understanding of Loneliness." *Social Work* 28, 2 (March-April 1983): 116–119.

BORENZWEIG, HERMAN. *Jung and Social Work*. Lanham, Md.: University Press of America, 1984.

BOSTON WOMEN'S HEALTH BOOK COLLECTIVE. *Our Bodies, Ourselves*. New York: Simon & Schuster, 1976.

BOTWINICK, JACK. *Aging and Behavior*. New York: Springer, 1973.

BOYD, JEFFREY H., and MYRNA M. WEISSMAN. "The Epidemiology of Psychiatric Disorders of Middle Age: Depression, Alcoholism, and Suicide." In Howells, 1981: 201–221.

BRIM, ORVILLE G., JR. "Theories of the Male Mid-Life Crisis." *Counseling Psychologist* 6, 1 (1976): 2–9.

BRODY, ELAINE M. "Aging and Family Personality: A Developmental View." *Family Process* 13, 1 (March 1974): 23–37.

———. "Women in the Middle and Family Help to Older People." *Gerontologist* 21, 5 (1981): 471–480.

BURROWS, GRAHAM D., and LORRAINE DENNERSTEIN. "Depression and Suicide in Middle Age." In Howells, 1981: 222–250.

CARTER, ELIZABETH A., and MONICA MCGOLDRICK. "The Family Life Cycle and Family Therapy: an Overview." In Carter and McGoldrick, eds. *The Family Life Cycle: A Framework for Family Therapy.* New York: Gardner Press, 1980: 3–20.

CATH, STANLEY H. "The Orchestration of Disengagement." *International Journal of Aging and Human Development* 6, 3 (1975): 179–213.

CHERRY, SHELDON H. "The Menopause and Post-Menopausal Years (50–65)." In Cherry, *For Women of All Ages: A Gynecologist's Guide to Modern Female Health Care.* New York: Macmillan, 1979: 201–219.

CHIRIBOGA, DAVID A. "The Developmental Psychology of Middle Age." In Howells, 1981: 3–25.

———, and MAJDA THURNHER. "The Concept of Self." In Lowenthal, Thurnher, Chiriboga, et al. 1975: 62–83.

CICIRELLI, VICTOR, G. "Adult Childrens' Attachment and Helping Behavior to Elderly Parents: A Path Model." *Journal of Marriage and the Family* 45 4 (November 1983): 815–825.

———. "Adult Children and Their Elderly Parents." In Timothy H. Brubaker, ed. *Family Relationships in Later Life.* Beverly Hills: Sage, 1983: 31–46.

CLAUSEN, JOHN A. "Men's Occupational Careers in the Middle Years." In Eichorn, Clausen, Haan, Honzik, and Mussen, 1981: 321–351.

CLAVAN, SYLVIA. "The Impact of Social Class and Social Trends on the Role of the Grandparent." *Family Coordinator* 27, 4 (October 1978): 351–357.

CLEVELAND, MARTHA. "Sex and Marriage at 40 and Beyond." *Family Coordinator* 25, 3 (July 1976): 233–240.

COHEN, FRANCES, and RICHARD S. LAZARUS. "Coping and Adaptation in Health and Illness. In David Mechanic, ed. *Handbook of Health, Health Care, and the Health Professions.* New York: Free Press, 1983: 608–635.

COHEN, JESSICA F. "Male Roles in Midlife." *Family Coordinator* 28, 4 (October 1979): 465–471.

COHEN, STEPHEN Z., and BRUCE M. GANS. *The Other Generation Gap: The Middle-Aged and Their Aging Parents.* Chicago: Follett, 1978.

COHLER, BERTRAM J., and ANDREW M. BOXER. "Middle Adulthood: Settling into the World—Person, Time and Context." In Daniel Offer and Melvin Sabshin, eds. *Normality and the Life Cycle.* New York: Basic Books, 1984: 145–203.

COOPER, CARY L. "Middle-Aged Men and the Pressures of Work." In Howells, 1981: 90–102.

DATAN, NANCY. "Midas and Other Midlife Crises." In W. H. Norman and T. J. Scaramella, eds. *Midlife: Developmental and Clinical Issues.* New York: Brunner/Mazel, 1980.

———, AARON ANTONOVSKY, and BENJAMIN MAOZ. *A Time to Reap: The Middle Age of Women in Five Israeli Subcultures.* Baltimore: Johns Hopkins Univ. Press, 1981.

———, and NANCY LOHMANN, eds. *Transitions of Aging.* New York: Academic Press, 1980.

DAVITZ, JOEL, and LOIS DAVITZ. *Making It from 40 to 50.* New York: Random House, 1976.

DEUTSCH, HELENE. *The Psychology of Women.* New York: Grune & Stratton, 1944.

DEUTSCHER, IRWIN. "The Quality of Postparental Life." In Neugarten, 1968: 263–268.

Diagnostic and Statistical Manual of Mental Disorders , 3rd ed. Washington, D.C.: American Psychiatric Association, 1980.

DOHRENWEND, BARBARA S., and BRUCE P. DOHRENWEND, eds. *Stressful Life Events: Their Nature and Effects.* New York: John Wiley & Sons, 1974.

DONOHUGH, DONALD L. *The Middle Years.* Philadelphia: Saunders Press, 1981.

DUVALL, EVELYN M. *Marriage and Family Development*, 5th ed. Philadelphia: J. B. Lippincott, 1977.

EICHORN, DOROTHY H., JOHN A. CLAUSEN, NORMAN HAAN, MARJORIE P. HONZIK, and PAUL H. MUSSEN, eds. *Present and Past in Middle Life.* New York: Academic Press, 1981.

EICHORN, DOROTHY H., JANE V. HUNT, and MARJORIE P. HONZIK. "Experience, Personality, and I.Q.: Adolescence to Middle Age." In Eichorn, et al., 1981: 89–116.

ERIKSON, ERIK H. *Identity and the Life Cycle: Psychological Issues.* Vol 1, 1. New York: International Universities Press, 1959.

———. *Adulthood.* New York: W. W. Norton, 1976.

FARRELL, MICHAEL P., and STANLEY D. ROSENBERG. *Men at Midlife.* Boston: Auburn House, 1981.

FISCHER, LUCY R. "Transitions in the Mother-Daughter Relationship." *Journal of Marriage and the Family* 43, 3 (August 1981): 613–622.

FISKE, MARJORIE. "Interpersonal Relationships and Adaptation in Adulthood." In Peter F. Ostwald, ed. *Communication and Social Interaction.* New York: Grune & Stratton, 1977: 265–275.

———. "The Reality of Psychological Change." In L. F. Jarvik, ed. *Aging in the 21st Century*. New York: Gardner Press, 1978: 97–111.

———. "Changing Hierarchies of Commitment in Adulthood." In Smelser and Erikson, 1980: 238–264.

FOGARTY, MICHAEL P. *Forty to Sixty: How We Waste the Middle Aged*. London: Bedford Square Press, 1975.

FRIED, BARBARA. *The Middle-Age Crisis*, rev. ed. New York: Harper & Row, 1976.

FRIEDMAN, HENRY J. "The Divorced in Middle Age." In Howells, 1981: 103–115.

FRIEDMAN, M., and R. H. ROSENMAN. *Type A Behavior and Your Heart*. New York: Fawcett, 1978.

FUCHS, ESTELLE. *The Second Season: Life, Love, and Sex for Women in the Middle Years*. Garden City, N.Y.: Anchor, Doubleday, 1978.

GALINSKY, ELLEN. *Between Generations: The Six Stages of Parenthood*. New York: Times Books. 1981.

GEORGE, LINDA K. *Role Transitions in Later Life*. Monterey, Calif.: Brooks/Cole, 1980.

———. "Models of Transitions in Middle and Later Life." In Felix M. Berardo, 1982: 22–37.

GERMAIN, CAREL, and ALEX GITTERMAN. *The Life Model of Social Work Practice*. New York: Columbia University Press, 1980.

GERSON, MARY-JOAN, JUDITH L. ALBERT, and MARY SUE RICHARDSON. "Mothering: The View from Psychological Research." *Signs* 9, 3 (1984): 434–453.

GIELE, JANET Z., ed. *Women in the Middle Years: Current Knowledge and Directions for Research and Policy*. New York: John Wiley & Sons, 1982.

GIESEN, CAROL B., and NANCY DATAN. "The Competent Older Woman." In Datan and Lohmann, 1980: 57–72.

GILLIGAN, CAROL. *In a Different Voice*. Cambridge, Mass.: Harvard University Press, 1982.

———. "Adult Development and Women's Development: Arrangements for a Marriage." In Giele, 1982: 89–114.

GLICK, IRA O., ROBERT S. WEISS, and C. MURRAY PARKES. *The First Year of Bereavement*. New York: John Wiley & Sons, 1974.

GOIN, MARCIA K., and RODNEY W. BURGOYNE. "Psychology of the Widow and Widower." In Howells, 1981: 26–35.

GOLAN, NAOMI. "Wife to Widow to Woman." *Social Work* 20, 5 (September 1975): 369–374.

———. *Treatment in Crisis Situations*. New York: Free Press, 1978.

_____. *Passing Through Transitions: A Guide for Practitioners.* New York: Free Press, 1981.

_____. "Shifts in Postparental Women's Ties to Their Husbands, Children, and Parents." Paper presented at International Interdisciplinary Congress for Women, University of Haifa, Haifa, Israel, December 28, 1981. Reproduced.

_____. "The Transition to Postparenthood: Ties Between Physiological and Psychological Changes in the Lives of Middle-Aged Couples." *Proceedings of the 5th World Congress of Sexology*, Jerusalem, June 21, 1981. Amsterdam: Excerpta Medica, 1982.

_____. "Transition to Postparenthood: A Challenge for Family Therapists." Paper presented at 4th International Congress on Family Therapy. Tel Aviv, July 5, 1983. Reproduced.

GOODMAN, ELLEN. *Turning Points: How and Why Do We Change?* New York: Fawcett Columbine, 1979.

GORLITZ, PAULA, and DAVID GUTMANN. "The Psychological Transition into Grandparenthood." In Howells, 1981: 167–186.

GOULD, ROGER. "Adult Life Stages: Growth Toward Self-Tolerance." *Psychology Today* 8, 9 (1975): 74–78.

GUTMANN, DAVID, JEROME GRUNES, and BRIAN GRIFFIN. "The Clinical Psychology of Later Life: Developmental Paradigms." In Datan and Lohmann, 1980: 119–131.

GUZINSKI, GAY. "Medical Gynecology: Problems and Patients." In Notman and Nadelson, 1978: 181–202.

HAAN, NORMA. "Common Dimensions of Personality Development: Early Adolescence to Middle Life." In Eichorn, et al., 1981: 117–151.

HALLBERG, EDMOND C. *The Gray Itch: The Male Metapause Syndrome.* New York: Warner Books, 1977.

HARKINS, ELIZABETH B. "Effects of the Empty Nest Transition on the Self-Report of Psychological and Physical Well-Being." *Journal of Marriage and the Family* 40, 3 (August 1978): 549–556.

HARTOG, JOSEPH, J. RALPH AUDY, and YEHUDI A. COHEN. *The Anatomy of Loneliness.* New York: International Universities Press, 1980.

HAVIGHURST, ROBERT J. *Human Development and Education.* London: Longmans, Green, 1953.

HENKER, FRED O. "Male Climacteric." In Howells, 1981: 304–327.

HENRY, JULES. "Loneliness and Vulnerability." In Hartog, Audy, and Cohen, 1980: 95–110.

HESS, BETH B. and ELIZABETH W. MARKSON. *Aging and Old Age.* New York: Macmillan, 1980.

HESS, BETH B. and JOAN M. WARING. "Parent and Child in Later Life: Rethinking the Relationship." In Richard Lerner and Graham B. Spanier, eds. *Child Influences on Marital and Family Interactions: A Life-Span Perspective*. New York: Academic Press, 1978: 241–273.

_____. "Changing Patterns of Aging and Family Bonds in Later Life." *Family Coordinator* 27, 4 (October 1978): 303–314.

HOFFMAN, DAVID L., and MARY L. REMMEL. "Uncovering the Precipitant in Crisis Intervention." *Social Casework* 56, 5 (May 1975): 259–267.

HOLLIS, FLORENCE, and MARY E. WOOD. *Casework: A Psychosocial Therapy*, 3rd ed. New York: Random House, 1981.

HOLMES, THOMAS H., and H. R. RAHE. "The Social Readjustment Rating Scale." *Journal of Psychosomatic Research* 2 (1967): 213–218.

HORN, J. L., and RAYMOND B. CATTELL. "Age Differences in Fluid and Crystallized Intelligence." *Acta Psychologica* 26 (1967): 107–129.

HOWELL, ELIZABETH. "Psychological Reaction of Postpartum Women." In Elizabeth Howell and Marjorie Bayes, eds. *Women and Mental Health*. New York: Basic Books, 1981: 340–346.

HOWELLS, JOHN G., ed. *Modern Perspectives in the Psychiatry of Middle Age*. New York: Brunner/Mazel, 1981.

HUNT, MORTON. *Sexual Behavior in the 1970's*. New York: Dell Books, 1974.

IGLEHART, ALFREDA P. "Wives, Husbands, and Social Change: The Role of Social Work." *Social Service Review* 56, 1 (March 1982): 27–38.

JANZEN, CURTIS, and OLIVER HARRIS. *Family Treatment in Social Work Practice*. Itasca, Ill.: Peacock, 1980.

JAQUES, ELLIOTT. "Death and the Mid-Life Crisis." *International Journal of Psychoanalysis* 46 (1965): 502–514.

JOHNSON, ELIZABETH S., and BARBARA J. BURSK. "Relationship Between the Elderly and Their Adult Children." *Gerontologist* 17 (1977): 90–96.

JOHNSON, RALPH E. "Marital Patterns During the Middle Years." Doctoral Dissertation. University of Minnesota, 1968. Reported on in Aldous, 1978.

JUNG, CARL G. *Collected Works*. Princeton: Princeton University Press, 1966.

KAHANA, BOAZ, and EVA KAHANA. "Clinical Issues of Middle Age and Later Life." In Felix M. Berardo, 1982: 140–161.

KALISH, RICHARD A. "Death and Survivorship: The Final Transition." In Felix M. Berardo, 1982: 163–173.

KAPLAN, DAVID M. "Interventions for Disorders of Change." *Social Work* 27, 5 (September 1982): 404–410.

KAPLAN, HELEN S. *The New Sex Therapy*. New York: Brunner/Mazel, 1974.

KERCKHOFF, RICHARD L. "Marriage and Middle Age." *Family Coordinator* 25, 1 (January 1976): 5–11.

KIRSCHNER, CHARLOTTE. "The Aging Family in Crisis: A Problem in Living." *Social Casework* 60, 4 (April 1979): 209–216.

KRYSTAL, SHEILA, and DAVID A. CHIRIBOGA. "The Empty Nest Process in Midlife Men and Women." Research Report, Langley Porter Institute, University of California, San Francisco, August 1978. Reproduced.

KUYPERS, JOSEPH A., and VERN L. BENGSTON, "Toward Competence in the Older Family." In Timothy H. Brubaker, ed. *Family Relationships in Later Life*. Beverly Hills: Sage, 1983: 211–225.

LEADER, ARUTHUR L. "The Relationship of Presenting Problems to Family Conflicts." *Social Casework* 61, 8 (October 1981): 451–457.

LESHAN, EDA J. *The Wonderful Crisis of Middle Age*. New York: McKay, 1973.

LEVINSON, DANIEL J. "Toward a Conception of the Adult Life Course." In Smelser and Erikson, 1980: 265–290.

_____. "The Midlife Transition: A Period in Adult Psychoosocial Development." In Laurence D. Steinberg, ed. *The Life Cycle*. New York: Columbia Univerity Press, 1981: 280–298.

_____, CHARLOTTE M. DARROW, EDWARD B. KLEIN, MARIA H. LEVINSON, and BRAXTON MCKEE. *The Seasons of a Man's Life*. New York: Knopf, 1978.

LEWIS, ROBERT A., PHILLIP J. FRENEAU, and CRAIG L. ROBERTS. "Fathers and the Postparental Transition." *Family Coordinator* 28, 4 (October 1979):514–520.

LIDZ, THEODORE. *The Person: His and Her Development Throughout the Life Cycle*, rev. ed. New York: Basic Books, 1976.

LIVSON, FLORINE B. "Coming Out of the Closet: Marriage and Other Crises of Middle Age." In Troll, Israel, and Israel, 1977: 81–92.

_____. "Paths to Psychological Health in the Middle Years: Sex Differences." In Eichorn, et al., 1981: 195–221.

LOEWENSTEIN, SOPHIE F. "Passion as a Mental Health Hazard." In Carol L. Heckerman, ed. *The Evolving Female: Women in a Psychosocial Context*, New York: Human Sciences Press, 1980: 45–73.

_____. "Toward Choice and Differentiation in the Midlife Crises of Women." In Heckerman, ed. *The Evolving Female: Women in a Psychosocial Context*. New York: Human Sciences Press, 1980: 158–188.

LOPATA, HELENA Z. *Women as Widows: Support Systems*. New York: Elsevier, 1979.

LOWENTHAL, MARJORIE F. "Psychosocial Variations Across the Adult Life Course: Frontiers for Research and Policy." *Gerontologist* 15 (February 1975):6–12.

_____, MAJDA THURNHER, DAVID A. CHIRIBOGA, et al. *Four Stages of Life: A Comparative Study of Women and Men Facing Transitions*. San Francisco: Jossey-Bass, 1975.

MALDONADO, DAVID, JR. "Aging in the Chicano Context," In Donald E. Gelfand and Alfred J. Kutzik, eds. *Ethnicity and Aging: Theory, Research, and Policy.* New York: Springer, 1979.

MALUCCIO, ANTHONY N., ed. *Promoting Competence in Clients.* New York: Free Press, 1981.

MASTERS, WILLIAM H., and VIRGINIA E. JOHNSON. *Human Sexual Response.* Boston: Little, Brown, 1966.

_____. *Human Sexual Inadequacy.* Boston: Little, Brown, 1970.

MAYER, NANCY. *The Male Mid-Life Crisis: Fresh Starts After 40.* New York: Doubleday Signet, 1978.

McCONNELL, ADELINE, and BEVERLY ANDERSON. *Single After Fifty.* New York: McGraw-Hill, 1978.

McGILL, MICHAEL E. *The 40-to-60-Year Old Male.* New York: Simon & Schuster, 1980.

MELAMED, ELISSA. *Mirror, Mirror: The Terror of Not Being Young.* New York: Linden Press/Simon & Schuster, 1983.

MENAGHAN, ELIZABETH. "Marital Stress and Family Transitions: A Panel Analysis." *Journal of Marriage and the Family* 45, 2 (May 1983): 371–386.

MILLER, DOROTHY A. "The 'Sandwich' Generation: Adult Children of the Aging." *Social Work* 26, 5 (September 1981): 419–423.

MIRKIN, PETER M., and ROGER E. MEYER. "Alcoholism in Middle Age." In Howells, 1981: 251–265.

MORSE, DONALD R., and M. LAWRENCE FURST. *Women Under Stress.* New York: Van Nostrand Reinhold, 1982.

MURRY, SAUNDRA, and DAPHNE HARRISON. "Black Women and the Future." *Psychology of Women Quarterly* 6, 1 (Fall 1981): 113–122.

MUSSEN, PAUL, JOHN J. CONGER, JEROME KAGAN, and JAMES GEIWITZ. *Psychological Development: A Life-Span Approach.* New York: Harper & Row, 1979.

NACHTIGALL, LILA, E., et al. "Estrogen Replacement Therapy: A 10-Year Prospective Study in Relationship to Osteoporosis." *Obstetrics and Gynecology* 53 (1979): 277–287.

NADELSON, CAROL C., DEREK C. POLONSKY, and MARY ALICE MATHEWS. "Marriage Problems and Marital Therapy in the Middle-Aged." In Howells, 1981: 337–352.

NADELSON, CAROL C., and MALKAH T. NOTMAN. *The Woman Patient.* vol. 2. *Concepts of Femininity and the Life Cycle.* New York: Plenum Press, 1982.

NEUGARTEN, BERNICE L. *Personality in Middle and Late Life: Empirical Studies.* New York: Atherton Press, 1964.

_____, ed. *Middle Age and Aging.* Chicago: University of Chicago Press, 1968.

————. "The Awareness of Middle Age." In Neugarten, 1968: 93–98.

————. "Adult Personality: Toward a Psychology of the Life Cycle." In Neugarten, 1968: 137–147.

————. "The Future and the Young-Old." *Gerontologist* 15 (1975): 4–9.

————. "Adaptation and the Life Cycle." *Counseling Psychologist* 6, 1 (1976): 16–20.

————. "Time, Age, and the Life Cycle." *American Journal of Psychiatry* 136, 7 (1979): 887–894.

————. "The Middle Generation." In P. K. Ragan. *Aging Parents*. Los Angeles: University of Southern California Press, 1979: 258–266.

————, and LORILL BROWN-REZANKA. "Midlife Women in the 1980's." In *Women in Midlife—Security and Fulfillment*, I. Compendium of Papers Submitted to the Select Committee on Aging, Subcommittee on Retirement, U.S. House of Representatives. Washington, D.C.: U.S. Government Printing Office, 1978: 25–38.

————, and NANCY DATAN. "The Middle Years." In Silvano Arieti, ed. *American Handbook of Psychiatry*. vol. 1. New York: Basic Books, 1974: 592–608.

————, and GUNHILD O. HAGESTAD. "Age and the Life Course." In Robert H. Binstock and Ethel M. Shanas, eds. *Handbook of Aging and the Social Sciences*. New York: Van Nostrand Reinhold, 1976: 35–55.

———— and KAROL K. WEINSTEIN. "The Changing American Grandparent." In Neugarten, 1968: 280–285.

————, VIVIAN WOOD, RUTH J. KRAINES, and BARBARA LOOMIS. "Women's Attitudes Toward the Menopause." In Neugarten, 1968: 195–200.

NEWMAN, BARBARA M., and PHILIP R. NEWMAN. *Development Through Life: A Psychosocial Approach*. Homewood, Ill.: Dorsey Press, 1975.

NOTMAN, MALKAH T. "Midlife Concerns of Women: Implications of Menopause." In Elizabeth Howell and Majorie Bayes, eds. *Women and Mental Health*. New York: Basic Books, 1981: 385–394.

————, and CAROL. C. NADELSON, eds. *The Woman Patient: Medical and Psychological Interfaces*. vol. 1. New York: Plenum Press, 1978.

NOWAK, CAROL A. "Does Youthfulness Equal Attractiveness?" In Troll, Israel, and Israel, 1977: 59–64.

NUDEL, ADELE. *For the Woman Over 50: A Practical Guide for a Full and Vital Life*. New York: Taplinger, 1978.

NYE, IVAN F., and FELIX M. BERARDO. "The Role of Grandparents." In Laurence D. Steinberg, ed. *The Life Cycle*. New York: Columbia University Press, 1981: 325–330.

O'RAND, ANGELA M., and JOHN C. HENRETTA. "Women at Middle Age: Developmental Transitions," In Felix M. Berardo, 1982: 57–64.

PALOMA, MARGARET M., BRIAN F. PENDLETON, and T. NEAL GARLAND. "Reconsidering the Dual Career Marriage: A Longitudinal Approach." In Joan Aldous, ed. *Two Paychecks: Life in Dual-Earner Families*. Beverly Hills: Sage, 1982: 173–192.

PARENT, MARY K. "The Losses of Middle Age and Related Developmental Tasks." In Elizabeth Prichard, et al., eds. *Social Work with the Dying Patient and the Family*. New York: Columbia University Press, 1977: 146–153.

PECK, ROBERT C. "Psychological Developments in the Second Half of Life." In Neugarten, 1968: 88–92.

PERLMUTTER, JOHANNA H. "A Gynecological Approach to Menopause." In Notman and Nadelson, 1978: 323–335.

PFEIFFER, ERIC, ADRIAAN VERWOERDT, and GLENN C. DAVIS. "Sexual Behavior in Middle Life." *American Journal of Psychiatry* 129 (April 1972): 1962–1967.

REID, WILLIAM J., and LAURA L. EPSTEIN. *Task-Centered Casework*. New York: Columbia University Press, 1972.

RHODES, SONYA L. "A Developmental Approach to the Life Cycle of the Family." *Social Casework* 58, 5 (May 1977): 301–311.

ROBERTS, CRAIG L., and ROBERT A. LEWIS. "The Empty Nest Syndrome." In Howells, 1981: 328–336.

ROBERTSON, JOAN F. "The Significance of Grandparents: Perceptions of Young Adult Grandchildren." *Gerontologist* 16 (1976): 137–140.

———. "Women in Midlife: Crises, Reverberations, and Support Networks." *Family Coordinator* 27, 4 (October 1978): 375–382.

ROGERS, RITA R. "On Parenting One's Elderly Parents." In Howells, 1981: 187–197.

ROSSI, ALICE S. "Transitions to Parenthood." *Journal of Marriage and the Family* 30, 1 (1968): 26–39.

———. "Life Span Theories and Women's Lives." *Signs* 6, 1 (1980): 4–32.

RUBIN, LILLIAN B. *Worlds of Pain: Life in the Working-Class Family*. New York: Basic Books. 1976.

———. *Women of a Certain Age: The Midlife Search for Self*. New York: Harper & Row, 1979.

RYFF, CAROL D., and SUSAN MIGDAL. "Intimacy and Generativity: Self-Perceived Transitions." *Signs* 9, 3 (1984): 470–481.

SALES, ESTHER. "Women's Adult Development." In Irene H. Frieze, Jacquelynne E. Parsons, Paula B. Johnson, Diane N. Ruble, and Gail L. Zellman, eds. *Women and Sex Roles: A Social Psychological Perspective*. New York: W. W. Norton, 1978: 157–190.

SCARF, MAGGIE. *Unfinished Business: Pressure Points in the Lives of Women*. Garden City, N.Y.: Doubleday, 1980.

SCHARLACH, ANDREW E. "Relief of Filial Distress Among Women with Aging Mothers." Paper presented at Annual Meeting of the Gerontological Society of America, San Francisco, November 1983. Reproduced.

SCHLOSSBERG, NANCY K. "A Model for Analyzing Human Adaptation to Transition." *Counseling Psychologist* 9, 2 (1981): 2–18.

_____. *Counseling Adults in Transition: Linking Practice with Theory.* New York: Springer, 1984.

SCHMIDT, MARY G. "Failing Parents, Aging Children." *Journal of Gerontological Social Work* 2 (1980): 259–268.

SCHORR, ALVIN. *Filial Responsibility in the Modern American Family.* Washington, D.C.: Department of Health, Education and Welfare, Social Security Administration, Division of Program Research, 1960.

SCHUERMAN, JOHN R. *Research and Evaluation in the Human Services.* New York: Free Press, 1983.

SCHWARTZ, ARTHUR N. *Survival Handbook for Children of Aging Parents.* Chicago: Follett, 1977.

SEELBACH, WAYNE C. "Correlates of Aged Parents' Filial Responsibility: Expectations and Realizations." *Family Coordinator* 27, 4 (October 1978): 341–350.

SHANAS, ETHEL M. "The Family as a Social Support System in Old Age." *Gerontologist* 19 (April 1979): 169–175.

_____. "Older People and Their Families: The New Pioneers." *Journal of Marriage and the Family* 42, 1 (February 1980): 9–15.

SILVERMAN, PHYLLIS R. "Transitions and Models of Intervention." In Felix M. Berardo, 1982: 174–187.

SIMON, ANNE W. *The New Years: A New Middle Age.* New York: Knopf, 1968.

SIMOS, BERTHA G. "Adult Chldren and Their Aging Parents." *Social Work* 18, 3 (May 1973): 78–85.

_____. *A Time to Grieve: Loss as a Universal Human Experience.* New York: Family Service Association of America, 1979.

SKOLNICK, ARLENE. "Married Lives: Longitudinal Perspective on Marriage." In Eichorn, et al., 1981: 269–298.

SMELSER, NEIL J., and ERIK H. ERIKSON, eds. *Themes of Work and Love in Adulthood.* Cambridge, Mass. Harvard University Press, 1980.

SPENCE, DONALD L., and THOMAS B. LONNER. "The 'Empty Nest': A Transition Within Motherhood." *Family Coordinator* 20, 4 (October 1971): 369–375.

_____. "Career Set: A Resource Through Transitions and Crises." *International Journal of Aging and Human Development* 9, 1 (1978–1979): 51–65.

SPREY, JETSE, and SARAH H. MATTHEWS. "Contemporary Grandparenthood: A Systemic Transition." In Felix M. Berardo, 1982: 91–103.

STARTZ, MORTON R., and CLAIRE W. EVANS. "Developmental Phases of Marriage and Marital Therapy." *Social Casework* 62, 6 (June 1981): 343–351.

STEIN, STEFAN, and CHARLES A. SHAMOIAN. "Psychosomatic Disorders in the Middle-Aged." In Howells, 1981: 266–278.

STEVENS-LONG, JUDITH. *Adult Life: Developmental Processes.* Palo Alto, Calif.: Mayfield, 1979.

STREIB, GORDON F., and RUBYE W. BECK. "Older Families: A Decade Review." *Journal of Marriage and the Family* 42, 4 (November 1980): 937–956.

STRICKLER, MARTIN. "Crisis Intervention and the Climacteric Man." *Social Casework* 56, 2 (February 1975): 85–90.

SULLIVAN, JOYCE, and KAREN G. ARMS. "Working Women Today and Tomorrow." In Howells, 1981: 71–89.

TAMIR, LOIS M. "Men at Middle Age: Developmental Transitions." In Felix M. Berardo, 1982: 47–56.

THOMPSON, GAYLE B. "Economic Status of Late Middle-Aged Widows." In Datan and Lohmann, 1980: 133–149.

THURNHER, MAJDA. "Midlife Marriage: Sex Differences in Evaluation and Perspectives." *International Journal of Aging and Human Development* 7, 2 (1976): 129–135.

––––––. "Turning Points and Developmental Change: Subjective and Objective Assessments." *American Journal of Orthopsychiatry* 53, 1 (January 1983): 52–60.

TREAS, JUDITH, and VERN L. BENGTSON. "The Demography of Mid- and Late-Life Transitions. In Felix M. Berardo, 1982: 11–21.

TROLL, LILLIAN E. "Family Life in Middle and Old Age: The Generation Gap." In Felix M. Berardo, 1982: 38–46.

––––––. "Grandparents: The Family Watchdogs." In Timothy H. Brubaker, ed. *Family Relationships in Later Life.* Beverly Hills: Sage, 1983: 63–76.

––––––, JOAN ISRAEL, and KENNETH ISRAEL, eds. *Looking Ahead: A Woman's Guide to the Problems and Joys of Growing Older.* Englewood Cliffs, N.J.: Prentice-Hall, 1977.

––––––, SHEILA J. MILLER, and ROBERT C. ATCHLEY. *Families in Later Life.* Belmont, Calif.: Wadsworth, 1979.

TURNER, JOSEPH G. "Patterns of Intergenerational Exchange: A Developmental Approach." *International Journal of Aging and Human Development* 6, 1975: 111–115.

U.S. BUREAU OF THE CENSUS. "Marital Status and Living Arrangements." *Current Population Reports*, Series P-20, No. 358. Washington, D.C.: U.S. Government Printing Office, 1979.

VAILLANT, GEORGE. *Adaptation to Life*. Boston: Little, Brown, 1977.

WARING, JOAN. "The Middle Years: A Life Course Perspective: The Importance of Health." In Alvin C. Eurich, ed. *Major Transitions in the Human Life Cycle*. Lexington, Mass. Heath, 1980: 449–511.

_____. "The Meaning of Work." In Alvin C. Eurich, ed. *Major Transitions in the Human Life Cycle*. Lexington, Mass.: Heath, 1980: 457–470.

WASSERMAN, SIDNEY. "The Middle-Age Separation Crisis and Ego-Supportive Casework Treatment." *Clinical Social Work Journal* 1, 1 (September 1973): 38–47.

WEG, RUTH. "More than Wrinkles." In Troll, Israel, and Israel, 1977: 22–42.

WEISS, ROBERT S. *Loneliness: The Experience of Emotional and Social Isolation*. Cambridge, Mass.: M.I.T. Press, 1973.

WEISSMAN, MYRNA M. "The Treatment of Depressed Women: The Efficacy of Psychotherapy." In Carol L. Heckerman, ed. *The Evolving Female: Women in a Psychosocial Context*. New York: Human Sciences Press, 1980: 307–324.

_____, and EUGENE S. PAYKEL. *The Depressed Woman: A Study of Social Relationships*. Chicago: University of Chicago Press, 1974.

WETZEL, JANICE W. "Depression and Dependence Upon Unsustaining Environments." *Clinical Social Work* (1978): 75–89.

WILLIAMS, JUANITA H. *Psychology of Women: Behavior in a Biosocial Context*, 2nd ed. New York: W. W. Norton, 1983.

WILSON, R. A. *Feminine Forever*. New York: Evans Press, 1966.

WINOKUR, GEORGE. "Depression in the Menopause." *American Journal of Psychiatry* 130 (January 1973): 92–93.

YOUNG, MICHAEL, and PETER WILLMOTT. *Family and Kinship in East London*. London: Routledge & Kegan Paul, 1957.

ZACKS, HANNA. "Self-Actualization: A Midlife Problem." *Social Casework* 61, 4 (April 1980): 223–233.

ZILBACH, JOAN J. "Separation: A Family Developmental Process of Midlife Years." In Nadelson and Notman, 1982: 159–167.

ZUBE, MARGARET. "Changing Behavior and the Outlook of Aging Men and Women." *Family Relations* 31, 1 (January 1982): 147–156.

Index

Adrenals, 44, 47
Adult children, relations with, 34,
      96–115
   grandparents, 111–113
   men, effect on, 107–109
   women, effect on, 99–107
Affective reactions, 57–74
Age-Fifty Transition, 5, 15
Aging parents, ties with, 34,
      116–134
   filial maturity, 117, 124–129
   filial responsibility, 117, 118–124
   significant others, involvement
      of, 129–132
Aging process
   in men, 39–41, 60
   in women, 41–43
Alcoholism, 60–64
Aldous, Joan, 98
Anima/animus, 11
Anterior pituitary gland, 44, 47,
      48
Archbold, Patricia, 122
Atchley, Robert C., 5, 88

Baldness, 38, 49
Ballinger, Barbara, 69
Barnett, Rosalind, 103
Bart, Pauline, 70, 100
Baruch, Grace, 103
Benedek, Therese, 69, 103, 112
Berardo, Donna, 148
Berkun, Cleo, 71
Bernard, Jessie, 86
Biophysical reactions, 34, 37–55
   aging process, 37–43
   climacteric, 43–53
Birren, James, 57
Black women
   adult children, relations with, 99
   grandparenthood, 112–113
Blau, Zena, 125
Blenkner, Margaret, 117
Block, Marilyn R., 43, 48, 51, 86
Botwinick, Jack, 57
Boyd, Jeffrey, 61
Breast cancer, 50–51
Brody, Elaine M., 125, 132
Burrows, Graham D., 65

Cancer, 38, 39, 49–51
Carter, Elizabeth, 18
Case histories
  first interviews, 163–165,
    173–175, 182–184, 190–192,
    200–202, 211–213
  implications for practice, 224–29
  professionals' opinions, 165–166,
    175–176, 184–185, 192–193,
    202–203, 213–214
  treatment, 166–172, 176–181,
    185–189, 193–199, 203–210,
    214–219
Change; see also Transitions
  disruptions of, 23–24
Chicano family, aging parents in,
    118
Chiriboga, David, 16
Cicirelli, Victor, 117, 125
Clausen, John, 79
Clavan, Sylvia, 112
Climacteric, 43–53
Cognitive changes, 56–57
Cohen, Frances, 40
Complementarity bonds, 141–142
Cooper, Cary, 82
Corbett, Sherry L., 88
Counseling Adults in Transitions
    (Schlossberg), 8
Crystallized intelligence, 57

Datan, Nancy, 4, 14, 70, 98
Dennerstein, Lorraine, 65
Depression, 38, 39
  in men, 60–62
  in women, 61, 65–74, 100, 102
Deutsch, Helene, 69
Developmental perspective on
    mid-adulthood, 12–16
Diagnostic and Statistical Manual
    of Mental Disorders—DSM-III
    (American Psychiatric
    Association), 68n
Divorce, 51, 146–149
Dohrenwend, Barbara S., 38
Dohrenwend, Bruce P., 38
Dowager's hump, 49
Dual career couples, 88, 89

Duvall, Evelyn M., 17–18, 96,
    99–100, 111
Dying process, 126–127

Eichorn, Dorothy, 4
Empty nest, 96–115
Endocrine functioning, changes in,
    43–45, 47–49
Environmental conditions,
    reactions to, 73–74
Epstein, Laura, 28
Erikson, Erik H., 5, 6, 11, 15
Estrogen, 47, 49–50, 65
Exhaustion crisis, defined, 6
Extramarital affairs, 142–145

Families in Later Life (Troll, Miller,
    and Atchley), 5
Father-son bond, 108–109
Filial anxiety, 125–126
Filial maturity, 117, 124–129
Filial responsibility, 117, 118–124
First interviews, 163–165, 173–175,
    182–184, 190–192, 200–202,
    211–213
Fischer, Lucy, 103
Fiske, Marjorie, 16, 83
Fluid intelligence, 57
Follicle-stimulating hormone
    (FSH), 44, 47, 48
For the Woman Over 50 (Nudel), 4
Freud, Sigmund, 10
Fried, Barbara, 5
Friedman, Henry, 149
Friedman, M., 39
Fuchs, Estelle, 4, 106

Galinsky, Ellen, 97
Generativity, 11
George, Linda, 151, 153
Giele, Janet, 19, 88
Gilligan, Carol, 18–19
Golan, Naomi, 28, 29, 147n, 150
Gonadotropins, 44, 47
"Good provider" role, 86
Goodman, Ellen, 23, 86, 180
Grandparenthood, 111–113
Gray Itch, The (Hallberg), 4

Gutmann, David, 58

Haan, Norma, 58
Hair, 38, 49
Hallberg, Edmond, 4
Harkins, Elizabeth, 100
Harrison, Daphne, 99
Havighurst, Robert, 12
Hearing, 56
Heart attacks, 38–41
Heavyweight changes, 23
Henretta, John C., 88
Henry, Jules, 71
Holmes, Thomas H., 38
Hormones, 44, 47–48
Hot flashes (flushes), 47, 49
Howells, John, 4
Hysterectomy, 50

Illnesses, 38, 43
Impotence, 45, 140
Individuation, 10–11
Intellectual abilities, 57
Intergenerational shifts: *see* Adult children, relations with; Aging parents, relations with
Interrupted career (women), 87
Introspection, 13

Jaques, Elliott, 60
Jewish families, aging parents in, 121
Job security, 79, 80
Johnson, Ralph, 142
Johnson, Virginia E., 45, 140
Jung, Carl Gustav, 10–11, 58

Kahana, Boaz, 64
Kahana, Eva, 64
Kalish, Richard A., 150
Kaplan, David, 23–24
Kaplan, Helen, 140
Kerckhoff, Richard, 142

Lazarus, Richard S., 40
LeShan, Eda J., 4, 97, 127, 136, 144
Levinson, Daniel J., 5, 15, 60, 79

Life cycle, theoretical approaches to, 10–21
Lightweight changes, 23
Livson, Florine, B., 58–59, 148
Loewenstein, Sophie F., 74, 92, 100, 144, 145
Lohmann, Nancy, 5
Loneliness, 71–72
Lonner, Thomas, 100
Luteinizing hormone (LH), 44, 47

MacLaine, Shirley, 3
Maldonado, David, 118
Marriages, mid-life, 34, 135–158
   alternatives to, 147–155
   areas of change, 137–147
   overall tone of, 136–137
Mastectomy, 51
Masters, William H., 45, 140
Material-arrangemental (instrumental) tasks, 30, 31
Mayer, Nancy, 5
McGill, Michael, 107, 108
McGoldrick, Monica, 18
Men; *see also* Marriages, mid-life
   adult children, relations with, 107–109
   aging process, 39–41, 60
   alcoholism, 60–64
   climacteric, 44–47
   depression, 60–62
   emotional reactions, 60–65
   work role, 78–86
Menopause, 44, 47–50, 68–71, 74, 140–141
Meyer, Roger, 62
Mid-adulthood, theoretical approaches to, 10–21
Middle-range changes, 23
Mid-Life Transition, 5, 15
Miller, Sheila, 5
Modern Perspectives in the Psychiatry of Middle Age (Howells), 4
Modified second career (women), 87
Mother-daughter bond, 103–105, 130

Mother-son bond, 105–107
Murkin, Peter, 62
Murry, Saundra, 99

Nadelson, Carol, 141
Neugarten, Bernice L., 6, 13–16,
    57, 69, 93, 112, 118
New Years, The (Simon), 4
Nontraditionals, 59–60
Nudel, Adele, 4

Oakland Growth Study, 58–59, 79
Occupational obsolescence, 82, 83
Oedipal conflict, 106
O'Rand, Angela M., 88
Osteoporosis, 49
Ovaries, 44, 47, 50

Paloma, Margaret, 87
Peck, Robert C., 11–12
Penis, 44
Perceptual changes, 56
Perlman, Helen, 161
Personality types, 58–60
    heart attacks and, 39–40
Present and Past in Middle Life
    (Eichorn), 4
Problem-solving, 23
Professionals' opinions on case
    histories, 165–166, 175–176,
    184–185, 192–193, 202–203,
    213–214
Progesterone, 47
Psychodynamic perspective on
    mid-adulthood, 10–12
Psychological reactions, 34, 56–77
    affective reactions, 57–74
    perceptual and cognitive
        changes, 56–57
Psychosocial (affective) tasks, 30–31
Psychosomatic illnesses, 38

Rahe, R. H., 38
Regular career pattern (women), 87
Reid, William, 28
Remarriage, 151, 153–155
Retirement, 83
Rhodes, Sonya, 135

Rogers, Rita, 129
Rosenman, R. H., 39
Rossi, Alice S., 58
Rubin, Lillian B., 4, 102, 108, 139

Same-sex partnerships, 153
San Francisco Transition Study,
    100, 136
Scarf, Maggie, 4, 71–72
Schlossberg, Nancy, 8, 26
Schorr, Alvin, 117
Seasons of a Man's Life, The
    (Levinson), 79
Second career (women), 87
Second Season, The (Fuchs), 4
Seelbach, Wayne, 118
Sexual functioning, 44–47, 139–141
Shamoian, Charles A., 38, 39
Shanas, Ethel, 116, 121
Shock crisis, defined, 6
Sibling rivalries, aging parents and,
    129–130
Simon, Anne, 4
Simos, Bertha, 121
Singlehood, 152–153
Skin, 38, 41, 43
Skolnick, Arlene, 137
Social class, 14, 27n, 35
Social clocks, 6, 14
Sociological perspectives on
    mid-adulthood, 17–18
Spence, Donald, 100
Stein, Stefan, 38, 39
Steinem, Gloria, 3
Stress, 38, 82
Stuck points, 25, 29
Suicide, 64–66
Support groups, 30

Task-centered model of treatment,
    28–29
Testes, 44
Testosterone, 44
Theoretical approaches to
    mid-adulthood, 10–21
Thurnher, Majda, 16, 60, 136
Traditionals, 59
Tranquilizers, 65, 66

Transition of Aging (Datan and
    Lohmann), 4–5
Transitional tasks, 30–31
Transitions
  assessment of elements, 25–28
  scope of, 5–7
  types of problems, 24–25
Treatment in case histories,
    166–172, 176–181, 185–189,
    193–199, 203–210, 214–219
Troll, Lillian, 5, 113, 116
Turning points, 15

Unfinished Business (Scarf), 4

Vagina, 48, 49
Vaillant, George, 15–16
Visual ability, 56

Waring, Joan, 78
Weight, 37–38, 41, 43

Weissman, Myrna, 61, 68
Wetzel, Janice, 74
Widowhood, 149–152
Women; *see also* Marriages,
    mid-life
  adult children, relations with,
    99–107
  aging process, 41–43
  climacteric, 47–53
  depression, 61, 65–74, 100, 102
  emotional reactions, 65–74
  on theoretical approaches to
    mid-adulthood, 18–19
  work role, 86–93
Women of a Certain Age (Rubin), 4
Women's movement, 103
*Wonderful Crisis of Middle Age,
    The* (LeShan), 4
Work role, 34, 94–95
  of men, 78–86
  of women, 86–93
Workaholics, 80